PRIMITIVE ART

THE BELLE SAUVAGE LIBRARY

PRIMITIVE ART

LEONHARD ADAM

CASSELL · LONDON

CASSELL & COMPANY LTD

35 Red Lion Square . London WC I
and at

MELBOURNE · SYDNEY · TORONTO · CAPE TOWN
JOHANNESBURG · AUCKLAND

————

Printed in Czechoslovakia

TO
MARY AND MARY-CLARE

CONTENTS

7

CONTENTS

LIST OF TEXT FIGURES

9

The text figures (except No. 12) are from pen drawings by the author, Nos. 2, 5, 10, 24, 27–35, 37, 40–3 being original drawings and the others made after illustrations in the various sources referred to in the above list or in the text.

LIST OF PLATES

(between pages 128–129)

1. (*a*) Bushman rock engraving in the pecking (intaglio) technique, representing an eland antelope. Length (nose to tail) 28.5 cm. Klipfontein (Style II). *South African Museum. After M. Wilman.*

    (*b*) West African pre-Islamic pottery figure of a man. Height 25 cm. Excavated at Tago (Lake Chad) by Jean-Paul Lebeuf and Mme A. Masson-Detourbet. *By courtesy of M. Sougez, Paris.*

2. (*a*) Ivory figure of a horseman. Height 14.3 in. Yoruba, Nigeria. *British Museum.*

    (*b*) Female ancestor figure. Wood. Bangwa tribe, Cameroons. Height 82 cm. *Formerly in the Museum f. Völkerkunde, Berlin. After E. v. Sydow, 'Die Kunst der Naturvölker'.*

3. Two chief's stools, combined with over life-size statues. Wood. From Bekom, Bamenda district, Cameroons. Height (left figure) 185 cm.; (right figure) 194 cm. *Museum f. Völkerkunde, Berlin. After E. v. Sydow.*

4. Carved door-frame. Wood. From Bamum, Cameroons. Width 2 metres. *Museum f. Völkerkunde, Berlin. After E. v. Sydow.*

5. (*a*) Wooden mask, painted black and white. Mpongwe, Gabun, French Equatorial Africa. *By courtesy of Heinz Hagen, late of Berlin.*

    (*b*) Wooden mask, wearing a plug in the upper lip. Makonde tribe. Portuguese East Africa. Height 9 in. *British Museum.*

6. Wooden stool, the seat supported by an ancestral couple. Baluba sculpture of the eastern Congo, illustrating the 'long-faced style of Buli' (F. Olbrechts). Height 53.5 cm.; upper diameter 45.5 cm. *Museum f. Völkerkunde, Berlin, III C. 14966. After E. v. Sydow.*

7. (*a*) Wooden vase with incised *buina* ('carving knife') pattern.

13

Bakongo tribe, Belg. Congo. Torday Expedition. Height 8 in. *British Museum.*

(*b*) Wooden figure. Baluba, Belgian Congo. Height *c.* 5 in. *British Museum.*

7. (*c*) Ivory statuette. Bapende, Belg. Congo. Height 13 cm. *By courtesy of Hanns Krenz, late of Berlin.*

(*d*) Bronze plaque with relief representing a woman holding a mirror or tray. Benin. Height *c.* 6 in. *British Museum.*

8. (*a*) Ivory armlet consisting of two interlocking cylinders, carved with figures of the king in his supernatural aspect, surrounded by armed figures. Benin. According to Miss M. A. Bennet-Clark, this piece is in the Yoruba style, probably of Owo. Height *c.* 6 in. *British Museum.*

(*b*) Bronze head representing a king wearing coral ornaments. Benin. Height *c.* 12 in. *From a private collection.*

9. (*a*) Bronze head excavated at Ife, Nigeria, in 1938. Height *c.* 12 in. Weight 10 lb. 5 oz.

(*b*) Bronze head excavated at Ife, Nigeria, in 1938. Height *c.* 12 in. Weight 11 lb. 11 oz. The heads are hollow, and each has a circular hole about 3 in. in diameter at the back of the skull. *Nos. 9a and 9b by courtesy of Mr E. H. Duckworth, Editor of* 'Nigeria'.

10. (*a*) Bronze head from Ife, Nigeria. Height *c.* 15 in. *By courtesy of Mr. E. H. Duckworth.*

(*b*) Ashanti gold weights ('*mrammuo*') of bronze cast in the *cire-perdue* process. Height *c.* 2–3 cm. each, (i) and (ii) *Pitt Rivers Museum, Oxford,* (iii) and (iv) *Mr and Mrs Paul Robeson's Collection.* There are many types of gold weights. Figures usually illustrate proverbs: (i), representing an oryx-antelope, is called *nim-sa,* that is: 'Had I known that has passed behind me'. This refers to the animals' backward-sloping horns. The meaning is that regrets are vain. (ii) represents the famous old men known as Amoako and Adu, two legendary friends who met again after many years of separation, both having encountered misfortune and become very poor. These interpretation were obtained and published by R. S. Rattray. ('*Ashanti*', Clarendon Press 1913, pp. 310, 312). For (iii) and (iv) no interpretation was available, but they undoubtedly illustrate other proverbs.

11. (*a*) Stone figures discovered at Esie, Ilorin Province, Nigeria, in 1934. Average height, 22 in. *By courtesy of Mr E. H. Duckworth.*

(*b*) Clay figures combined with pieces of fabric made by Tallensi children (Northern Territories of the Gold Coast). *Phot. by H. V. Meyerowitz. Copyright by K. and M. Lubinski, London.*

12. (*a*) Ancient Chinese bronze statuette of a man carrying a tray. Green patina. Ts'in dynasty (255–207 B.C.). Height *c.* 15 cm. *Courtesy of Mr Edgar Worch, late of Berlin.*

(*b*) Clay figures from ancient tombs. Nilgiri Hills, S. India. Height 6.9 and 3.8 in. *British Museum.*

13. (*a*) Amulet box of horn, with carved wooden lid. Batak. *Collected in Deli, Sumatra,* 1868-69.

(*b*) Dagger from Balige, a Toba-Batak village, Sumatra. Haft and sheath of wood, the eyes and armlets of the squatted human figure carved on the haft are of metal. The sheath set with bands of sheet copper. Length 24.5 cm. (*a*) and (*b*) *Museum f. Völkerkunde, Basel.*

(*c*) Ancestor post, *batugur*, from the Siang district, upper Barito river S.E. Borneo. Carving in black wood. Height 2 metres. A buffalo is tied to such a post and is eventually killed as a sacrifice. *Collected by Dr P. Wirz,* 1926. *Museum f. Völkerkunde, Basel.*

14. (*a*) Three wooden ancestor figures from Nias (Indonesia). Height 26 cm.; 30.5 cm.; 22.5 cm. Note that the mouth is missing in the face of the figure on the right. *Coll. Max Fröhlich, Berlin.*

(*b*) Wooden statue representing 'Bolli Atap', a charm to keep off sickness. Kelamantan tribe, Baram River, Sarawak. Height 14.8 in. *British Museum.*

15. Wooden statue. Phillippine Islands. Height 65 cm. *Municipal Museum, Brunswick, After E. v. Sydow.*

16. (*a*) Calabash for holding chunam or lime for betel chewing. Height 9.7 in. Massim area, New Guinea. Made before 1870. *British Museum.*

(*b*) Skull of an ancestor, the soft parts modelled in clay. White and red paint. Sepik River area, New Guinea. *Coll. Dr P. H. Cook, Melbourne.*

17. Stool with image of an ancestor. Carved in one piece, painted red and white. Height 3 ft. 2 in. Sepik River New Guinea. *National Museum of Victoria, Melbourne.*

18. (*a*) Wooden mask, illustrating conventional style typical of the Sepik area, New Guinea. Height 31 cm. *National Museum of Victoria, Melbourne.*

(*b*) Large pottery urn with plastic decoration and red and white paint. Ramu valley, New Guinea. Height 60 cm.; diameter 50 cm. *Ethnological Museum, Bremen. After E. v. Sydow.*

19. (*a*) and (*b*). Stone sculpture, found near Annaberg, Atemble district, Ramu valley, New Guinea. (*a*) front view; (*b*) back view. Height 44 cm. *Australian Museum, Sydney.*

20. (*a*) Statuette carved from a slab of chalk in memory of a deceased relative. Southern New Ireland. Height 69 cm. *National Museum of Victoria, Melbourne.*

(*b*) Wood carving in open-work, illustrating the *malanggan* style. Spirits and mythical beings are represented. Red, black, and white decoration. Northern New Ireland. Height *c.* 4 ft. *British Museum.*

21. (*a*) Ancestor figures, carved from a fern-tree trunk. Ambrym Island, New Hebrides. Height 7 ft. 8 in. *National Museum, Melbourne.*

(*b*) Carved board flanking the entrance to a chief's hut. New Caledonia. Height 7 ft. 6 in. *British Museum.*

22. (*a*) Wooden statuette of a woman, Buka, northern Solomon Islands. The wood is stained black, the head-gear and part of the stand are painted a dark red. Height 64 cm. *Melbourne University Collection.*

(*b*) Detail showing the treatment of the hands and legs.

23. (*a*) Bowl in the shape of a bird. Wood inlaid with shell. Palau Islands, Micronesia, *British Museum.*

(*b*) Wooden bowl in the shape of a bird. Admiralty Islands. *Museum f. Völkerkunde, Berlin.*

24. (*a*) Prow of a canoe. Maori, New Zealand. Height *c.* 3 ft. *British Museum.*

    (*b*) Feather box, wood, inlaid with haliotis shell. Length 21 in. *University Museum of Archaelogy and Enthnology, Cambridge.*

25.   Wooden door-frame of a decorated store-house, Maori. The high relief carvings represent mythological figures. The protruding tongues are symbols of energy and fierceness. The eyes were originally inlaid with green *paua* (haliotis) shell. Height *c.* 1.50 metres. *Museum f. Völkerkunde, Berlin.*

26. (*a*) Wooden spittoon ('Ipu Kuha'). Oahu Island, Hawaii. Height 8 in. *British Museum.*

27. (*a*) Feather-cloak of King Kamehameha II of Hawaii (1827). Colours: scarlet red, light yellow, black (with metallic lustre). Length *c.* 1.50 metres. *Museum f. Völkerkunde, Berlin.*

27. (*b*) Feather cape of a Hawaiian nobleman. Colours: scarlet, yellow, black. Width *c.* 89 cm. *By courtesy of the Royal Scottish Museum, Edinburgh.*

28. (*a*) Monumental sandstone sculpture, Easter Island. Height *c.* 8 ft. width *c.* 3 ft. The name of the figure is Hoa-Haka-Nana-Ia. Brought to England by H.M.S. *Topaze* in 1869 and now in the British Museum. *By courtesy of the Trustees.*

    (*b*) Part of the rock engravings at Ko Te Kari Kari, Easter Island. *By courtesy of Professor H. Lavachery.*

29. (*a*) Statuette of toromiro wood. Easter Island. Height *c.* 48 cm. *British Museum.*

    (*b*) Polychrome wooden statuette, representing the 'Elder Wauwelak sister', from Yirrkalla, N.E. Arnhem Land, Northern Territory of Australia. Height. *c.* 91.4 cm. *Collected by Ronald and Catherine Berndt. Department of Anthropology, University of Sydney.*

30. (*a*) Monumental wall painting in a rock shelter in the Kimberleys, north-western Australia. Height of the

17

largest figure approximately 1.80 m. *Photograph by Fox. By courtesy of the Frobenius Institute, Frankfurt a. M.*

(*b*) Rock engravings representing a shoal of fish on the horizontal rock surface of a site in the Kuringai Chase, a Natural Reserve in the Sydney District. Length of illustrated section *c.* 1.20 metres. *Photograph by J. Mary Adam.*

31. Bark painting from Groote Eylandt, Gulf of Carpentaria, Northern Territory of Australia. Height *c.* 3 ft. *University of Melbourne Collection. Photograph by courtesy of the Department of Information, Commonwealth of Australia.*

32. Bark painting from Groote Eylandt. Height *c.* 3 ft. *University of Melbourne Collection. By courtesy of the Department of Information, Commonwealth of Australia.*

33. (*a*) Pipe, carved in walrus ivory, decorated with hunting scenes and animal figures in three different techniques, viz., engraving, carving in relief, and carving in the round. Length 33.6 cm. Alaska Eskimos. *D. L. Adam coll. Melbourne.*

(*b*) Totem pole. Haida Indians, Queen Charlotte Islands, British Columbia. Height 39 ft. British Museum. The legend illustrated in this pole has been published by Capt. T. A. Joyce in the *Journal of the Royal Anthropological Institute,* vol. xxxiii.

34. (*a*) Haida mask, Queen Charlotte Islands, British Columbia. Height 29 cm. *Collected between 1881 and 1883 by Capt. Adrian Jacobsen. Museum f. Völkerkunde, Berlin.*

(*b*) Dish of cedar wood in the shape of a seal, inlaid with haliotis shell, opercula of sea snails, and tiny glass beads. Length 41 cm. *Museum f. Völkerkunde, Berlin.* (*a*) *and* (*b*) *after L. Adam,* 'Nordwestamerikanische Indianerkunst', (*Orbis Pictus Series*), *Berlin, 1923.*

35. (*a*) Wooden mask representing the mythical thunder-bird. Partly painted in black, red, and blue. Bilxula Indians, British Columbia. Length 21 in. *Museum f. Völkerkunde, Berlin. After L. Adam, Nordwestamerikan. Indianerkunst, pl. 25.*

(b) Antler pendant carved in the form of a killer-whale. Height 2.2 in., Length 6.3 in. Haida or Tsimshian, British Columbia. *British Museum.*

36. (a) Upper part of a realistic statuette of cedar wood, polychrome. Total height of the statuette 12 in. Haida Indians, Queen Charlotte Islands, British Columbia. *British Museum.*

(b) Wooden mask of the Iroquois, representing a spirit. Painted dark red. Real human hair. *British Museum.*

37. (a) Sandstone pipe-bowl, from a mound in Kentucky. *British Museum.*

(b) A *kachina* doll, representing a rain-god. Wood, with polychrome decoration in bright colours. Hopi Indians. Height 8.3 in. *British Museum.*

38. (a) Archaic Mayan figure of greenstone. Chimaltenango, Guatemala. Height 8.7 in. *Dr Thomas W. F. Gann Coll., British Museum.*

(b) Two marble vases. Late Maya period. Rio Uluá, Honduras. *Museum f. Völkerkunde, Berlin. (First published by the author in the art magazine* 'Cicerone', 1927).

39. (a) Wooden statuette of a European, dressed in the fashion of the first half of the nineteenth century. Coat painted blue. Height 12.5 in. This is a so-called *nuchu* of the Cuny Indians of San Blas, northern Panama. *British Museum. Nuchus* are used for magical treatment by medicine men. I am indebted to Prof. David B. Stout, University of Syracuse, N. Y., for the following information: The *nuchus* are classified according to the kind of wood they are made of, not according to whether they are male or female, or the style of clothing. The original medicines were made from different woods and were so classified; so now these figures. Dr Stout is of the opinion that these statuettes, with the idea: magic wood — magic image of wood, were adopted from African Negroes.

(b) Clay figure with gold nose-ring. Cauca Calley, Colombia Height 7.6 in. *British Museum.*

40. (a) A modern sculpture in wood from Nigeria, by B. C. En-

wonwu. Height 18.5 in. *Colonial Department Institute of Education, University of London.*
(*b*) Art students at Achimota College, Ghana. *Phot. by H. V. Meyerowitz. Copyright by K. & M. Lubinski, London.*

ACKNOWLEDGEMENTS

The majority of the objects already illustrated in the first edition are in the British Museum, and I wish to thank Mr H. J. Braunholtz, M. A., Keeper of the Ethnographical Department, for his kind permission to reproduce them. I also appreciate the valuable co-operation of Mr Adrian Digby, M. A. (now Keeper).

For permission to illustrate a large proportion of the new photographs and line-blocks in this revised and enlarged edition I am indebted to the Director of the National Museum of Victoria, Mr R. T. M. Pescott, M. AGR. SC. I am much obliged to Dr A. B. Walkom, Director of the Australian Museum, Sydney, for his kind permission to reproduce the piece shown on Pl. 19, and to the Rector of the Pallottine Missionary College at Kew (Melbourne), Very Rev. Fr Ernest Worms, P.S.M., for his kind permission to illustrate the clay figures Fig. 41.

The photographs illustrating objects in the British Museum were taken by Dr Albert Hahn, except Plates 20(b), 21(b), 23(a), 24(a), 26(b), 28(a), 33(b), which are official photographs of the British Museum. Plates 10 (b), (c), (d) were taken by Mr C. W. James (London); Plates 16(b), 17, 18(a), 20(a), 21(a), 33(a) by Mr C. J. Frazer, ('Frazer Studios') Melbourne; Plates 31, 32 by a staff photographer of the Department of Information, Commonwealth of Australia.

Text figures Nos. 27, 34, 35, 37, 40 have been previously published in my guide-book to the Primitive Art Exhibition, Melbourne, 1943 (now out of print), which I arranged for the National Gallery and National Museum of Victoria.

Foreword to the First Edition (1940)

By R. R. Marett,

D.SC., D.LITT., LL.D., F.B.A.

(1866—1943)

Dr Adam is to be congratulated on having completed just before the outbreak of war – as may be deduced from his useful list of references – a compact and readable manual which in war-time bound to prove a godsend to those of us who would devote their spare moments to the contemplation of the constructive, rather than the destructive, energies of the human race. True, the book deals solely with primitive man, in the double sense of old and old-fashioned. But at present nobody can be feeling particularly proud of being civilized. Indeed, it is even possible to be somewhat envious of the world's simpler peoples, more concerned as they are to make friends with Nature than so seek to overcome their fellow-man. Nor has the artist himself any special reason to rejoice in civilization in its most recent phase; for nowadays private persons have too little money, and public bodies too little taste, to provide him with a living wage.

Fine art, however, is by no means bound up with any one type of human culture. It is, on the contrary, a hardy plant that blossoms in all climates and at all seasons. The evolutionist is, in fact, greatly puzzled by a constitutional tendency of ours that throughout its long history shows little sign of changing either for better or for worse. Whether one chooses to label it primitive or advanced, the cult of beauty in one or another of its myriad manifestations is ever there to cheer humanity on its way. In all ages the talented few achieve certain masterpieces, while a wider public shows itself in varying degree susceptible to their charm. For such amenities of existence it may be hard to find any utilitarian justification, whether we seek to apply the biological test of survival-value, or are content to think more loosely in terms of relative wealth or political power. Yet, like a glint of sun on a dull day, a vision of perfect form, however momentary, enlarges the promise of life, by helping to establish its higher and more enduring values. It provides the nearest thing to a pure plesasure, to a like extent

21

sublimating that sensuous element which gives what we call the soul, as distinguished from the mind, its richer content. Unfortunately, individuals and whole peoples are somewhat unequally endowed in respect to creative and even appreciative genius of the aesthetic order. Yet education can do much to bring out in most of us a power of nice perception though almost latent hitherto, or narrowed and stifled by convention. My prescription would be for those who would teach themselves to enjoy beauty on a worldwide scale: find a good ethnological museum, and use Dr Adam's text-book as your guide.

Now it is not for me to attempt here to examine, much less to criticize, the contents of a work that, without wasting a word, fulfils the twofold task of analysing principles and describing results. Suffice it to say that so concrete a treatment will appear to everyone who likes facts; and some of Dr Adam's facts, notably those relating to various modern representatives of the primitive, will have been previously known to few. Speaking for myself, and being chiefly interested in Social Anthropology, I have nothing but praise for his insistence on the connexion of fine art with the other functions of the body politic. For instance, one can never afford to ignore the religious or magico-religious significance of much that, regarded apart from its context, might easily be credited with a purely decorative purpose. Or, again, the primitive artist merges with the artisan, so that he cannot turn out a useful tool or weapon without introducing the ornamental as a finishing touch. I might go on to note how the psychological interest is maintained throughout. Thus something, yet perhaps enough, is said about the obscure but real relation between the artistic and the sexual impulses. So, too, the rather dangerous analogy between the savage and the child is handled with caution; nor is the civilized artist forgotten whose only change of reaching the primitive is, in default of innocence, by way of repentance. But what need to say more? The reader will find in this handy volume a wealth of information, and what is even more important, a wealth of suggestion. The fact that genuine beauty is revealed to the simple-minded has wide implications that are worth thinking out.

Preface to the Third Edition

FOR the present edition, the text and the number of illustrations have been enlarged, while the arrangement of the Hind edition has been retained. Eight plates with fifteen new half-tones, and one line drawing, have been added, whereby a careful selection has been made in order to fill certain gaps and also to illustrate a few examples of important recent discoveries, such as one of the wooden statuettes of Yirrkalla (north-western Arnhem Land), which were first published by Ronald and Catherine Berndt a few years ago; and one of the very interesting clay figures excavated by Jean-Paul Lebeuf and Mme A. Masson-Detourbet south of Lake Chad recently. Needless to say, there are still many gaps in the list of illustrations, but the limitations of a concise introduction into so vast a subject are obvious. Additions have been made to several chapters, but as it was intended to leave the bulk of the text intact, much that would normally be said in the text will be found in the notes at the end.

For constructive criticism I have to thank Professor Georg Höltker, who kindly reviewed the second edition and the Spanish translation (*Arte Primitivo*, Lautaro, Buenos Aires, 1947) in *Anthropos*. If not all of the valuable references suggested by my friendly critics appear in this new edition, this is due not only to lack of space but also to my wish not to overwhelm the beginner, especially the young student, with too much specialized literature. Furthermore, this little book is, generally speaking, not the place to discuss theories, in particular those about the origins of certain primitive art styles. This will be done, to some extent, in another book which I hope to publish shortly.*

Our knowledge of the early stages of some primitive arts has been enriched by archaelogical research recently, notably in

---

* *Arts of the Primitive Peoples* (The Pelican History of Art, edited by N. Pevsner). This volume will be complementary to the present book.

north-western Alaska (and here especially by H. Larsen and F. Rainey) and West Africa (excavations carried out by Bernard Fagg, M. Griaule, J.-P. Lebeuf, and others), and reference has been made to some of those important discoveries. Probably the greatest scientific achievement for the study of archaeology and the early stages of primitive art was the American invention of *radiocarbon dating* (the so-called 'carbon-14 method'). This method, which was developed by Williard F. Libby in collaboration with E. C. Anderson and James R. Arnold only a few years ago, makes it possible to establish, within the limits of an upper and lower margin, the *absolute* date of a fossil find if it consists of a material (such as wood, charcoal, bone, etc.) which has been affected by cosmic radiation.* Some of the available results have been quoted. Radiocarbon dating is also bound to affect most, if not all, of the theories dealing with the relative chronology and origins of art styles of recent primitive peoples, especially those which are probably derivatives of the higher civilizations. For this reason it seems to be advisable for the time being to treat genetic theories with still more reserve than before.

It has been found necessary to remind beginners that still surviving primitive art forms occupy only a more or less obscure place in countries like India, Ceylon, and (partly) Indonesia, which, in the past, have been the centres of some of the highest developments in religious sculpture and architecture and that, of course, we are not here concerned with either Brahmanic or Buddhist art but with earlier stages.

It has been possible for me to keep the book fairly up to date, largely through my research work and other activities at the University of Melbourne, including the building-up of a small museum of ethnography and primitive art and an archive of photographs and slides. I wish to take this opportunity to express my gratitude to the academic authorities of the University of Melbourne, and also personally to Professor R. M. Crawford, Head of the Department of History.

The Director of the Museum für Völkerkunde in Basel

* Willard F. Libby, *Radiocarbon Dating* (The University of Chicago Press and Cambridge University Press, 1952).

(Switzerland) (Professor Alfred Bühler) has generously helped me with a large number of photographs, for which I am very grateful.

I am much obliged to Dr H. D. Skinner of the Otago Museum (Dunedin, N.Z.), for his helpful advice, and to Professor Joseph Burke, O.B.E., 'The Herald' Professor of Fine Arts in the University of Melbourne, for his valuable hints and for having called my attention to Viktor Loewenfeld's *Nature of Creative Activity*.

My friend, Mr John Harrison Thompson, of London, has assisted me by keeping me informed of exhibitions of primitive art in the United Kingdom.

I also wish to thank Miss Mary Lugton and Miss Margaret MacMillan of the Central Library, University of Melbourne, for their kind assistance, especially by procuring for me some literary sources not otherwise available.

Mr Geoffrey Best has been kind enough to read the proofs of the index, a difficult task because of the numerous additions and changes of references.

LEONHARD ADAM

Department of History
University of Melbourne
January 1953

CHAPTER I

What Do We Mean by Primitive Art?

THE oldest works of art in the world which can be traced to-day belong to the Upper Palaeolithic period. Until recently there was only a relative chronological order of prehistoric fossil finds, based on the geological strata. The age of the cave paintings of the Upper Palaeolithic of southern France and eastern Spain, for example, could only be estimated, and the date suggested was somewhere between 20,000 and 10,000 B.C. Nowadays it is possible, under certain favourable circumstances, to ascertain the date of a fossil find within a certain margin through radiocarbon dating. The date worked out in this way for the Lascaux Cave near Montignac, Dordogne, lies between the thirteenth and the middle of the fifteenth centuries B.C., which shows that the estimate was at least approximately accurate.

The works concerned are examples of 'primitive art' – art in its earliest stages. They were made by 'primitive' men who lived in the Old Stone Age, and from the skulls and skeletons of these men which have been unearthed it would seem that they belonged to racial stocks which are now extinct.

But 'primitive man' is also a general term for the native races of Africa, the South Seas, America, and certain parts of Asia. It is only between the end of the fifteenth and the end of the nineteenth centuries (in some cases even in the twentieth century) that these peoples were discovered by Europeans, and a considerable number of them are our contemporaries.

All the primitive races of modern times are physically distinct, both from prehistoric man and from the modern European. Their classification as 'primitive', however, is based on the stage of their cultural development rather than on their somatic features. These stages vary from the simplest possible type to comparatively high developments which some writers have called 'barbarian' or 'semi-civilized'. The terms, however, are extremely vague, and better avoided.

It is difficult, if not impossible, to give a satisfactory definition of 'primitive man' as distinct from 'civilized man'. Even if we take our own civilization as a standard, the question arises which side or feature of that civilization should be considered as decisive. Three elements have been suggested; Christian morals, scientific knowledge, and technical achievements. But a close examination of primitive cultures shows that in these things they differ from ours not in kind but only in degree. Many primitive tribes have been famous for their high (though not Christian) moral standard. The Polynesian seafarers acquired a considerable knowledge of astronomy which must have called for a good deal of scientific observation. The technical achievements of the Eskimos enabled them to make the best of the poor resources of their inhospitable country. Modern Europeans living under the same conditions could hardly produce better equipment for the struggle for life in Arctic regions, and in fact when they go there they have to adopt the habits and apply the methods of the Eskimos.

On the sociological side, primitive life is in general less differentiated, but there are many tribal organizations which are even more complicated than the social structure of a 'civilized' state. There is no fundamental difference between the organization of a State as defined by constitutional law, and the organization of a tribe as defined by custom, and some primitive peoples have been able to establish States in the proper sense of the term (Iroquois, Dahomey, Ashanti, Benin, the Hausa States, Lunda, Hawaii, Tahiti, etc.). Similarly, primitive law is a genuine form of law, endowed with sanctions no less effective than those of the great legal systems.

It is only in the religious sphere that primitive man appears to be clearly distinguishable. Admittedly, the various forms of primitive religion are from our point of view predominantly irrational (though not illogical), and magic plays an important part in them. But even in civilized communities various superstitions such as belief in witchcraft and magic still survive, so that here, too, there is no clear-cut line of demarcation.

The best way, then, to define 'primitive' peoples would be to say that they comprise all those tribes who are outside the spheres of (*a*) modern European civilization, and (*b*) the great Oriental

Fig. 1. Bushman Painting in a Rock-shelter near Orange Spring, about $\frac{1}{2}$ metre from the ground. Here a mask dance scene is represented, the men wearing heads of antelopes and the women and other men clapping their hands. After M. Helen Tongue. By courtesy of the Clarendon Press.

civilizations – in other words, peoples representing *comparatively* low cultural stages. The theory is that these cultural stages are 'earlier' in the development of ideas.

There is no reason to assume that the culture of prehistoric man in Europe, some ten to twenty thousand years ago, was identical with that of the recent primitive tribes outside Europe. But it has been proved by prehistoric find that they must have had many features in common. Prehistoric man is in fact' primitive' in terms of comparative anthropology, as well as from the purely chronological point of view.

The various periods of the Stone Age are represented in many parts of the world. But when similar types of stone implements are unearthed in different continents, that does not necessarily mean that they are equally old. The Palaeolithic stage of culture in India, for instance, cannot be assumed to be contemporary with the Palaeolithic period in Europe, unless the chronological coincidence is proved separately by geological stratigraphy. Some peoples have been practically Stone Age men up to the twentieth century.

In some areas inhabited by primitive tribes, prehistoric finds have been made, and prehistoric art, such as rock engravings, has been discovered which is not the work of the present natives but belongs either to their ancestors or to a different tribe inhabiting the same region in the past. Such finds enable us to carry the study of primitive art beyond the narrow scope of mere description and analysis into the sphere of historical research.

There is no question yet of linking up the scattered facts and studying them on a universal scale. For such a gigantic task the material available to-day is still too small. Moreover, outside Europe prehistoric research is only beginning. For a long time to come the work done must be confined to single tribes or groups of tribes.

Art is not an isolated phenomenon. It is part of a culture, linked up with the history of the culture and with the history of the people. Consequently, the understanding of every national art is helped by a knowledge of history, and there are important historical conclusions to be derived from the study of art. An insight into these interrelations is one of the lasting results of the intellectual research of this century.[1]

No nation has produced its own culture quite independently of influences from outside. Much has been written in the anthropological literature about the predominant part played in the development of human culture by either evolution or diffusion. As far as I can see, nobody has ever suggested that every culture has been entirely evolved from within, without borrowing cultural elements from other peoples. On the other hand, some schools of enthnology are inclined to minimize the rôle of independent origination and to over-estimate the importance of diffusion. According to one extreme 'diffusionist' school, all human cultures are even derived from one single source, namely, Egypt; but this theory has been rejected by the overwhelming majority of anthropologists, including diffusionists. The fact is that, ever since the very first groups of human beings emerged from a pre-human stage at a far remote geological period, there must always have been both discoveries and inventions on the one hand and adoption of the achievements of others on the other hand. The history of the later ages of mankind up to the present time shows that, in all ages, the peoples of the earth have invented for themselves, creating new forms and remoulding older devices, at the same time acquiring cultural wealth from other peoples. But a great deal must have been invented several times independently, in different ages and in different parts of the world.

What has been said of culture in general applies particularly to the development of art. There is no unified history of art. As one of our outstanding prehistorians, M. C. Burkitt, puts it: 'There art with a capital A, which, starting in prehistoric times, developed in various directions, among different people, with periods when special heights of skill and beauty were attained.'[2]

'Primitive art', then, is merely a general term covering a variety of historical phenomena, the products of different races, mentalities, temperaments, historical events, and influences of environment. Every people, however primitive, has developed a specific style by giving preference to certain objects and patterns or certain arrangements of lines and spaces.

Fashion plays an important part in primitive communities just as in civilized countries, and sometimes results in changes of art styles. But there is also a strong conservative tendency and a sense of tradition. Costumes, and ornaments of the olden times, may still appear as sacred attributes of demons, gods, and heroes in mask dances or other ceremonies. Obsolete types of weapons may now serve as maces or ceremonial clubs or adzes. Religion and conservatism are responsible for the prevalence of replicas as distinct from new creations. Even an exceptionally good carving like the statuette in Pl. 36 (*a*) is not unique, except for the individual features of the face. It represents a type, though not a frequent type. The need for replicas arises periodically when wooden masks or images get worn and have to be replaced by fresh carvings of the same kind. As in Christian or Buddhist art, however, there is always room for an artist to show his talent and creative force.

Scientifically speaking, there is no one element common to all the various branches of primitive art; but their mere foreignness in form and content serves to link them together in our mind for the purposes of art criticism. The link, however, is extraneous to the works themselves. It depends on us and our attitude to them.

This strangeness in itself can exercise an aesthetic charm. At the same time it can repel us. It seems as though a complete enjoyment of beauty is possible only when we are confronted with a work of art which either belongs to our own kind of culture, or is at least superficially related to our own ideals of artistic beauty. The combinations of form and colour evolved by foreign civilization may have many attractions, but they remain shrouded in an uncanny, mysterious atmosphere which is entirely alien to us. Works of art like those shown on Pls. 9 and 10 (*a*) arouse familiar, intimate feelings because they have been influenced by Egyptian (or Mediterranean) civilization, so that although they are the work of primitive artists, they cannot be regarded as genuine examples of primitive art.

Since the first stage of anything is usually undeveloped and unfinished, a popular meaning has grown up for the word 'primitive', denoting something crude, lacking that certain accord of lines, spaces, or colours which is the source of our emotional sensation when we look at a real work of art. The originator of the work either had insufficient means of expression at his disposal, or else lacked the ability to use them in such a way as to express what he wanted to portray. Actually this is not so much a work of art as an unsuccessful attempt to produce one – the decision will, of course, always be a judgement of value. The 'primitive work', in this sense, may be simply the work of a bungler who lacks both artistic inspiration and technical skill, in which case it has nothing to do with real primitiveness but is simply bad art without even a documentary value to recommend it. On the other hand, if it is the work of a savage or a child, it will have some importance at least as genetic or psychological evidence.

A more interesting use of the word 'primitive' applies to genuine works of art, and is by no means depreciatory. The critics use it to describe a certain naïveté of inspiration and simplicity of vision. Primitiveness in this sense appears in some of the art of every period and of every people. It is especially associated with Egyptian, Babylonian, Assyrian, and Byzantine art, and with the 'primitive Italians' who were the forerunners of the Renaissance.

An art style is not a static but a dynamic phenomenon, bound up and changing with a specific period of cultural development. It is an established fact that there is something like a periodicity of art styles, corresponding to a periodicity of tastes. It is not certain to what extent the style and the emotional reaction to it are conditioned by each other. The most obvious characteristic of modern artistic taste is simplicity. Living in a highly complicated world, noisy and mechanized to breaking point, and caught up in a speed of living far too fast for him, twentieth-century man has developed a strong tendency towards simplicity – simplicity in the external forms of daily life, a distaste for ornamentation in architecture, furniture, and utensils, and a preference for primitiveness and spontaneity rather than refinement and sophistication. That is why the simplicity of many primitive arts appeals to him so strongly.

'From a study of the Negro and the Bushman,' says Sir Herbert Read, 'we are led to an understanding of art in its most elementary form, and the elementary is always the most vital.'[3] G. A. Stevens offers a similar but more specific judgement: 'Primitive art is the most pure, most sincere form of art there can be, partly because it is deeply inspired by religious ideas and spiritual experience, and partly because it is entirely unselfconscious as art; there are no tricks which can be acquired by the unworthy, and no technical exercises which can masquerade as works of inspiration.'⁴ Such a judgement, however, is only justified by comparatively limited sections of the art of primitive races. In point of fact the 'primitive' artist is not always as naïve as one would like to think.

As there is such a great variety of types of primitive art — variety of character as well as of artistic merits we should try to be objective in our appreciation. This is possible only if we temporarily detach ourselves from any trend predominant, or fashionable, in our own art at present. For example, the majority of contemporary art critics does not think very highly of naturalism in the sense of visual truth to nature as the ideal of representative art. But there can be no doubt that truth to nature was ambition of the masters of the cave paintings in the Dordogne during the Upper Palaeolithic fifteen thousand, or more, years ago; and it is obviously also the ideal in some – though not by any means in all – of the more recent primitive art provinces. Thus the primitive artist may strive after an end which offers no attractions to us because it has been achieved long ago in the history of our own art. Comparisons like this are out of place. It does not matter so much what the primitive artist might have aimed at; what really matters is the way he did it.

CHAPTER II

Characteristics of Primitive Art

1. Technique

INADEQUATE technical means are not necessarily characteristic of primitive art. On the contrary, the materials in which the primitive artist works – stone, ivory, bone, wood, clay, and metal – are largely the same as those of the European artist. Even in painting, the mineral colours and vegetable and even animal dyes are in many cases similar.

The means at the disposal of the primitive artist belong to his cultural level, and to his surroundings. In an African shrine or temple an oil painting on canvas would be both historically untrue and aesthetically unpleasing. Primitive methods vary considerably; yet we find similar techniques applied in altogether different areas. The method of sculpture in wood, for example, is predominantly chopping, not carving. The tool is a kind of adze. The result in the finished piece is a faceted surface showing the unplaned marks of the tool. This technique is prevalent in Western and Southern Africa, New Guinea, and North-west America.

The aim of the primitive artist is good craftsmanship. The conditions under which he works are different from those of his 'civilized' colleague. Before he can begin an artistic work he has first to collect, manufacture, and prepare his tools and his material, and usually he has to do all this single-handed.

Take, for example, the North American Indian painter. Among the Plains Indians it is the women who are responsible for the geometric type of decorative art. The men confine themselves to representative paintings. In both cases plants or minerals must be collected to provide the paints. They must then be boiled or ground and mixed with size or fat to set the pigment. A buffallo hide must then be carefully prepared and the surface made as smooth as possible for the painting.

Even after a very complicated preparatory process the surface

35

FIG. 2. Polychrome
Painting on a Buffalo Hide.
Oglala Tribe, North
America.

The horse of the rider is red, the wild horses

is still so rough that outlines must first be pressed into the ground
before the drawing proper can be carried out, and the drawing
must be repeated several times to press the pigment thoroughly
into the hide. Consequently, a polychrome picture like the hunting scene shown in Fig. 2 is actually a coloured engraving rather
than a simple drawing. Fixing requires another complicated process, but this is applied only in geometric designs.[5]

All this preparatory work requires skilled craftsmanship and is
largely mechanical. So was the work of a European painter in
former times. To-day art material of every description can be
bought ready made. It is only the sculptors who are still tied to
any considerable amount of mechanical craftsmanship.

Generally speaking, the primitive artist is faced with a difficult
technical task. That does not mean, however, that he is not a true
artist with ideas of his own and sometimes genuine artistic inspiration. Many years ago Professor Franz Boas of Columbia
University met an Indian from Vancouver Island who had been
a good painter, though his works were in the traditional style of
the North-west coast (Figs. 11 and 44). This Indian was so
seriously ill that he was confined to his bed. But during his illness
he used to sit up 'holding his brush between his lips, silent and
apparently oblivious of his surroundings. He could hardly be
induced to speak, but when he spoke he dilated upon his visions

36

are yellow (2), red, and blue. British Museum.

of designs that he could no longer execute. Undoubtedly his was the mind and the attitude of a true inspired artist.' [6]

This intimate connexion with solid craftsmanship seems to be the reason why the primitive artist is so frequently successful. Eric Newton has a sentence in one of his exhibition reports which can perhaps be appreciated in its full significance only by artists themselves: 'The true test of an artist's power is surely that he should have sufficient stamina to enable his first frenzy to survive the process of "finishing".' [7] This is even more true of the primitive artist than of his civilized colleague to-day. The primitive artist not only knows from the beginning exactly what he wants, but continues with unwavering constancy until it is attained.

2. *Vision*

It has been suggested that the absence of perspective values and other aesthetic devices 'makes even primitive arts of high quality tend to seem either grotesque or monotonous to us on first contact with them'. [8] This may hold good for some primitive art, but it cannot be accepted for all. In view of the great variety of altogether different types, generalizations are dangerous.

Similarly, violent deviations from reality cannot be taken as characteristic of purely primitive vision, for they are found also in the art of hi ghly developed cultures. This is especially true of the lack of perspective which one finds in Egyptian, Byzantine, and Gothic art, but it is also evident in the arbitrary proportion of limbs in such figures as Botticelli's or Greco's. On the other hand, palaeolithic and Bushman art have produced remarkable attempts at fore-shortening, overlapping colours, linear perspective, and colour shading (Figs. 18, 19, 22).

Some primitive arts have attained the highest level in realistic portrayal. Bushman paintings, and drawings like those shown in Figs. 2 and 42, appeal to us strongly because we have no difficulty in understanding them. This type of graphic art is reminiscent of our own. It is simple, plain, and unsophisticated. Consequently, we find these works naïve and 'primitive' in an appreciative sense. We do not have to apply any new or unaccustomed kind of vision; for, in the long run, the primitive artist, like the European artist, works from life.

It is true that a large proportion of primitive art has obviously been worked from memory, and that gods, demons, and fantastic creatures are products of the artist's imagination, though some details may be derived from real forms. But innumerable works of art, particularly sculptures, from Africa, the South Seas, and America, are so realistic and individual that one can assume with certainty that the artists were actually working from nature. Above all, the sculptors of ancient Mexico and Peru (who were, of course, far from being really primitive) must have been looking directly at nature, and some of their works are in fact masterpieces of portraiture. [9]

In Africa the beautiful heads from Ife (Pls. 9 and 10 (a)) are no doubt life portraits, though some foreign influence may be responsible for this extraordinarily high standard of sculpture. But we find life portraits among even more primitive African tribes, in the Ivory Coast, the parkland of the Cameroons (Pl. 3), and the Congo Basin. Portraiture exists also in the Pacific area. The Maori of New Zealand have developed what may be called 'schematic' portraiture, whereby 'the patterns of tattooing, that infallible means of identification, rendered it possible to preserve the memories of the individual ancestors through pictorial representation'.[10]

The terms 'realistic' or 'naturalistic' art are usually applied to work which is done from the life and hence is true to nature. But their meaning, though definite enough in sculpture, tends to become ambiguous when applied to the graphic arts. If we speak of a naturalistic painting we mean that it is true to the optical impression of the model as observed at a given moment from a given angle. But in a different sense of the term we may speak of naturalism or realism if an artist represents all the details actually in existence, not only those he can see at the moment, but those he knows are there as well.[11]

In most primitive arts realism is of this kind; but we are used to looking on any deviation from our visual impression as artistically inferior, and are inclined to classify this variety of realism as 'primitive' in a sense of benevolent indulgence. It might perhaps be called 'intellectual' as opposed to purely optical. It reaches its highest development in the 'X-ray drawings' of Australia, Melanesia, and the coastal regions of British Columbia and southern Alaska (Figs. 3, 8, and 38). Here the artist depicts every detail of the body, including backbone, ribs, and internal organs, because he regards these as no less important than the characteristic features of a man's outward appearance. This amazing method often comes from the artist's material interests in particular details, rather than from any aesthetic appreciation. In Fig. 3, No. 1, for instance, the edible flesh of a fish is expressly indicated.

In North-west America there are monumental wall-paintings representing killer whales (or other animals), fabulous monsters and men, which are distinguished by the rendering of vertebrae and ribs. Typical of all North-west American graphic art is the stylized representation of the joint. This strange visual method is restricted to a few regions in the Pacific area, and is supposed to be one of the indications that this district may have been affected by Western influences at some remote period in the past. Intellectual realism of this sort cannot claim to be either naïve or simple. It is (paradoxically) a sophisticated kind of primitiveness.

The accentuation of certain features in a figure often leads to the disregard of others, so that realistic representation is gradually abandoned. It is eventually replaced by symbolism, where a few characteristic traits suffice to convey the idea of an object, and may be stylized and transformed into conventional signs. In an extreme stage of development an isolated claw and a single wing may symbolize a raven (Fig. 45). But here we have already left the realm of naturalistic art and entered the sphere of abstract or conventional design.

Geometric forms are found both in decorative drawings and as

FIG. 3. 'X-ray Drawings.'

1. Pencil drawing representing a fish, from New Ireland (after E. Stephan): (a = head; b = dorsal fin; c = ventral fin; d = caudal fin; e = scales; f = spine and bones; g = eatable flesh; h = intestines.)

2. Pencil drawing by an Alaska Eskimo, representing a white whale (after H. Himmelheber, *Eskimo-Künstler*). Artist: Timothy of Nunivak Island.

3. Detail from a monumental wall painting in a house of the Kwakiutl Indians, Brit. Columbia. Mythological scene: a wolf (showing vertebrae) swallowing a human figure. (After L. Adam. *Nordwestamerikanische Indianerkunst*, pl. 25.)

patterns in textiles and basketry. The variety of these patterns is endless, though some of them, such as zigzag bands, frets, triangles, various types of crosses, etc., are frequent among altogether different peoples. They are, in fact, almost universal, and do not necessarily indicate any historical relation between the several arts in which they occur. We find four-square frets, for example, not only in ancient Greece and China, but also among South American Indians, Melanesians, African Bantus, and other African peoples. But by a certain combination of patterns, how-

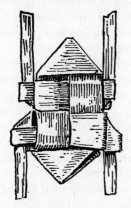 

FIG. 4. Animal Figures in Plaited Basket-work.
(a) Toad; (b) Deer. Bakaïrí Indians, Upper Xingú area, Central Brazil.

ever common the individual elements may be, the artist produces a specific style of marked national colouring which makes it possible for us to ascribe a decorated object to a certain people and often to a certain period. This, of course, holds good for the study of art in general, and is not confined to primitive art.[12]

In many cases decorative patterns are supposed to symbolize the material objects – animals, plants, etc. – after which they are named. The connexion between the pattern and its symbolic meaning arises in two ways: either by the deliberate simplification of a representative design, as in North-west America, or else, conversely, by the observation of incidental resemblances between the geometric pattern and its naturalistic interpretation.

In the decorative designs of the Indian tribes on the upper Xingú of the Matto Grosso (Brazil) two peculiar patterns are predominant: a simple equilateral black triangle called *uluri* and

41

a parallelogram with the four angles marked by small triangles. The latter pattern is called *mereshú*. This is the name of a fish which is almost square in shape, like a plaice. The four black triangles in the angles would then represent the head, dorsal fin, caudal fin, and ventral fin. *Ulurí* is the name given to the only dress worn by the women of the tribe, actually a hygienic protection against insects rather than a garment. It consists of a folded piece of palm leaf in the shape of an equilateral triangle, covering barely two square inches, and ending in a perineal band tied to a string which serves as a belt.

Professor Max Schmidt (late of the Ethnographical Museum at Berlin) has shown that both the *ulurí* and *mereshú* patterns come about incidentally in plaited basket-work, which is the principal craft among the Xingú tribes. They arise particularly from the use of light and dark strips of palm leaf crossing each other in various combinations. It is clear, then, that both names must have been applied to them later, after the association of ideas had been aroused by the appearance of the patterns.[13]

In some such way, the particular technique used by the craftsmen has often led to the development of symbolic design and of a specific ornamental style. Incidental resemblances can easily produce associations which give a susceptible artist the impulse either to elaborate a natural object into a more complete representation of something which it already resembles, or simply to take it as a model. It has been suggested that the first artists of the Stone Age may have been inspired by strange natural forms, such as curiously shaped stones or rock promontories.[14] One day in London an antiquary showed me a stone in the shape of a bull's head, about 2½ in. long, which he held to be an example of palaeolithic carving. This object actually had an amazing resemblance to a bull, but it proved on closer inspection to be a natural formation, and the resemblance was purely accidental.

Not only the form but also the colour of the material used in sculpture may influence the artist's inspiration. To take an example from a high cultural sphere: the Chinese, who have a special taste for working on hard stone of various colours (jade, agate, chalcedony, rose quartz, etc.), often adapt the incidental form and colouring of the stone in an incredibly skilful way to their carved vessels and figures. If by chance a piece of white agate reveals a red patch or vein, the stone-cutter may produce a white vase surrounded by a cherry spray, and he so arranges it that the red patch gives the effect of the cherry. Similarly, a green vein may inspire him to represent a frog or a lizard.

Generalizations are particularly dangerous when it comes to the suggestive effect of technical forms. Among the Indians of Guiana we find the same type of plaited basket work as in other

FIG. 5. The *mereshú* (I) and *ulurí* (II) patterns.
Upper Xingú area, Central Brazil.

parts of South America, but here dark and light strips are deliberately and very skilfully arranged to represent animal figures (usually jaguars and snakes), so that it is no longer a question of accidental effects and their subsequent interpretation.

'An appreciation of the effects of artificial decoration to a certain degree extends beyond the limits of the human race. ... There are various birds which love to adorn their nests or bowers with various bright objects – shells, paper, bleached bones, silver spoons and other articles foreign to the elements required for mere construction.' But this is 'no true operation of the intellect which characterizes the use of decoration as a fine art'.[15] Similarly, man in his earliest uncultured state may have been impressed by beauty as it occurs in nature, long before he started to produce artistic forms himself or to imitate the lines and figures

43

occurring in his natural environment. Certain primitive peoples of to-day have an obvious appreciation of the beauties of nature, and there are some tribes in Melanesia who, in their decorative art, attempt to depict even such phenomena as the rainbow and the luminosity of the sea by symbolic ornaments, and not in a naturalistic style.[16]

For the full appreciation of a work of art it should be seen as far as possible in the setting for which it was created. This is particularly true of primitive art because of its strange and altogether different cultural background. The statue of an ancestor or of a deity under African conditions of light, and intended to remain always in the gloom of a shrine or temple, cannot be expected to produce the same effect when it has been removed from its original surroundings and displayed in a glass cabinet in a European room. Other light and shade effects may appear and they may be no less attractive, but they are not original and add a foreign note to the statue.

Some years ago I received a letter from the late H. V. Meyerowitz, then Art Supervisor at the Prince of Wales College, Achimota, Ghana, who has distinguished himself not only as a student of primitive art but also by his successful combination of native tradition with modern art education. Mr Meyerowitz wrote about a certain author – we will call him X – who some twenty years ago went into ecstasies about 'Cubism' in Negro sculpture: 'Poor X! if only he were here and could realize that his "cubism" is simply due to the conditions of deep shadow in which every sensible person works – so that one has to work in simple shapes if one wants to see anything at all – he would not have written all this pathetic nonsense.'

It is obvious that, for an analysis and balanced aesthetic appreciation of any art, especially of a foreign culture, we must try to detach ourselves, for the time being, from present-day tendencies or fashions in our own contemporary society. Instead we should try to understand the artists' intentions as they may be manifest in their works. It will be seen that, generally speaking, the African sculptor's intention was evidently to represent animals and human beings as he saw them in real life – that is to say, not only in their every-day life but also in the emotions of

44

social, religious, or magical ceremonies. In other words, the artist's vision and basic tendency are, or were, naturalistic. This is modified by an emphasis, or exaggeration, of those details which are particularly characteristic or in which the artist was interested. If we recognize their fundamentally naturalistic – sometimes almost caricaturistic – attitude, we must consider it in our critical appreciation of the work, and, in our judgement of value, we have to examine to which extent, and how, the artist has succeeded in the realization of his ambition. Now in the European civilization at the present time, there is – for various reasons – hardly any interest in naturalistic art, plastic or graphic, while it is impossible to attempt an unambiguous definition of "modern art" since it includes many different types of vision and design, most of which, however, may be described as opposed to naturalism. For this reason, modern artists will probably prefer the non-naturalistic, expressionistic forms of primitive art. But we have to bear in mind that art styles are not static but dynamic; in fact, art styles come and go and sometimes come again, perhaps in a modified form, according to a mysterious law of periodicity, which seems to be linked with, or conditioned by cultural changes generally, especially technical and social development. A well-known example is the sequence of an archaic, a classical, a baroque, a rococo, and perhaps other styles in the history of Chinese art. The conclusion is that the attitude towards naturalism, too, is bound to change one day. In the meantime, at least in a museum, the public, the art lover, and, of course, the historian of art should, at any time, view each type of art independently of current tendencies and even of personal taste. It is amusing that, in the younger generation of modern art lovers, the aversion to any truth to nature is so strong that we can speak of a kind of snobbery, which makes it impossible for the student to take the objective attitude of the historian and to appreciate the fact that a substantial part of African art is decidedly naturalistic and has to be recognized as such. This recognition does not mean that an expressionistic statuette or mask would not arouse a greater sensation in our mind and could not impress us as a deeper experience of the soul, or a more vigorous rhythm of form.

CHAPTER III

Utilitarian Art and 'L'art pour l'art'

IT is often said that primitive art differs from modern European art by being always utilitarian. But in primitive communities there are many fewer human activities than in more highly developed stages of civilization. The life of primitive people, and the social life of the past in general, was much more of a unity, its component parts much more closely interconnected, than in modern civilized communities. In the simpler social structure of primitive tribes the word utilitarian has an altogether different meaning. There is no clear contrast between 'art for art's sake' and art in the service of a practical purpose.

In any case, the definition of 'purpose' opens a wide field for speculation. There is a sense in which all portraits can be called utilitarian, and the innumerable European masterpieces representing Christian saints and heroes are not without their purpose. Is the beautiful wooden portrait statue of Shamba Bolongongo, the Bushongo King of the Congo State – incidentally one of the outstanding masterpieces of African art in the British Museum – any more utilitarian because this great African ruler is now revered by his people not only as a patron of the arts and crafts but also as a man of peace, who is said to have abolished the use in war of dangerous weapons and to have instructed his soldiers only to wound and not to kill?

Various forms of primitive art have, of course, a practical purpose. The desire to convey information led to pictographic art, and the urge to record important events developed into what may be called historical art. (Compare the prehistoric picture shown in Fig. 15, the Australian paintings in Figs. 7 and 38, and the North American Indian painting in Fig. 2. The latter, however, may perhaps be merely decorative.)

Pictographic art must be regarded as the preliminary stage of writing. The classical examples are the oldest kinds of Egyptian

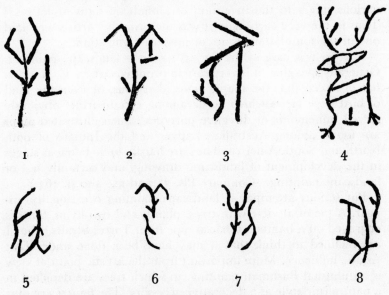

FIG. 6. Chinese Pictographs, after H. E. Gibson (see Note 25).
Shang period (2nd millennium B.C.).

1 = bull	2 = ram	3 = boar	4 = stag
5 = cow	6 = ewe	7 = ewe (other type)	8 = sory

FIG. 7. Bark drawing of a Kangaroo Hunt. Kakadu Tribe, Northern Territory of Australia. After Baldwin Spencer, *Native Tribes of the Northern Territory* (Fig. 87). By courtesy of Messrs Macmillan & Co. Ltd, London.

hieroglyphs and Chinese characters (Fig. 6). Pictographs are pictures or actual representations of objects. They are followed by ideograms, i.e., pictorial symbols which are used to suggest objects or abstract ideas. Further development leads through various stages to the invention of alphabetic signs or letters.[17] Thus in the very early days it was the primitive artists who laid one of the foundation stones of modern civilization.

A good test case of art for art's sake is landscape painting. Generally speaking, it is very rare in primitive art. A. C. Haddon has observed that the maps, plans, diagrams, or even the kind of bird's-eye views which occur among certain tribes obviously served 'mnemonic or directive purposes'. Such illustrated maps are found among Australian natives and the Indians of both North and South America. They are hardly to be taken as stages in the development of landscape drawing, and certainly not of landscape painting. (Compare Pls. 31 and 32, also p. 163.)

But serious attempts at landscape painting occasionally appear. A pictorial view with trees, plants, and two flying birds is engraved on a bamboo tobacco pipe from Torres Straits,[18] but I am inclined to think that it may have been done under East Asiatic influence. More important from the artistic point of view is an unusual Bushman painting, in which trees are depicted in a naturalistic style as a decorative accessory. The figures are thus detached from the plain rock, which is the usual ground of Bushman wall pictures, and the scene acquires the colouring of the specific locality.

Even in European art pure landscape painting is a comparatively recent development. The lack of it – apart from a few rare exceptions – cannot be regarded as a distinct feature of primitive art.

CHAPTER IV

Primitive Religion

RELIGIOUS emotion has always been one of the principal sources of artistic inspiration, and has provided the creative force for artistic productivity. Christian art covers almost two millennia, and includes various epochs and national art provinces. It involves the whole of Europe, a large part of the Near East, and considerable areas in other continents where Christianity has been spread by missionaries.

Buddhist art has also a large range of subdivisions, which have in common the symbols of the Buddhist doctrine and the characters of Buddhist legends, but differ from each other in their traditional styles. They cover the huge period from the time of the Indian king Aśoka (third century B.C.) to the beginning of the eighteenth century, and they still survive in millions of replicas.

The oldest of the religious arts still in existence is Hindu art. It is not only the art of the Aryan-speaking population but a syncretism between brahmanic art and the local or regional styles of various autochthonous ethnic groups. Since the discovery of primitive statuettes of Hindu gods and symbols, dating as far back as the early part of the third millennium B.C., in the excavations at Mohenjo-Daro in the Indus valley, it has been realized that this art is considerably older than was recently supposed.

Other principal provinces of art were predominantly, if not entirely, of a religious character, as for instance the art of Babylon and Assyria, Egypt, Greece, Mexico, Central America, and Colombia. Only the art of ancient Peru was to any large extent secular. The relation between art and religion is thus a universal feature, and by no means limited to primitive cultures. Moreover, the archaic stages of highly developed arts usually retain marked primitive traits.

In the primitive sphere, we must first of all become used to the idea of religion in a far wider sense than is understood by the monotheist creed of our own world.

Associated with the earliest forms of religion, but even with the ritual of highly developed religious systems, is magic. Magic is based on the belief in supernatural forces intervening in the lives of men and wholly or partially determining their fate. As primitive man is not yet capable of objective observation of the causal connexion between phenomena, his belief in magic may be conceived as a pre-scientific interpretation of the connexion between cause and effect. It is true that these supernatural (imaginary) forces can (or, in some cases, must) first of all be set in motion by men. But there are other supernatural forces controlled by gods and demons, which can be evoked or resisted through ritual – prayer, miming, or sacrifice.

A belief in divinities is by no means essential as a basis for religion. We first find gods, especially those conceived as having a physical form, in cultures which no longer rank as primitive. Before men believed in individual gods, they believed in natural forces or superior beings, which they thought of as manifest in sun, moon, fire, storm, or rain. It was only later that they attempted to portray them in images. The oldest Aryan Indians, whose religion is to be traced in the Veda, worshipped invisible gods. Individual deities did not appear until a later date. The Hindu pantheon of to-day is therefore of varying origin, and Śiva, who has become a figure of surpassing importance, is a comparatively recent addition.

The few really primitive races of the modern world are culturally thousands of years older than even the Aryan Indians of 1500 B.C. The Pygmies and the natives of Tierra del Fuego believe in an invisible 'supreme being', the author of man and of civilization, who rules over the destinies of the world. Professor Wilhelm Schmidt sees in this a proof that monotheism was characteristic of the first eras of humanity, and that all human creeds are a deviation or degeneration from it.

This theory is, however, not universally accepted. It is doubtful whether a parallel can be drawn between the supreme being of the present-day primitive races and our idea of God. It is also not quite certain that even most primitive races to-day are properly representative of the earliest stages of human development. It is impossible to say whether the first man, emerging (as we have always been led to suppose) from a pre-human stage, was already infused with an instinctive belief in the existence of God, before the various experiences and misinterpretations of natural events and the many fears and anxieties of an unintelligible world gave rise to a belief in magic, demons, etc.

When we come to the less highly developed civilizations which fall within the limits of historical research we are able to study their religious forms, and to reconstruct fairly accurately some thousands of years of their religious development. It becomes clear that the belief in divinities does not take the place of magic, but that magic appears in various forms in all communities, even in our own civilized world. Where a highly developed dogmatic religion has evolved, magic is opposed to religion. It is no longer needed to satisfy certain metaphysical demands, and it degenerates into mere superstition.

Frequently, however, magic is combined with a belief in divinities, particularly in the so-called Agrarian religions. Art then enters the service of ritual. It is used in magical ceremonies for the purpose of humouring the gods, and of begging or even compelling them to grant fertility to the fields.

One example can be found in the religion of the Pueblo Indians of New Mexico, which has been described in an exhaustive monograph by Elsie Clews Parsons.[20] The Hopi Indians, who believe in a pantheon of gods and demons, perform a number of rituals which are to all intents and purposes sympathetic magic. They go through certain mimic performances which symbolize a desired result, in the conviction that in this way the actual result will be brought about. One of their agricultural deities is reproduced in Pl. 37 (b). He has a design on his cheeks with curved lines to represent rain-clouds, serpentine lines winding upwards to symbolize lightning, and vertical strokes below to show the falling rain.

Many races believe in culture-heroes, whom they suppose to have brought fire, water, or other indispensable blessings to man. Frequently these culture-heroes are treated as gods – that is, worshipped through ritual. But in other cases no divine attributes are ascribed to them, and they are regarded as great men of the past, and sometimes as ancestors of a particular tribe. Yet, whether as gods or not, these culture-heroes usually play the principal part in a whole cycle of myths or legends. A dramatic performance of these legends is often given at feast-times, and various artistic forms are pressed into service. There is dramatic art itself (as in the mystery plays of antiquity), there is instrumental and vocal music, and there are various kinds of plastic art – dance-masks, carved rattles, dancing-shields, and ritual painting of the face and body.

The distinction between religious and profane legends is not always clear. When heroes and legendary figures are not actually worshipped, but merely represented from time to time in an historical celebration, the religious significance may be lost altogether. Very often there are a whole host of subsidiary figures – good and evil spirits which play a part as masks in the ceremony, either alone or in conjunction with divinities and heroes.

The principal territories where manifold mask representations of this kind are to be found are North-west America, West Africa, Ceylon, Melanesia, and Tibet (where Lamaism is amalgamated with the old Bon religion). Even at the present day some old heathen customs still exist side by side with Christianity. In Alpine districts, such as the Tyrol and the regions of the Upper Rhine, masks of devils and the ceremonies connected with them still survive.

On Pl. 35 (a) we see a mask from the Bilxula tribe of North America – the head of a gigantic eagle, which, according to the belief of these Indians, produces thunder through the beating of its mighty wings, and is therefore called the thunder-bird. This is an excellent example of North-west American sculpture. There are two styles, one naturalistic, the other strictly traditional with a number of heraldic forms. The piece reproduced harmonizes both.

Pl. 14(b) shows an entirely different type: a benevolent demon from the Kelamantan tribe of Borneo called Bolli Atap, and used as a charm to keep off sickness. It is one of the most impressive works of primitive sculpture in our series of illustrations. Although one arm and one foot are missing, the torso that remains

is infused with an incredibly rhythmical movement. It is reproduced here from two angles so as to give as complete a view as
possible. Its aesthetic charm depends on the fact that it is a representation of a supernatural being and its movement has a magic
significance.

With primitive works of art, which originate in a world so entirely foreign to us, a knowledge of their meaning is essential. Sir
Michael Sadler has pointed out that we Europeans can only
appreciate 'the strange beauty of the masterpieces of West
African sculpture' if we 'put ourselves as near as may be in the
place of those for whom the artist carved his figure'. This is only
possible if we make use of the key to the symbolical and hieratic
meanings of primitive art which has been supplied by the students
of primitive religion.[21] Without such a knowledge, the European,
though he may not be left entirely unimpressed, is bound to make
his own personal interpretation, which in the case of religious
figures is usually a misinterpretation.

Another type of primitive religion closely related to art is ancestor worship. Statues representing ancestors are held to be the
habitat of the souls of the dead, and are an object of worship with
many races. Offerings are brought to them to feed them in the
other world and to retain their favour. Many primitive peoples
hold a prejudice about the dead and try in this way to prevent
them from harming those still living. Ancestor worship is, or was,
practised in all parts of the world, but in West Africa, New
Guinea, Melanesia, and North-west America the sculpture of ancestor figures reached a particularly high stage of development.

A deep respect for the forefathers, however, is not always connected with a religious cult. Some ancestor figures are merely
memorials. In very rare cases they have developed into real portraits with individual features. The Kwakiutl tribe on Vancouver
Island and on the mainland opposite possess wooden statues of
ancestors handed down from father to son. While the old tribal
culture still existed they had a particularly strict property law.
When a man died, his son inherited not only his material belong-
ings, but also his name, rank, crest, and even his clan legends.
The son then personified entire ancestry right back to the chieftain who won or established the name, the crest, and the legends

of the clan. There is a story of a chief delivering a speech to the Indians assembled at one of the winter ceremonials. He placed himself behind a hollow statue and spoke through the hole representing the mouth, thus giving the impression that it was the ancestor himself who was speaking.

Then there is the question of *mana*. *Mana* is a Melanesian word first recorded by R. H. Codrington, one of the pioneers of modern anthropology, but later more generally applied, and recognized by R. R. Marett as a universal element of primitive religion. It has been described as a specific type of supernatural power analogous to the soul-substance which is also a feature of primitive metaphysics. It is a sort of spiritual fluid without which no magical or supernatural result can be obtained.[21] A medicine-man or *shaman** must have *mana* to carry on his occupation. He can only obtain it, first by being predestined for it, and then by submitting himself to certain rituals.

But *mana* can also belong to material objects. Possibly the suggestive power radiating from many strong personalities is felt to be supernatural and is interpreted as *mana*. The figure of a god or demon has to be infused with this supernatural power, so that it is fit to fulfil a religious function only after it has been 'consecrated'. In West Africa a wooden fetish must be ceremonially smeared with colour before it ceases to be a mere carving and is looked on as an inspired object. In Tibet and China statues of the various Buddhas and Bodhisattvas do not acquire their proper religious significance until their eyes and mouth have been painted and their interior filled with small rolls of paper or silk inscribed with fragments of the sacred writings.

Even a so-called *fetish*, which is believed to be inhabited by a spirit, is ultimately nothing but an object endowed with *mana*. Anthropologists of to-day are inclined to eliminate fetish and fetishism from their vocabulary, since the words suggest so many different meanings that it is better to abolish them altogether.

---

* In Anthropology, the word *shaman* now denotes especially the medicine-men of Siberian, North-west American, and Eskimo tribes. It is derived from an ancient Central Asiatic language, Sogdian. The Sanskrit word *śramana* is related to it. A *shaman* is supposed to be endowed with supernatural gifts, acting as a mediator between man and the supernatural world.

The institution of *totemism*, which is scattered over a large part of the earth, has both a religious and a social significance. The word 'totem' comes from the tribal group of Algonkin in North America. Its approximate meaning is supernatural friend or helper.

Most primitive races live very close to nature. They know the characteristics of the animal world, for their own subsistence depends essentially on animals. They begin to regard the animals not as inferior creatures, but as equals, and to judge them according to the same standards as themselves. They see the qualities of their own nature as common also to the animal world.

Most primitive men have no conception of 'humanity' as embracing all races and tribes, but think of it only in terms of their own tribe. At any rate, this view must have been fairly widespread at the time when their languages assumed their present form. The majority refer to their own tribe by words which simply mean 'man'. The various species of animals are tribes and peoples – the bear tribe, the wolf tribe, the eagle tribe, and so on.

Moreover, these animals have many qualities – strength, speed, cunning – which man both fears and admires. Admiration leads to the desire to imitate, and to the appropriation of individual names derived from the animals which display the quality admired.

The aborigines of Australia must frequently have asked themselves, 'How can I learn to run and jump as well as the kangaroo?' Eventually the men of the clan, who always clung together, may have thought, 'We will turn ourselves into kangaroos'. With this idea in mind they would assemble at the place where they had often seen kangaroos gather. In time they would begin to believe that they were actually relatives – say, cousins – of the kangaroo family. Consequently they would have to treat the kangaroos as kinsmen. However much they had relished kangaroo stew in the past, there would no longer be any question of killing a kangaroo, much less of eating it. Other clans would do the same thing with other animals, until the whole tribe was divided into groups who considered themselves cousins of various animal species.

This explanation is admittedly sheer conjecture. A number of different theories have been put forward for the origin of totemism, and it has been pointed out that most peoples who believe in totems do not consider them as relatives, but only as friends.[22] But whatever the exact process may have been, it is the admiration of the animal's qualities which leads to the respect almost always shown to it when it becomes a totem.

The totem, then, is not one individual animal, but the species as a whole. It is supposed to be somehow superior to man, but it is not a god. There are no sacrifices. The most common features of the behaviour of the tribe towards the totem are a prohibition of the species as food, and a certain respect for the animal in its natural state. But there are cases where these forms are not observed, or have fallen into disuse.

The origin of totemism has long been a problem for anthropologists and sociologists. The literature is voluminous, but Sir James Frazer's *Totemism and Exogamy* remains the standard work. The practice appears in so many different forms all over the world that it has been suggested recently that it would be better not to speak of it as a general concept at all. Nevertheless, all its manifestations have one common element: a belief in the existence of intimate and special relations between a human group and a class of animals (or even of other objects such as plants or minerals). Beyond this, generalizations are apt to be misleading. The belief that the totem is the ancestor of the clan, for instance, is by no means universal. The origin of totemism can never be definitely ascertained. My own view is that the wide variations can best be explained by assuming a different origin in different parts of the world.

Where a tribe is divided into a number of totem clans, the members of each group may decorate their bodies with paintings or tattooings representing or symbolizing their totem. They may personify their totems by wearing masks and performing ceremonial dances, which are either sympathetic magic or simply dramatizations of clan legends.

Marriage within the totem group is strictly prohibited, and the wife must always be taken from another group. This institution, exogamy, appears illogical: common sense would suggest that

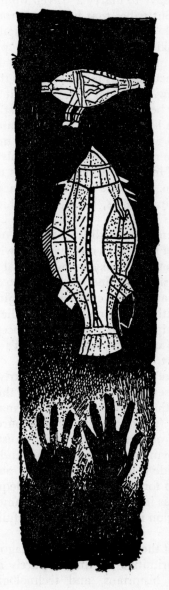

FIG. 8. Bark Drawing representing a pigmy goose, a Barramunda fish (both 'X-ray' drawings showing backbone, intestines, etc.). and stencilled hands. Kakadu tribe, Northern Territory of Australia. After Baldwin Spencer (Fig. 88). By courtesy of Messrs Macmillan & Co. Ltd, London.

a 'raven man' would have to marry a 'raven woman' instead of a 'bear', 'wolf', etc. But tribes that have a totemistic organization are not necessarily incapable of logical thought. There is a theory that the thinking of primitive man is 'pre-logical', as shown in his belief in an altogether irrational relationship between cause and effect, such as magic; but this theory confuses the process of thinking with the aim which it has in view. Primitive man, simply because he is human, must try to find an explanation for all the happenings in his environment. He does not know the physical and physiological which modern science has discovered, and he can account for them only by irrational explanation. His belief in magic and witchcraft is to some extent a substitute for science. It is due to his ignorance of real facts and his belief in imaginary facts, but it has nothing to do with his mental processes as such.

Primitive logic, then, is not different from our own. The psychological process of linking an observed fact with an imaginary cause is the same as that of linking it with a real cause grasped by scientific study. A similar principle applies to primitive art. All the strange beings and forms created by primitive artists are the outcome of primitive imagination and belief, but not of a different mental equipment or a different process of thought. In this, primitive art (and incidentally children's art) is fundamentally unlike the art of neurotics.

A large proportion of primitive art, particularly sculpture, is religious in the widest sense of the word. Besides this, there is the art which arises from the desire to convey information or to record interesting events (pictographic art), and purely decorative art, such as geometric ornamentation, which must have originated in the simple enjoyment of attractive lines and forms. But in general the religious side is so important that a purely aesthetic approach, restricted to formal qualities, is inadequate. It is Sir Michael Sadler who has insisted that a certain amount of knowledge of primitive religion is indispensable for a full appreciation of primitive art.

It is unfortunate that there should be any antagonism between those who approach primitive art from a purely aesthetic view and the ethnologists, historians, and technological students.

58

Mr J. J. Sweeney, for instance, suggests that 'in the end ... it is not the tribal characteristics of Negro art, nor its strangeness that are interesting. It is its plastic qualities. Picturesque or exotic features as well as historical and ethnographic considerations have a tendency to blind us to its true worth. This was realized at once by its earliest amateurs. To-day, with the advances we have made during the last thirty years in our knowledge of Africa, it has become an even graver danger. Our approach must be held conscientiously in quite another direction. It is the vitality of the forms of Negro art that should speak to us, the unerring emphasis on the essential, the consistent, three-dimensional organization of structural planes in architectural sequences.' [23] No doubt this judgement on the aesthetic merits of African sculpture will be very helpful for those who have no innate susceptibility to art. Socrates taught us that virtue may be acquired – why not, then, the aesthetic enjoyment of a work of art? But can it be achieved by deliberate disregard of the cultural background and especially of the religious meaning?

If we look, for example, at the 'Venus of Willendorf' (Fig. 13), would not a merely formal approach leave us completely helpless, and is not our sensation entirely different when we learn that this is not a caricature of a fat woman but a goddess of motherhood?

CHAPTER V

Primitive Art and Psycho-analysis

THE clue to the mysteries of the subconscious is the dream. In the dream, the mind can 'let itself go', free from the fetters of conventional rules of behaviour, the burden of inhibitions, but also temporarily deprived of the benefit of reasoning.

Man has always taken a keen interest in dreams, but the attitude towards dreams has not always been the same throughout the ages and cultural stages. The modern psycho-analytical approach, since Freud, is rational: once you have untwisted the maze of your dream world and exposed the causality of your emotions, there is nothing to worry about. The dream is essentially a reflection of our own personality and experience, although the psycho-analyst has to discover a symbolic significance in dreamed figures and events before he can identify them with phenomena as they actually are. A different attitude is represented by what we may call the Oriental approach, which is best illustrated by the interpretation of Nebuchadnezzar's dream in the Book of Daniel. The Oriental conception of dreams is entirely symbolic, but here the significance is referred to the future rather than the past, and the symbolic paraphrase ascribed to events coming from outside, and thus not to the psychic life of the individual. We are principally concerned with the third attitude, that of primitive man. While symbolism plays an important part in primitive art, the primitive interpretation of dreams is not symbolic; in fact, we cannot really speak of an interpretation, because primitive man regards dreams as a reality. We have seen in the preceding chapter that primitive man makes no distinction between real and imaginary facts, and this holds good, not only for dreams, but also for illusions and hallucinations, which play an important part in the experiences of youths during the initiation ritual. Among many tribes of North America, a young man who was desirous of obtaining a guardian spirit had to spend some considerable time in the forest, living there quite by himself, fasting and concentrating upon his sole object, to meet his guardian spirit. Gradually his senses became overexcited, until he eventually reached a stage where he saw, or heard, real things amplified, or otherwise in a different light (illusions); or he might even imagine figures, or voices, which were not really there (hallucination). Thus he would imagine that an owl talked to him, or the like. Among the Plains Indians, these imaginary adventures did not reflect upon art of any kind, but on the north-west coast, similar experiences stimulated representative sculpture to a high degree. Here the large number of mythical beings, represented by masks, or in the wall paintings, and associated with their individual legends, songs, and dances, can often be traced back to more or less imaginary adventures of Indians. Once a mask had been carved for the first time by the man who met the spirit, or supernatural being, and introduced his ritual, it became incorporated in the hierarchy of secret societies and made its appearance periodically during the winter ceremonies. The mask-dancer was not regarded as an actor, but as the personification of the spirit himself. To the primitive mind the mythical world is a reality. On the north-west coast of America, however, this does not mean that the Indians lived in a mythical atmosphere all the time. On the contrary, the rituals were confined to a certain period, whereas the summer season was profane. The carver of a ceremonial mask was able to produce altogether different, profane carvings if he wanted to do so.

An entirely different mental attitude of a primitive artist was observed among the Australian aborigines by Mr C. P. Mountford some years ago.[91] There was an aboriginal boy living at a White settlement who used to make pencil drawings on paper, depicting practically everything he saw in his environment, such as European tools, cars, aeroplanes. These drawings were very similar to those done by European children. Later, however, the boy 'went bush' and became initiated according to the customs of his tribe. Then the experiences of his initiation 'wrought a major psychological change in the youth'. This became manifest in the drawings made by him after his return. From then on he no longer represented European persons or objects, but exclusively objects associated with the tribal life of the aborigines – that is to say, ritual objects and patterns. This development is in agreement with Professor A. P. Elkin's description of the effect of initiation in his book *Aboriginal Men of High Degree* (Sydney, 1946), p. 11: 'In an unforgettable ceremonial manner, he is taken from the camp and scenes of his irresponsible early years. He becomes the subject of a series of rites, extending with intervals over several years.' – 'He "dies" to the former life of childhood and of ignorance of esoteric knowledge, and "rises" or is "reborn" to a new life. The latter is not merely adult life, for which he has meanwhile been disciplined and instructed. It is much more: it is a life of knowledge and power. At the end of the ritual journey, with its trials, loneliness, "death", revelations, and rejoicing, he can say: "Whereas previously I was blind to the significance of the seasons, of natural species, of heavenly bodies and of man himself, now I begin to see; and whereas before I did not understand the secret of life, now I begin to know."'

Among many primitive peoples the initiation ceremonies of age-classes and secret societies reveal a symbolic interpretation of biological facts and provide an outlet for instincts which in civilized communities are kept down by inhibitions anchored in our moral principles and sanctioned by tradition, custom, law, and education. Rules of moral conduct in primitive society are different from our own unwritten code; nevertheless they are often very strict. The sexual life of primitive peoples is more closely tied up with the social life of the community than in civilized countries.

Eckart von Sydow has suggested a sexual background to the arts of primitive peoples, as a parallel to Freud's theory of sexual complexes underlying primitive institutions and customs.[24] But he goes too far, and reads sexual ideas into objects which have obviously nothing to do with sex. He admits that he does not agree with all the theories of Freud's school, but he has not been able to avoid its characteristic mistake of exaggerating the part played by sexual elements in the subconscious mind. It is absurd to see a phallic symbol in every long-shaped object, or an emblem of motherhood in every semi-globular hut.

Most primitive men do not regard any part of the body as indecent. The genital organs are considered as natural emblems of sex, and their representation in sculptures and drawings has nothing to do with obscenity. The primitive 'X-ray' method described in Chapter II, whereby the artist represents details which he cannot see but knows to be there, is generally employed by primitive draughtsmen in portraiture. Both Karl von den

FIG. 9. Pencil Drawings by South American Indians. After Th. Koch-Gruenberg. (*a*) An Indian of the Hianákoto-Umàua tribe, N.W. Brazil. By a member of this tribe. (*b*) A flying bird (Karará); drawn by a Kobéua Indian, N.W. Brazil.

Steinen and Th. Koch-Gruenberg had this experience among altogether different tribes of Indians in South America, when the natives tried to portray their European visitors and marked their genital organs by crude symbolic forms. To them this was simply the natural emblem of manhood which, consequently, could not be omitted. This is also the significance of certain details in Fig. 9(*a*). Even in higher civilizations we find a similar frankness and naïvety. For example, the earliest known Chinese characters, used during the Shang dynasty (1766–1123 B.C.), which were still to some extent true pictographs, had certain symbols indicating male and female (Fig. 6). The forms are very simple. The male consists of two strokes, one horizontal and one vertical; the female of a curved vertical line with an attached short stroke set at an angle. The symbols appear in early inscriptions at the side of the ideogram, which may thus denote either a bull or a cow, a ram or a ewe, a dog or a bitch, etc.[25]

The attitude of primitive man would not be sufficiently well characterized by the formula *naturalia non sunt turpiai* since, to him, those *naturalia* are most essential. Still, they would not be unnecessarily emphasized. Thus we find, for example in plastic portraiture in West Africa as well as in the Sepik area of New Guinea, naturalistic statuettes carved in full details, but subsequently dressed as is the custom of the tribe, in a loin-cloth. When it comes to representations of mythical beings, however, certain organs and functions of the body may have a symbolic significance. This symbolism is sometimes obvious; for example, in the mask dances of certain agricultural tribes genital organs are represented as symbols of fertility. Or a plastic representation of childbirth occurs as a head-gear of a mask in the Congo basin (among the Bayaka, if I am not mistaken). A more cryptic symbolism of *sexualia* is frequent in the plastic art of the Sepik and Ramu areas of New Guinea and in northern and central New Ireland. It is here that we find hermaphroditic figures which have given rise to various speculations. They have been interpreted as cosmogonic symbols of the male and female principles as the creative forces of the universe. A fascinating but much-criticized book on the mythological significance of the 'bisexual being' has been written by J. Winthuis. It goes without saying that a correct analysis of symbolic works of primitive art cannot be derived from the sculptures or drawings alone, but requires the study of the illustrated myth, or legend.

The first to combine the psycho-analytical approach with anthropological field work has been Dr Géza Róheim. So far, however, his researches have been mainly devoted to customs, rituals, and myths, but only incidentally to primitive art.[26]

CHAPTER VI

Social Implications

HOWEVER much indebted an artist may be to his environment for impressions, ideas, and technical methods, his creative act is something altogether personal. But once a work of art is in existence, society alone can provide the public who will make use of it. The greater part of primitive art production is designed for practical application in the social life of the community. It furnishes the formal arrangement of design for a large number of co-operative activities – religious rites, warfare, politics, work, and sport. In this sense, art, of course, includes music, dancing, poetry, and drama.

It is remarkable that a large proportion of decorative art is a monopoly of women. Among the North American Plains Indians it is the women who prepare the buffalo hides for pictoral decoration, and who carry out the conventional geometric designs, while the men are responsible for representational paintings such as the example shown in Fig. 2. The same division prevails among the otherwise entirely different tribes on the north-west coast. A number of important crafts, such as weaving and pottery, were introduced by women. It was natural, therefore, that they should acquire a monopoly of the conventional forms of decoration associated with them. Sculpture, on the other hand, is everywhere the monopoly of men.

The older schools of anthropology held the view that in primitive society there was practically no individual life at all. Individuals functioned simply as members of a social unit. Recently, however, it has been established that there is a good deal of individual activity in primitive society. There is documentary proof from various parts of the world that individual artists were appreciated for their talent and achieved fame even beyond the limits of their own tribe. Craftsmen and artists on the Ivory Coast, for example, sometimes accept and train apprentices.[27] There are

Fig. 10. Engraved Ornament from a Bamboo Pipe. Baram River, Sarawak. British Museum, 1900, 873.

records of individual artists on the north-west coast of America, especially among the Haida in the Queen Charlotte Islands. The name of Edensaw, inherited through several generations of sculptors and draughtsmen, is outstanding in the history of Haida art.[28]

The north-west coast, before the indigenous cultures were disintegrated by European civilization, appears to have been the birthplace of whole nations of artists. Talented sculptors in wood and other materials are found not only among the Haida, but also in the neighbouring tribes – Tlingit, Tsimshian, and Kwakiutl.

This region provides an interesting example also of a number of artists co-operating in the production of single works, namely, totem poles. (The largest of these in the British Museum is reproduced on Pl. 33(*b*).) When a totem pole was erected, the trunk of a huge cedar was divided into as many sections as there were figures, and the execution of each figure was allotted to a separate artist.

Division of labour between the different sexes and age-groups is found to some extent in most primitive communities. In more advanced stages various separate occupations and social classes develop. But in all primitive tribes there is greater homogeneity than among the citizens of a highly civilized community. There is no diversity of religions. All the adult members of the tribe take part in the same ceremonies. The work of tilling the soil, harvesting, sailing, fishing, hunting, etc., is co-operative. Usually (but not always) the land is held in common, and the rights of cultivation, grazing, and hunting are communal. Everyone is familiar with the formalities of public life, and knows exactly what is going on in the tribe.

There is one important exception. The activities and mysteries of secret societies are reserved to those who have been selected for membership, and who have undergone the elaborate and often painful ceremonies of initiation. The uninitiated, and especially the women, are strictly forbidden to attend the secret meetings. They are not even allowed to look at ritual objects, such as masks, bull-roarers (Fig. 39), etc. Sometimes, however, the women have their own secret societies.

So vital is the necessity for guarding the mysteries, that here and there special organizations or clubs are instituted for the sole purpose of keeping away the uninitiated. It is in the secret societies that most of those terrifying masks originate which are largely responsible for the popular prejudice that primitive art is essentially grotesque and repulsive.

The co-operative character of primitive society is most clearly seen in the periodic performance of ceremonies by all the members of a tribe, or group within the tribe. The winter ceremonies of the Kwakiutl tribe of Vancouver Island and the mainland opposite are an outstanding example. The tribal organization is suspended during the winter season to provide full freedom for traditional performances of all descriptions.

Some of the dances and songs are imitative of the movements and voices of animals. They are designed either to attract game by witchcraft or to put a spell on dreaded beasts of prey. These are objects which concern the whole community, and this type of magic dance is not confined to any individual group.

The mimetic dances peculiar to the separate totem clans are similarly examples of co-operative expression. Myths and legends, common to the whole tribe, may be dramatized by any of the groups with or without a special application to the group itself. Whether the dances are performed by the whole attendance or by individuals with the others acting as chorus, the mass character is obviously the same.

Any mass movement, however, requires rhythm as its ordering principle. The rhythm is not merely a technical expedient. It is something at once fundamental and irrational, to which primitive peoples – so much more irrational than civilized men – appear to have a more direct approach.[29] Travellers and anthropological field workers bear witness to the predominant part that rhythm plays in primitive performances. The same delight in rhythmical arrangement comes out strikingly in the contours of wooden vessels and pottery (Fig. 35; Pl. 7 (a); Pl. 23), the ornaments of pottery and textiles (Figs. 46, 48; Pl. 18 (b)), and the form of representational sculptures (Pls. 14 (b), 26).[30]

Art – and thus primitive art also – has its economic side. A work of art is potentially at least an article of trade, and may establish a relation between producers and consumer. Among most primitive tribes artistic production is not a permanent or exclusive occupation. Craftsmen and artists work only occasionally, and for their own requirements. Even where we find professional artists, they are at the same time farmers (West Africa), fishermen (Northwest America), etc. An art or craft offers the possibility of obtaining other commodities by barter or such primitive currency as shells, knives, or blankets. On the Ivory Coast a young man may become a carver purely in order to make enough money to get married.

A work of art may be made to order, like the fetish figures in West Africa. In this case the purchaser would be an individual customer. But we also find industries engaged in the mass production and distribution of such things as textiles, basketry, pottery, carved and decorated wooden trays, etc. The exchange of these goods may be confined to the members of one tribe; but it may also take place over a distance, so that the production of craftsmanship and art typical of one district may be found among totally different tribes. It has been proved by archaeological research that even in prehistoric times, commercial relations extended over distances as wide as from the Mediterranean to Sweden. Glass beads from ancient Egypt and other parts of the Mediterranean area found their way almost all over Africa, Europe, and Asia. New Guinea and the neighbouring islands undertook the mass production of certain wood carvings, especially wooden vessels, for export. It is a mistake to assume that the European demand for 'curios' is entirely responsible for these native industries and for a consequent degeneration of indigenous arts and crafts, though in many cases this is undoubtedly true.

Finally, there exists, strangely enough, a relation between primitive art and primitive law. Property, as Huntington Cairns puts it, is 'basically conceived of as a part of the personality or self; it is a relation between the person and the thing. Something that the individual has touched or handled becomes imbued with a portion of his personality.'[31] The creative act of manufacturing an object brings about an intimate bond between the maker and his work, involving the right to prevent others from putting their hands to the object, because it is part of its owner's personal sphere, or an emanation of his personality. This feeling is strongest where works of art are distinguished by marked individual features. Some primitive peoples have developed a high appreciation of the artist's rights in the product of his own creative skill, and this is especially strong when the works concerned are of a religious character. Many of the beautiful boat-shaped wooden bowls made in Tami Island (off the north coast of New Guinea) bear the engraved mark of the maker in the centre of the bottom.

Among the North-west American Indians the various clans are distinguished by crests, clan legends, and songs. These they regard as their property because they inherited them from their ancestors who invented or introduced them. Usually the elder of the clan or family is invested with the ownership during his lifetime (see p. 53). The ownership of a crest implies the right to use it, and the right to carve, say, a new mask representing it. Property in legends and dances is correspondingly exclusive. Nobody but the owner is allowed to tell the legend: nobody but the owner may perform the dance. It was even possible to sell or bequeath such property. In other words, we are faced with a well-developed copyright system among a group of tribes who practised cannibalism as a ritual up to the eighties of last century. Other primitive peoples, such as the natives of the eastern Torres Straits Islands and the Central Eskimos, have developed incorporeal property on the same or very similar lines.[32]

There is no indication of an historical connexion between these primitive institutions and their civilized parallels. It would seem that human society feels an innate need for the legal protection of works of art both material and non-material. Its psychological source is the belief in magical ties between man and the products of his activities. But when such belief is sanctioned by custom it has already been incorporated in the sphere of law.

CHAPTER VII

Peasant Art

BEFORE the introduction of European civilization, the majority of primitive tribes were either hunters, fishermen, or peasants, and many tribes combined these occupations. Those who lived on an agricultural basis developed a belief in gods and demons of fertility, or in magic rites designed to secure rich harvests and to deter evil spirits. The art of such tribes is usually a reflection and practical application of their agricultural beliefs (Pl. 37 (*b*)). Similarly, fishing tribes, like the Indians of the north-west coast of America, developed what we may call a marine art, incorporating all the creatures, real and fabulous, with which their imagination populated the sea (Fig. 11).

By 'peasant art', however, we usually mean the art of the peasant population in the civilized countries of to-day. Compared with sophisticated art in the urban centres it is apparently 'primitive', and no doubt it has preserved from remote heathen times a number of genuinely primitive traits. This applies to decorative rather than representative art. Professor Strzygowski of the University of Vienna has made a special study of the various ornamental styles in use among the modern peasant populations of Europe and Asia, and has traced back their historical connexions to very early periods.

The bulk of modern peasant art, however, is composed of entirely different elements. Reflections of the religious art of the towns are to be found in even the remotest villages. They take the form of replicas of sacred images – in Europe, images of Christ, the Virgin, and the various saints; in Asia, of Buddha, the innumerable Bodhisattvas, or the deities of Hinduism. Direct copies of works of art from the central churches and temples found their way into simple village shrines. Further copies were then made, not from the originals, but from the replicas. In time the peasant craftsmen began to paint or carve images with the aid of their imagination. Thus a peasant art developed displaying primitive characteristics, but actually derivative – Professor Kroeber calls it 'derivative primitive art'.[33]

Examples are to be found in almost every country, but they are particularly common on the Upper Rhine and in the German and Austrian Alps. Wood carvings in the local churches in these districts often provide admirable examples of Gothic, Renaissance, and Baroque art.

Fig. 11. Painting representing a Dog-fish. Haida Indians, Queen Charlotte Islands. After F. Boas.

In India the mass production of crude replicas of well-known temple statues was continued until quite recently, and accompanied by a whole selection of bronze, brass, and clay figures of local village gods. Similarly in China, since the introduction of Buddhism (first century A.D.), and particularly after the T'ang dynasty (seventh to ninth centuries) a prolific peasant art has developed in both Buddhist and Taoist images. We find traces of Chinese influence on ornamentation even as far as Siberia, and especially clear in the Amur region.

The peasant arts, therefore, cannot be completely identified with primitive art. Even on the decorative side they are inclined to show less vitality. Kroeber's description is that they 'tend to geometric or floral design, or to a naïve, somewhat inept realism. They please but hardly stir.'

CHAPTER VIII

Children's Art

THE spontaneous drawings of young children are genuinely primitive. The younger the child, the more primitive the drawings. The most interesting are the first attempts of children under school age. They are quite different from the work of older children who have had lessons and who have gained impressions and inspiration from works of art in their immediate environment. A number of quite advanced pictures of this kind have been published by Evelyn Gibbs in her book, *The Teaching of Art in Schools*.

By contrast, the attempts of younger children are very rudimentary. Often it is not even clear what the child is trying to portray, and he has to be asked to explain. Yet in other details there may be an unexpected observation of nature, a surprising grasp of essentials, and considerable power to express them.

The drawing here shown (Fig. 12) was produced by a small boy from Beaconsfield, Bucks, who was only four years and three months old, and not yet at school. His mother describes him as an imaginative child with a strong character, and she illustrates the early development of his powers of reasoning by telling how he once asked the question, 'Mummy, you can't stop time, can you?'

The drawing is supposed to represent 'Man shaving, watched by dog'. The most outstanding feature is the way in which the slant of the head and the movement of the arm have been reproduced. On the other hand, the left arm hardly shows, and perhaps does not even exist. The legs are also missing, though it is possible that feet are marked at the lower corners of the square body. The boy has found three strokes on the head a sufficient indication of hair. He has shown the mouth clearly, but only one eye is marked by a dot. Ears and neck are completely missing.

The smaller figure on the right represents the dog, but it would be unrecognizable without an explanation. On the left we can clearly see the head, while the stroke on the right is supposed to be

73

the tail. I can recall more finished drawings by older children, who would, however, have been quite incapable of reproducing the movement of the arm so convincingly.

Here we come to an important distinction between European children's art and the art of primitive adults. The primitiveness of children's art is a transitory phenomenon in the life of the individual, a mere stage in his development, and in complete contrast to the primitiveness conditioned by an entire culture of which it

FIG. 12. Man Shaving, Watched by Dog. Pencil drawing by Doyne North (Beaconsfield, Bucks), age 4 years 3 months.

forms a part. As the child grows up he reaches a cultural stage entirely different in character from his temporary undeveloped outlook. But just as the physiological development of the human individual from conception to birth has been said to reflect the phases in the physical development of the human race, it may also be said that the child in his mental growth shows many psychological traits similar to those of primitive man. Like the savage, he often interprets the incidents of his environment irrationally.

Sometimes, though not always, his imagination is ruled by the idea of magic. Children who have not done their home-work may think they can tell by means of secret signs whether they will 'get through' or not. For instance, they may count the paving-stones, and if the last stone they tread on before going into school has an even number they decide that everything will be all right. In fact, it would seem from Lovett's entertaining little book, *Magic in*

Modern London, that many adults also cling to the same primitive notions.

Just as the savage believes in good and evil spirits, so children have their fairies, gnomes, and pixies – that is, if their golden dreams of childhood have not been rudely shattered by enlightenment at too early an age. But there is no indication that the first stages of juvenile art are concerned with these supernatural beings. Children's drawings seem rather to begin with the desire to give a realistic representation of life and objects in their environment.* Similarly, the primitive artist does not paint or draw from religious or magical motives only. In reality a large part of primitive art owes its existence to the sheer urge to create, a delight in representation, and occasionally even in beauty.

From a purely technical point of view the drawings of young children have often a strong resemblance to certain representative drawings of the primitive races. This is particularly true of the drawings of South American Indians in Professor Koch-Gruenberg's collection (Fig. 9).[34]

In common with primitive artists, children have considerable powers of accurate observation. They reject everything that is not entirely characteristic, and they often bring out the essential features with surprising clarity. They completely disregard perspective, and observe lines rather than surfaces. Frequently also they do not confine themselves to what they see, but add details which they know to exist, although they are not actually visible.

The primitive art which is purely decorative, however, has no parallel in children's art. The young European child never occupies himself with decorative art, unless he has been taught to do so by adults. An interest in sculpture is less common with children than a taste for drawing. It appears, however, in their independent fabrication of toys, and in their use of clay and plasticine.

It has been argued that, since children grow up surrounded by pictures and images, their art cannot be accurately described as primitive. But only older children seem to be influenced at all by

* As an example I may mention our own daughter, Mary-Clare (born 1945). She was four when she first attempted to draw human and animal figures, but it was not before she was seven that she began to depict fairies, pixies, and witches.

the works of art in their environment. It is only in the rarest cases that smaller children are affected: they have to learn to observe pictures before they can be influenced by them.

So far we have spoken of children's art only among civilized people. But what about children's art in primitive races? Is the art of primitive children different from that of primitive adults? Not very much material exists for comparison. Some of the art of primitive children is of an amazingly high standard – as, for example, the figures in clay combined with pieces of fabric from West Africa, some of which are reproduced in Pl. 11(b). Lack of experience, and often also of suitable material and tools, is no doubt responsible for the cruder features of children's art as compared with the art of primitive adults, but it is remarkable that in some tribes there are characteristic features of vision which children and adults have in common. In some cases children have developed a special technique, such as drawing in snow, which is a favourite hobby among Eskimo girls on the west coast of Alaska.

CHAPTER IX

Primitive Art in Prehistoric Europe

THE oldest known art comes from the Upper Palaeolithic period, and dates roughly from between 20,000 and 10,000 B.C. Before the Upper Palaeolithic, and much earlier, were the Middle and Lower Palaeolithic periods, but from these no works of art have been preserved – unless we regard stone implements as works of art. This does not mean, however, that no art existed then. Plastic works in anything but the hardest material would inevitably have decayed.

The Upper Palaeolithic is divided into various stages, of which the earliest is the Aurignacian.* This is the period to which the oldest traceable drawings, paintings, and sculptures belong. We know from their skeletons that the men of that time were at least closely related in both intellect and psychology to the present human races, particularly the Europeans. The physique of *Homo aurignacensis* was not exactly the same as that of any living race, but the difference is comparatively slight. On the other hand, *Homo mousteriensis*, † of the Middle Palaeolithic period, was an entirely different being. He was undoubtedly human, since he was always capable of manufacturing stone implements and of burying his dead, but the dimensions of his bones, particularly the proportions of his skull, indicate an earlier stage in the development of the human race. His intellectual abilities must have been much more primitive than those of the living human race (*Homo sapiens*). For all these reasons he is considered by anthropologists to be representative of an earlier species, *Homo primigenius*. Thus *Homo aurignacensis* and not *Homo mousteriensis* was the direct ancestor of the present human race, and consequently the art of the Aurig-

---

* From the cave of Aurignac, Haute Garonne, France.
† From the prehistoric site at Le Moustier, Dordogne, France.

nacian period can be regarded as the earliest art created by human beings of our own kinship.

Of this the oldest examples are small human figures carved in hard materials in the round, together with a few stone reliefs of larger dimensions. No individual traits can be recognized in these

FIG. 13. The 'Venus of Willendorf'. Limestone. Height 135 mm. Upper Palaeolithic. (After H. Obermaier.)

figures. Prehistoric sculptors paid no attention to faces; they were interested only in the characteristic features of the body. Female characteristics, such as breasts and thighs, are strongly accentuated. It is generally believed that these statuettes were idols – images of goddesses of motherhood or childbirth. But it is possible that primitive artists merely liked to portray a principal object of their appreciation, either sexual or aesthetic – probably both.

Eight ivory statuettes have been found at Brassempouy (Grotte du Pape, Landes, France), and six of soapstone and one of bone in the Grimaldi caves near Mentone. The most beautiful figure is the female ivory statue, 147 mm. long and 66 mm. wide, which was discovered by Count Saint-Périer in the Grotte des Rideaux, near Lespugue (Haute Garonne), in 1922.

Another important find was the limestone statue, 135 mm. high, reproduced in Fig. 13. It was unearthed during the excavations carried out by Professor Obermaier near Willendorf, on the Danube, in 1908. Although this is not perhaps the most beautiful piece from our aesthetic point of view, it is certainly the most important. It is in excellent condition, and has various very interesting details. It is known as the 'Venus of Willendorf', because it probably illustrates the ideal of female beauty held by men of that particular region in the stone age.

The piece is distinguished by two crudely marked bangles round the forearm, and by the extraordinarily rich growth of hair arranged in concentric circles. The hair may be in plaits, or it may be kneaded with clay into a plastic form such as is still customary among certain African peoples. The bangles and the hair style show that these Stone Age men must have been comparatively highly advanced in the decoration of the body. Red paint, obviously used for cosmetic purposes, was found with the skeleton of *Homo aurignacensis*.

Other female statues, notably the specimen from the Grotte des Rideaux, are slimmer, especially in the upper part of the body and the neck. But both here and in Palaeolithic rock painting the thighs and the buttocks are still very strongly developed. This feature, called *steatopygia*, is common also among the Bushmen and Hottentots of South Africa (cf. Fig. 1). It provides one of the arguments for those scholars who maintain that the prehistoric race responsible for the Stone Age art of France and Southern Spain must themselves have been either Bushmen or closely related to Bushmen. This theory, however, is not generally accepted.

Plastic art was widely spread in Europe during the very early period. A male figure in ivory which is probably Aurignacian has been excavated near Brno in Czechoslovakia. The most eastern example hitherto discovered in Europe is a female ivory figure without a head found at Kostienki in Southern Russia, but more statuettes of the same type have been found as far east as Irkutsk, in East Siberia, recently. It does not follow, however, that any statue was necessarily made on the site of its discovery. There is ample evidence that some sort of primitive trade existed in prehistoric times.

Palaeolithic statues of human beings are very primitive to our aesthetic feeling. If we compare them with certain West African Negro sculptures, we find the same masterly, fully plastic representation of the body with its curves and surfaces, and the same

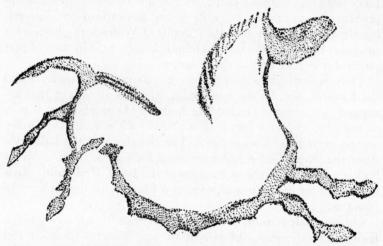

FIG. 14. Galloping Horse. Colour: red. (After H. Breuil and H. Obermaier, *The Cave of Altamira*; Madrid, 1935.)

accentuation of those traits in the body which are the artist's principal interest. But no Negro scuptor has ever gone so far as to omit the face entirely, like the Stone Age man who created the Venus of Willendorf. Here the artist has succeeded very well in avoiding any representation of the face, by inclining the head forward, so that the front part of it lies in deep shadow.

Animal sculpture developed greatly at a later period, known as the Magdalenian period. Sculpture in the round began more and more to give place to engravings, but both sculpture and engravings were much more naturalistic, as we understand it, that the human figures, and consequently make a stronger appeal to us. There is a haut-relief of a lion in clay, 160 cm. long and 70 cm.

high, in the Caverne de Montespan (Haute Garonne), where the lion appears to be walking towards the entrance of the cave, and the whole work shows an astonishing animation.[35]

The productions, however, which we can enjoy even to-day as works of art, unimpeded by the feeling that we are dealing with scientific specimens, are the wall paintings in the various caves of France and Spain. Here we must distinguish between a number of geographical, chronological, and stylistic groups. The first has been called the Franco-Cantabrian group by both Obermaier and Burkitt, and Obermaier divides it into three phases.[36]

In the first or Lower Aurignacian phase there are engravings drawn with the finger on soft clay walls. They are either simple spirals and frets, or crude representations of animals. There are paintings of animals, the crude contours done in black, yellow, or red. And there are stencilled silhouettes of human hands, produced by laying the hand on the wall and blowing colour over it or tracing the the outline. Examples of similar stencilled hands are found in the rock art and bark paintings of Australia (Fig. 8).

In the second or Upper Aurignacian phase we find engravings and paintings of animals represented with remarkable adherence to nature. The colours used are red and black, and the most essential details of the body are reproduced as well as the contours.

In the third or Lower Magdalenian phase both engravings and paintings reach the highest stage of their development.[37] Proportions and details are masterfully portrayed. In the engravings spaces are often rendered by hatching. Paintings are black, partially filled in with brown or red, and there is expert use of shading. The most famous are those of bison, but I have preferred here to reproduce another piece – a galloping horse from the cave of Altamira (Fig. 14). It is obviously not in a complete state of preservation, but the essentials are clearly recognizable. We must imagine a shaggy kind of horse, perhaps something like a Shetland pony, with short legs, a thick mane, and long coarse hair growing from the lower curve of the body. Note that the artist has worked in spaces, not in lines. The technique of this, and of the other animal pictures at Altamira, is therefore painting in the proper sense of the term, and not drawing. In the original the colour is red.

81

A new discovery of cave paintings of the Aurignacian period, superimposed by others of the Magdalenian period, has been made in a grotto at Lascaux, near Montignac, Dordogne, quite recently. The principal representation is that of a gigantic aurochs, measuring 16 ft. 5 in., painted at the bottom of the grotto. The whole animal is painted in admirably vigorous strokes, but the head is the greatest masterpiece. This and other figures from the ceiling and walls of the cave were first published in the *Illustrated London News* of February 28, 1942. There is also a number of horses, with conspicuous manes and short legs, like the type we know from other caves. Here we see, among other scenes, a wild mare and foal hunted by bowmen, a scene full of life and movement. It is interesting to note that, according to the report, 'minute particles of lime have formed tiny crystals, which have acted as a protection to the frescoes and have glazed them with a thin veneer'. A radiocarbon test of charcoal taken from the occupation level in the north-western portion of the grotto by Abbé Breuil and M. Severin Blanc in 1949 yielded the age of 15.516 ± 900 years.* i.e., a date between 14.463 and 12.663 B.C.

Naturalistic representations of man are characteristic of another group, in Eastern Spain. Quite apart from their artistic interest, these representations give us an idea of the life of these Palaeolithic men. We see them in their principal occupation, hunting, and we can study their weapons, tools, and ornaments. The Stone Age painters were complete masters in the art of rendering movement. A large number of their pictures are full of excitement and animation, as for instance the fighting scene from the Galeria del Roble shown in Fig. 15. I think it will be generally agreed that we are completely unconscious of the lack of perspective. Is there, indeed, a lack of perspective at all? Does it not appear as if the artist had looked down from a high rock on this handful of men attacking each other with bows and arrows? And in that case would not the representation meet even our demands in the matter of perspective?

Both the galloping horse and the fighting scene show one characteristic feature of Stone Age painting at its highest development:

* Willard F. Libby, *Radiocarbon Dating* (Chicago, 1952), p. 72.

FIG. 15. Fighting Scene. Palaeolithic wall-painting in dark red from the Galería del Roble, near Morella la Vella, Prov. Castellón, Spain. Total height of the group *c.* 12 in. After a photograph first published by F. Benítez and reproduced by H. Obermaier.

concentration on what is absolutely essential, and omission of all unnecessary detail. This is in accordance with at least one recognized principle of artistic draughtsmanship to-day. The definition of drawing as the art of omitting details has been ascribed independently to more than one modern artist. But while the modern artist has trained himself to concentrate on the indispensable characteristics, his colleague in remote prehistoric times may not have yet learned to visualize details, and may have unconsciously arrived at similar effect from an entirely different approach. The original purpose of pictures like Fig. 15 may not have been aesthetic, but rather pictographic, to record personal experience as a warrior or as a hunter. Perhaps that is why the human bodies are reduced to a few skilful and animated lines, which Obermaier describes as 'an expressionistic interpretation seeking to render life and movement'.

It is now almost certain that the pictures representing animals and hunting scenes were intended to fulfil a magical function. On certain animal pictures marks have been found which suggest that arrows had been shot at them. There are also pictures of men wearing stags' heads, and thus obviously masquerading as animals. In other words, the Stone Age hunters must have been practising sympathetic magic. They probably performed the same kind of magic dances with the animal masks as savages in historical times. Fig. 1, for example, shows Bushmen dancing in animal masks while their women-folk beat time with their hands. The dancer identifies himself with the desired animal, executing its movements in order to attract it and lure it into his power. Similarly, the Indians of the North-west Coast of America imitated in one of their dances the leaping salmon which constituted their main food.

European primitive art is not confined to the very early periods but continues in a variety of styles through the later prehistoric epochs (New Stone Age, Bronze Age, Iron Age) right to the Middle Ages. The remnants of ancient paganism provide examples of typically primitive arts in many parts of Europe. It is probable that certain Oriental elements were introduced with the western migrations in the Bronze Age, and exercised an influence as far as the British Isles.[38] But as we are not primarily concerned with prehistoric art, the above brief observations on the art of the Old Stone Age must suffice to show the aesthetic, psychological, and technical resemblances between the earliest art of prehistoric Europe and those of some modern primitive peoples.[39]

CHAPTER X

Northern Africa

THE prehistoric art of Europe is hidden in subterranean caves. In Northern Africa it has survived on the surface of the ground. No prehistoric sculptures have been found, but rock walls in the Atlas region and in various parts of the Sahara are adorned with pictures which date largely from the Stone Age onwards.

The rock drawings in the Atlas Mountains are mostly engraved or chipped linear figures representing animals. The age of the pictures is to some extent indicated by the species of animal. For example, drawings of the giant buffalo (*Bubalus antiquus*) are probably earlier than the Neolithic period, because this type of buffalo is believed to have become extinct by that time. Similarly, drawings of elephants, rhinoceroses, giraffes, and ostriches, which no longer live in the northern areas, must belong to the period when there was a considerably warmer climate in the Atlas region. Representations of the horse and the camel are always of a much later date, and belong to the historic 'Libyan-Berber' group. Accounts of the camel nomads first appear in history at the time when the Roman Empire was already on the decline. It is thus generally assumed that the camel was not brought from Asia into Africa until Roman times. Curtius, however, says that Alexander the Great's expedition to the Ammon oasis was made possible only by the use of camels from western Asia,[40] so that there are grounds for thinking that the camel must have been introduced into Egypt at least as early as the fourth century B.C. However, this is still a relatively late date, compared with prehistoric periods.

The rock pictures in the Atlas region of Algeria were first investigated by Leo Frobenius in 1913.[41] They are almost all engravings: only two pictures painted in ochre were discovered, and these belong to earlier periods.

Three principal art groups may be distinguished. There are first the very early naturalistic drawings of animals which are now

FIG. 16. The Lion of Djattou. Atlas Region. Naturalistic style (Palaeo-lithic?). Height over 4 ft; length over 6 ft. After Frobenius and Obermaier *Hadschra Maktuba.*

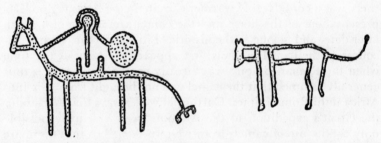

FIG. 17. Rock Engravings near Taghit (Atlas). Libyan-Berber style (late period). After Frobenius and Obermaier.

either extinct in this area, or belong to a very remote geological period. The huge impressive design of a lion at Djattou shown in Fig. 16 is a good example. Next comes a group of somewhat less naturalistic drawings, of slightly more recent date. Finally, there are the comparatively late Libyan-Berber designs, described as 'in part rather crude animal outlines, in part designs that are of a purely geometric and schematic character'. The chipped figures reproduced in Fig. 17 are examples of this schematic style. The animal shown in (*a*) is supposed to be older than the rider in (*b*).

In the central Saharan area paintings are commoner. The style is naturalistic, animated, and entirely different both from the con-

FIG. 18. Outlines of Two Human Figures (with Bows?) from a Polychrome Wall Painting in the Ahaggar Region (Central Sahara). After a photograph (pl. xxii) in *Art Rupestre au Hoggar*, by Count de Chasseloup Laubat.

ventionalized Lybian-Berber style, and from the early naturalistic group of the Atlas.[42] They seem to be much more closely related to Bushman art. Of particular interest are several polychrome paintings in the Tasili mountains representing graceful human figures with dappled cattle close by.

To the south-west of this region the French Ahaggar expedition discovered in 1935 another site with the same kind of polychrome wall paintings, showing various animals, but chiefly cattle. A few human figures are distinguished by extraordinarily animated and often graceful movements. Fig. 18 gives at least a faint idea of the artistic quality of these pictures. The work is carried out entirely in spaces, so that they are genuine paintings and not linear drawings. At the same site, however, there are also a number of engravings similar to the type in the Atlas region.[43]

Count de Chasseloup Laubat recognizes the strong similarity between the Ahaggar paintings and Bushman art, but suggests that they have also a striking resemblance to the art of Ancient Egypt. On the strength of this similarity, supported by linguistic arguments, he has put forward a fascinating theory about the prehistoric population of the Ahaggar plateau. When a change of climate in that region led to desiccation and soil erosion, the old civilization came to an end, and the people were dispersed in various directions. The suggestion is that one division may have migrated east to become one of the ethnic elements composing the ancient Egyptian race.

But, however attractive this theory may be, there are strong objections to it. The material available on the Ahaggar plateau is too slight to support an elaborate argument, and many more pictures of apparently the same style have been discovered farther east, so that the Ahaggar district may never have been the centre of the civilization. In any case, we can trace the development of Egyptian paintings in Egypt itself from very primitive beginnings.[44] As far as we know, strong influences have spread in exactly the opposite direction – that is, from Egypt to the West and South-west, but even this took place in the dynastic period, and not in prehistoric times. In the Atlas region the engraved figures of bulls and rams with sun discs between their horns show an obvious Egyptian influence, but they are not older than the New Stone Age, and may be even more recent. The paintings of the Ahaggar plateau, then, appear to be only a link – though probably the most beautiful one – in the chain of Saharan art centres 'parallel in age to pre-dynastic and dynastic Egypt'.[45]

CHAPTER XI

Bushman Art

THE yellow-skinned Bushmen to-day number only a few thousand, and live in the most uninviting parts of South Africa. They are not Negroes, but they are now partially intermingled with a Negro strain. They are a race apart, with their own form of primitive culture, and their own language split up into various dialects. Physically they are unique – strikingly small, even dwarf-like. They are the oldest known natives of South Africa, and were probably the aborigines.

Exactly when the Bushmen made their appearance there, and how far their history dates back, remains a mystery. It is not even certain if it was their ancestors who were responsible for the palaeolithic instruments which have been found at various prehistoric sites in the country. The Bushmen were driven back into the desert areas, not only by the white man, but also by the Hottentot invaders. The Hottentots are also a yellow-skinned race, so closely resembling the Bushmen that, according to C. G. Seligman, 'it is inadvisable to separate them'. There remains, however, an enormous difference between their artistic achievements. None of any consequence can be attributed to the Hottentots, but the old Bushmen have to their credit some of the finest examples of primitive art – in fact some of the most important 'schools' of art in the world.[4]

To-day the artistic production of the Bushmen is negligible. It consists largely of rather crude geometric engravings on ostrich eggs. For this reason some anthropologists are of the opinion that the so-called Bushman art cannot be the work of the Bushman race. Professor von Luschan suggests that the Bushman pictures may have some connexion with the wanderings of the Hamites.[47] The majority of anthropologists, however – H. Balfour, A. Kroeber, C. G. Seligman, and others, including the present writer – have no doubt that they are the work of the ancestors of the present Bushmen, and therefore rightly called 'Bushman art'.

FIG. 19. Two Bull Elands. Bushman painting on the ceiling of a cave at Glengyle, Barkley East District. Length c. 22 in. After *Bushman Paintings*, by M. Helen Tongue. By courtesy of the Clarendon Press.

We have already pointed to strong similarities between Bushman art and the prehistoric art of the Franco-Cantabrian group. The problem arises whether the prehistoric artists of the south-western part of Europe were also Bushmen. The similarity is most noticeable in the representation of human figures. Although there are marked resemblances in a few of the animal figures, the majority seem to me to be different in style, though it would be difficult to define this difference in writing.[48]

In any case, a proof of racial origin cannot be based on a similarity of art style alone.[49] Assuming that there are artists with a clear vision of nature and a high degree of technical skill, then similar implements, similar or even identical colours, and the same sort of ground (i.e., a rock surface) will in the majority of cases bring about stylistic resemblances, and these will be even more marked if the paintings are pictographic, so that human bodies are represented chiefly by lines and dots.

Bushman art proper is found all over South Africa. Sites in the Saharan area have already been mentioned, and there are further examples in the cave at In-Guezzam, south of the Ahaggar plateau. Similar pictures have been discovered in the neighbourhood of Lake Tanganyika by F. T. Bagshawe, and as recently as 1934–36 by Ludwig and Margit Kohl-Larsen. It is generally believed that the Bushman culture originated somewhere in the region of the East African lakes, and at one period extended over the whole continent.

There can be no doubt that the rock pictures in South Africa are the work of the ancestors of the modern Bushmen. G. W. Stow reports that he once showed copies of wall paintings to two old Bushmen on the Caledon river. They immediately recognized what was portrayed, explained several details, and declared that these paintings were the work of their own countrymen. One of the most beautiful of Bushman paintings shows a herd of ostriches of various colours. A close inspection, however, reveals that one of the birds has human legs, and peeping out from among the feathers a bow and arrow can be seen. It is a Bushman out on an ostrich hunt, disguising himself in an ostrich skin in order to get nearer to the birds. Stow showed a copy of this picture to a Bushman, and his explanation ran thus: 'Ostriches, three black males, two blue females.[5] The 'nusa Bushmen, not the 'kham Bushmen, are said to hunt in ostrich skins.'

These stories show at least that the Bushmen have a considerable knowledge of the wall paintings, though they give no actual proof that the painters themselves were Bushmen. The representa-

Fig. 20. Bushman Chipping representing an Elephant. Filling the surface of a rock near Luckhoff, Orange Free State. After M. Helen Tongue. By courtesy of the Clarendon Press.

tion of the human figure, however, leaves no doubt on the subject. Some of the pictures show clearly the little yellow Bushmen fighting with tall black figures, obviously Bantus. These paintings are somewhat later in date, but they clearly belong to the same tradition. In any case, the discussion is pointless, because Moszeik reports that he met an old Boer who actually watched the Bushmen at work.

The general character of Bushman art is naturalistic. The large majority of the figures are men and animals, but there are a few other objects which are probably symbolic, although their meaning is not always clear. In some regions the pictures are painted in

FIG. 21. Bushman Painting in White, Ochre, and Brown. Height 8 in. Liappering, Thaba Bosigo District, Basutoland. After a sketch by M. Wilman (1909), now in the Pitt Rivers Museum, Oxford. By courtesy of the Curator.

colour; elsewhere only chippings occur. The difference is due to the natural conditions of the country. The Bushmen living in the western corner of the Orange River Colony could not paint, because they had no smooth and sheltered surface to work on. Instead, they used flat boulders, and cut a picture on the rock itself with a stone. Of the four groups which can be distinguished – eastern, central, southern, and western – the central group is the most highly developed, and includes polychrome paintings, while the southern group (which Burkitt calls the Wilton group) is confined to monochrome pictures in red.

FIG. 22. Bushman Rock Painting. Height 5.2 in. Nibbetwan Valley, Bushman's River, Natal. After a copy by L. Tylor (1893). By courtesy of the Curator, Pitt Rivers Museum, Oxford.

It is generally assumed that chippings are more archaic than paintings. African paintings have been preserved only when overhanging rock have protected them from the weather, but the European cave paintings have survived even from Palaeolithic times. The art of engraving or chipping is often supposed to be more difficult than painting, provided the ground is a flat or weather-worn surface. Koch-Gruenberg, however, in his book on South American rock drawings, has pointed out that once an incision has been made into the rock surface it is comparatively easy to extend it.

Detailed information about the colours used by the Bushmen has been collected by Moszeik, who flaked small pieces off the

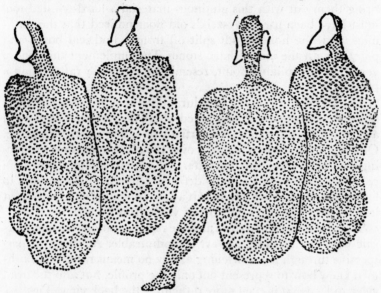

FIG. 23. Bushman Painting from Nibbetwan Valley, Bushman's River, Natal. Four men sitting on the ground. Height *c.* 3 in. Colours: (bodies) reddish brown; (faces and ears) flesh colour; (ground) greyish brown. Copy by L. Tylor (1893), now in the Pitt Rivers Museum, Oxford. By courtesy of the Curator.

rock and had them carefully analysed by Dr Wagner in Sondershausen. This analysis proved that the colours were earth pigments. Red and brown consist of bole or haematite; yellow was made from iron ochre; white from zinc oxide; black from charcoal or soot; blue shows iron and silicic acid; grey and violet were not examined. The blue is unusual, and (as has pointed out by Dr Kühn) does not occur in the Stone Age art of Europe. Red and brown were by far the most frequently used.

In one cave Moszeik discovered a hollowed-out stone slab, which was used for pounding the colours. Near it lay a mortar of hard stone. The pulverized colour was to have been mixed with animal fat. In this way a viscous, fatty paint was produced, of the consistency of our oil paints. The fine lines frequent in Bushman paintings are drawn with admirable precision, and to bring them out with this glutinous material a hard-pointed tool must have been used. Moszeik's old Boer noticed that the Bushmen used fine hollow rods split off from cylindrical bones and pointed with the aid of sharp stones. The implement thus had a very thin and pliable point, resembling a spatula rather than a brush.

The colours are of varying durability; white disappears most quickly. Many pictures have faded where the stone has been worn away by the weather, and are partially or entirely unrecognizable. Often new pictures are painted over the older ones, thus producing several layers of different date. Unfortunately, many Bushman paintings have been wantonly defaced, often in a vain attempt to loosen part of the rock and take it away. In Southern Rhodesia, at least, a stop has been put to this vandalism by law.[50]

The observation of nature and the representations of characteristic contours in Bushman art are admirable. Attempts at perspective through foreshortening are by no means rare. The Bushmen knew how to represent not only the profile, but also the front view and – what is even more difficult – the back view (Figs. 19, 22, and 23).

In the colouring the gradual shading is remarkable. This art, however, was not universally mastered. Some of the pictures place light and dark colours immediately next to each other in crude contrast. The birds reproduced in Fig. 21 are white against a grey rock background, with reddish-brown crests and yellowish legs – obviously supposed to be wading through water. As Roger Fry has pointed out in *Vision and Design*, they are reminiscent of Japanese art, but the association may arise merely because of the frequent appearance of cranes in Japanese pictures.

Perhaps the greatest achievement of the Bushman painters is composition. It is so outstanding that A. R. Willcox[46] thinks that Bushman art is not really 'primitive': 'The chief difference from primitive art (in Fry's sense) is the *unity* of a Bushman painting; it is whole, not merely the sum of its parts. And this is true also (where several figures, form a group or scene') (loc. cit. p. 83).

CHAPTER XII

Negro Art

NEGRO art is predominantly plastic. There exist several centres of Negro sculpture, most of them in the western half of Africa. One principal area is the region stretching from the Senegal eastwards to Lake Chad, with the exception of the entirely Mohammedan countries, where artistic inspiration is limited to practical arts and crafts and ornamental decoration. The Benuë, joining the Niger, forms the border of another region of sculpture stretching eastwards and south-eastwards, with the grassland of the Cameroons as its centre. Thus these two areas are both situated round the Gulf of Guinea, and may be described as the Sudan sphere. To the east and south-east, between the Atlantic and the Great Lakes of East Africa, lies the Congo sphere. A southern extension of it is the important art centre of Angola, between the Congo basin and South-west Africa. In East Africa we find an isolated group of plastic artists, the Makonde nation of southern Tanganyika and northern Portuguese East Africa. The Bantu tribes of South Africa, who are highly developed both mentally and physically, show considerable artistic talent, but their plastic art is unimportant compared with that of the Congo basin and the western Sudan sphere. However, they possess a marked talent for decorative geometric patterns, and the shapes and carved decorations of some of their wooden utensils, especially the head-rests (Fig. 24), reveal good taste. Occasionally we also find animal figures of interest.

It is the work of the western region which has made the Negro famous as a sculptor in wood. Wood sculpture is the classical art of Africa in the purest sense of the word. To some people the Benin bronzes represent even finer work, but it would probably be wrong to consider these as purely African, because the technique of bronze casting is believed to have been introduced from abroad.

The principal merit of African wood sculpture has been defined by Roger Fry as 'complete plastic freedom'. African artists 'really conceive form in three dimensions' and 'seem to have no difficulty in getting away from the two-dimensional plane'.[51] There is a simple explanation of the ease with which the African sculptor has grasped the round, and hence cylindrical, form of the human body. It lies in the material and in the technique imposed by it. The sculptor starts with a section of tree-trunk – a round block of wood. If the construction is simple, the block of wood remains clearly recognizable as a cylinder. The classical examples are the roughly fashioned ancestor figures of the Bari, and the colossal pole sculptures of the Azande, both in the eastern Sudan. If further cubic forms, similarly arrived at, are applied to this basic cylinder, the result is an almost geometric style. The trunk is one solid cylinder, the arms are smaller cylinders running parallel to the body, and the head is strongly stylized. Geometric sculptures of this type have been produced in their highest artistic form by the Habe tribe in the western Sudan.

The style is by no means confined to Africa; the same development is found in the South Seas, Siberia, Indo-China, and America. The principle of pole sculpture is also applied to masks. In the nature of things the mask is always half-cylindrical, and the artist has so little opportunity to elaborate this half-cylinder that it remains the predominant form. The head of the statuette on Pl. 37(b) illustrates this style as developed by the Hopi Indians in North America. In Africa masks of this kind are to be found on the Ivory Coast and in the Nilotic region.

It is obvious that cylindrical pole sculpture can develop from any long-shaped material, not necessarily from wood. An excellent variant is elephant-tusk (Pl. 2(a)). It is clear, too, that if an artist wants to retain the unity of a slender unbroken line in his sculpture, working from a single block without the addition of any other piece, he will not be able to portray any detail exceeding the limits of the original cylinder. From this arises a further characteristic of African sculpture: its lack of proportion. It is only in the parklands of the Cameroons that we find human statues of absolutely correct proportions, as, for example, in the admirably sculptured figures reproduced on Pl. 3, both over life-size. The ivory carving illustrated on Pl. 2(*a*) shows a striking contrast. It represents a rider on horseback and comcs from Nigeria. In comparison with the rider, the horse is so small that some people might think it was meant as a caricature. But the artist had no such intention. It was simply that within the limits of his tusk he had no means of making the horse large enough to be in proportion to the rider, and since he was principally concerned with the rider, the size of the horse did not trouble him.

Not all African wood sculpture is based on this principle. The round block can be more extensively elaborated into a progressively more realistic form which has no resemblance to the original shape of the material. Sculpture of this kind is found in the parklands of the Cameroons (Pl. 2(*b*); Pl. 3), through the whole of the Congo region (Pl. 7(*b*)), and in the east among the Makonde tribe.

The forms of African masks are extraordinarily varied. Some are purely realistic (Pl. 5(*b*)), others rigorously stylized. The majority are highly coloured, but this is not unique. There are very few peoples in history who left their sculptures unpainted. Greek statues were painted, chiefly on the eyes and mouth, to give a realistic appearance. Egyptian sculptures, the Buddhas of Gandhara, and the figures of divinities in ancient Mexico were all painted. In Africa the colouring ranges from the simple black statues and masks in the hinterland of the Cameroons to the brilliant yellows, reds, whites, and blues of the Nigerian figures and the Yoruba masks. On the Ivory Coast the Atutu cover the most precious of their statues with gold-leaf.[52] Sometimes the sculptor himself does the gilding, and sometimes he passes the work on to a specialist. One artist, who made only ungilded sculptures, said that if he ever had two sons he would teach one carving and the other gilding so that they could co-operate.

In many parts of Africa indigenous art is on the decline, but on the Ivory Coast it is still flourishing. It is even undergoing further development – not through European influence, but through the inventiveness of the artists themselves. Thus we hear of a carver who produced an innovation by carving the loin-cloth together with the figure out of the same piece of wood, where formerly the naked figure had been finished first, and a real piece of cloth added afterwards. This man did good business, and still does to-day, for rumours of his inventiveness have spread and attracted many purchasers.

The artist's occupation in Africa is so extraordinarily re-munerative that his European colleagues might well grow green with envy, and even consider emigrating to the Ivory Coast and settling among the Guro or Atutu. Generally speaking, the capacity of these tribes as craftsmen is not high, and their productivity is small. Their practical ability as sculptors and smiths is therefore all the more striking.

The Atutu, unlike other African tribes, have neither social dis-tinctions nor social prejudices. They greatly appreciate true skill in any form. They realize the value of the artist, and consequently allow him sufficient leisure to devote his life to his art. Thus when the inhabitants of a village are called out for public work, such as road-making, the artists are always exempted.

Among these tribes, too, many works of art have a religious significance. The Atutu are not ancestor worshippers, but they have a certain number of ancestor figures. These are carved at the time of a man's death, the body serving as a model. When the statue is completed the soul of the dead man is supposed to enter into it for a period, after which it passes into the beyond. In the meantime the ancestor figure is used as a fetish. If someone is in trouble, the village magician whose advice he asks may recom-mend him to have a fetish made. To the carver this is a job like any other. To make the fetish effective the owner must bring it an offering. It is usually sufficient to sprinkle it with flour or even white chalk, but in special cases a fowl may be killed. If it proves ineffective, the fetish has no value and may be destroyed; if, how-ever, it proves effective, it can be used again for other purposes. A barren woman will sometimes have a magic doll made re-presenting a child, and carry it round on her back 'to bring home to her body that she now wants a child like that'. If this effort is fruitless, she may use the doll as a mere profane toy, or even sell it at a reduced price. Dr Himmelheber got one for two francs, when the woman herself had paid fifteen.

The Atutu have other wooden dolls, carefully carved and ranging from 8 to 20 cm. in height, which have no magic or religious significance, but are used as toys by adults as well as children. There are also occasional carved portraits, 40–60 cm. high, made by order of the person represented, and given to his friends as souvenirs.

Among the southern Atutu tribes there is even something which might be described as 'art for art's sake'. These people make a number of carved objects which have no practical use and no religious significance – solid wooden vessels, models of singal horns, and carved animal figures. On feast days the owner fetches his art treasures out of his strong-room, lays them out on the veranda, and contemplates them affectionately.

Among some tribes of French West Africa, especially the Baoule and Habe, rigidly stylized figures are predominant, while the parkland of the Cameroons is distinguished by large realistic ancestor figures and dance masks, some of them larger than life size, astonishingly animated, and usually blacked over with soot. The various tribes of the Congo have developed a realistic type of statuette and mask (Pl. 5(a)) side by side with stylized, almost geometric carvings. Their statuettes and miniature masks in ivory are often of great beauty (Pl. 7(c)). The most artistic tribes in the Congo are the Bayaka, the Bakuba or Bushongo (where carving of ceremonial objects is a privilege of the aristocracy), the Baluba, the Bapende, and in the south the Vatchivokoe.[53]

Between the Ivory Coast and the Congo lie Ife, in the Yoruba country, and Benin, in Southern Nigeria, where African sculpture has reached its highest level. Benin was visited in the fifteenth century by Alfonso d'Aveiro (1485–86), and subsequently by several Portuguese, Dutch, and English travellers. A few ivory objects made their way to Europe, but it was only with the British conquest in 1897 that the bronzes were discovered and that Benin art in general became known to a wider circle.

The bronzes are of two kinds. There are figures – either life-size human heads or complete models of animals or human beings – and there are reliefs of complete scenes, animals, human beings, and mythological or magical symbols. One of these reliefs from the British Museum is reproduced in Pl. 7(d). Actually it is smaller than most, and the shape is unusual. The male heads seem somewhat stiff, on account of the high neck decoration

(Pl. 8(b)). The faces are bare of expression, and almost impersonal. The general effect is interesting rather than beautiful. Some of the women's heads are more individual and indeed remarkable works of art. The decoration on the neck is so slight as to be almost unnoticeable, and the hair is trained upwards in a high horn-like style.*

The principal ivory products are large elephant tusks carved in relief, goblets and tankards decorated either in relief or open-work, and armlets and other ornaments in the same style. The goblets and tankards are often European in shape, usually after the Renaissance style, and there is no doubt that they were carved from European patterns to the order of Portuguese travellers. Other pieces are purely or predominantly African. In the bracelet reproduced in Pl. 8(a), some of the details show a European influence, but the form and most of the figures are typically African. European soldiers and merchants in sixteenth-century dress appear occasionally on the bronze plaques.

The head-dress and the rings round the neck of bronze heads (Pl. 8(b)) represent the traditional coral decoration still worn by the kings or *obas* of Benin.[54] Coral beads were an important part of the crown treasures, and when a ruler ceased to wear them it was a sign of bad financial policy. Chief Egharevba reports that Ahenzae, the great-grandson of Oba Orhogbua, lost his wealth in this way. He was only sixteen when he came to the throne, and his inexperience was exploited by self-seeking courtiers. 'The long-stored treasure of the former kings was wasted, and the royal coral beads were gambled away in games of dice with Osuan.'

According to Bini tradition, brass casting was introduced into Benin from Ife (Uhe) under Oba Oguola in about 1280. The Oba wanted works like those imported from Ife to be produced in Benin itself. 'He therefore sent to the Oghene of Uhe for a brass-smith and Igue-igha was sent to him. Igue-igha was very clever and left many designs to his successors and was in consequence deified and is worshipped to this day by brass-smiths. The practice of making brass castings for the

* An example from the British Museum is reproduced in the *Handbook to the Ethnographical Collection*, 2nd ed., Pl. xvii.

preservation of the records of events was originated during the reign of Oguola.' Esigie (*c.* 1504) encouraged and improved the brass work, and it is generally recognized that the art of Benin reached its prime in the sixteenth century. Ivory and wood carving were introduced by Oba Ewuare the Great (*c.* 1440), while ivory flutes (*akohen*) were invented some time after 1735 by a man called Eresoyen.[55]

The bronzes are produced by what is known as the cireperdue process. This is essentially a peculiar method of making the mould. Here the original work is modelled in bee's wax. It is done on a model, or nucleus, of clay, unless the object is very small (e.g. Pl. 10(*b*)), in which case the original work consists entirely of wax. The pliable medium enables the artist to model practically every possible form he wishes to represent, and to bring out even the smallest details. Also modelled in wax are duct rods, which are necessary in the casting process. The completed wax sculpture is then carefully covered by successive layers ("investments") of wet clay. When the clay mould is dry and hard, it is heated, causing the wax to melt and to run out through the holes resp. pipes left by the molten duct rods. The liquid metal is then poured into the empty mould. When the metal has cooled, the shell of clay is carefully broken off. The surface of the bronze is often rough and has to be finished off with chisel and file. In cases of bad craftsmanship holes may be left where the metal did not entirely fill the cavity. Brass figures from the parklands of the Cameroons for instance, frequently show such holes filled with white metal (tin?), and on certain Buddhist and Taoist bronzes of China, especially of the Ming period, we find holes closed on the inside with small pieces of fabric, which are pasted over the opening, or the whole bronze may be coated with thin paper and then painted over or gilded. The *cire-perdue* method was and is still known in many parts of the world, and the procedure is not exactly the same everywhere. It was practised in ancient Babylonia and Egypt as well as in the old civilizations of Central and South America. In Asia, the chief centres are India and the Malayan archipelago. The method has been known in West Africa for centuries, it is the method employed in all West African bronze and brass industries. There is a set of models in the British Museum showing various stages of the work.

This technique has been recorded in many books, and there is a set of models in the British Museum showing various stages of the work. It is the method used in all West African bronze and brass industries. The great brass pipes, decorated with human and animal figures, produced by some tribes in the parklands of the Cameroons, are made in this way; so are the miniature brass figures which have been used by the Ashanti as gold weight (*mrammuo*) since at least 1760 (Pl. 10(*b*)). The *cire-perdue* process is not exactly the same everywhere,[56] but it is known in many parts of the world. In Asia the chief centres are India and the Malayan archipelago. It was also practised in ancient Egypt, and in the old civilizations of Central and South America.

It is clear from the date of the earlier Benin bronzes that the Bini practised this art before the arrival of the Portuguese, so that the theory that it was first learned from European sources is ruled out. There is another theory that it came by a round-about route from India; there is no reason, however, to reject the tradition that bronze casting was introduced to Benin from Ife. The question, therefore, is where the Yorubas learnt the technique.

There is a vast difference between the ancient sculpture of the Yorubas and their present-day work. Modern Yoruba art consists chiefly of wooden figures and masks. With its striking polychrome paints, it is certainly very decorative, but it is on a lower artistic plane than the old classic art in stone, terra-cotta, and bronze. The old carvings in hard stone, such as quartz, and the old bronze castings, are distinguished by an astonishing fidelity to nature, absolutely correct proportions, and a lack of conventional features. The technique was excellent, and the figures show a marked sense of beauty.

It is probably centuries since work of this kind was produced at Ife, but the antique masterpieces have never been forgotten. Bronze heads still stand in the palace of the Oni. On certain festivals they are removed by the priests and carried to the shrines. Dozens of beautiful terra-cotta heads were kept in a shrine outside the town until only a few years ago, when they were all stolen or broken.[57] In Ife there is still a ram's head in granite, almost life-size, and ceremonial stools carved in single pieces from solid pieces of quartz. (A similar stool is in the British Museum.) But it is the portrait heads in terra-cotta and bronze which show the art of ancient Ife at its best. Even the Benin heads cannot compare with them.

It is only recently that these most beautiful of all African sculptures have been known in Europe. Leo Frobenius brought back a number of terra-cotta heads about thirty years ago. There were comparatively few bronze heads known even in Ife until early in 1938, when seven splendid examples covered with green paitna were unearthed during the digging of foundations for a house, and four more at another site. Some of these (Pl. 9(a)) have tiny holes symmetrically arranged round the lower half of the face and along the border of the scalp for fixing hair and a beard, as in the wooden masks of Japan and North-west America. Professor Melville J. Herskovits rightly suggests that the holes over the face might have served for attaching a wig. Other heads (Pls. 9(b) and 10(a)) have furrows representing the vertical stripes which are still used as tribal marks among the Yorubas. The head on Pl. 10(a) wears a short crown in the form of a head-band with a high ornament in the centre, and is supposed to be the portrait of Olokun, wife of Odua, and mother of Obalufon I, second Oni of Ife.[58]

The age of the Ife heads has not yet been ascertained, but since it is practically certain that the bronze art of Benin was derived from Ife, there are some data to work on. P. Amaury Talbot has reproduced a series of heads found at Benin, two of which are supposed to have been brought originally from Ife.[59] These, however, are far cruder and much less realistic than those recently unearthed at Ife. If they represent the type which first came from Ife to Benin about 1280, then it must have taken some time for this crude art to develop into the masterpieces which we know, so that the bronze art of Ife cannot have reached its zenith till the thirteenth century at the earliest.

In recent years, several authors have claimed that it is wrong to speak of Ife and Benin "bronzes" and that they are actually all brass. Bronze is an alloy of copper and tin, whereas brass is an alloy of copper and zinc. However, if the alloy consists essentially of copper and tin, an additional admixture of a certain percentage of zinc or any other metal does not change the character of the alloy as 'bronze'.[59a] It is therefore quite legitimate to speak of the Ife and Benin bronzes, while the term 'brass' may probably be applied to metal work from Dahomey and a few other areas.

Although both in terra-cotta and bronze the racial character-istics of the models are admirably portrayed, the works give the impression of being products of ancient Greece or Egypt, rather than of Negro Africa. Frobenius considered a connexion with the Mediterranean sphere, and Sir Flinders Petrie in his book on an-cient Egypt remarks that if any of the Ife heads had been exca-vated in the foreign quarter of Memphis, they would have been accepted as larger examples of the local type. He adds: 'The Memphite work cannot have come from the Niger, it is too close in touch with Persia and India; but the idea, and even the work-men, may have come from Egypt to West Africa. The work of the fifth century B.C. may be the source; but nothing so late as the Roman age. Here there is, then, an indication of date for the early civilization. Was it an outlier of the Ethiopian Kingdom, like some other sites?' I wish to point out one striking peculiarity of some, if not all, bronze heads from Ife: on the back of the head there is a fairly large circular hole. This hole is not a necessary technical device associated with the *cire-perdue* technique. Now, exactly the same type of hole occurs on the back of ancient Greek and South-Italian–Greek statuettes and human portrait heads; but there the hole has a distinct technical function, in that it is designed to ensure the drying of the inner surface of the hollow clay sculptures and also to prevent cracks during the firing. The conclusion is that, if the original models of the Ife bronzes were Greek pottery sculptures, the hole was simply copied in bronze, although, technically, there was no need for it in metal-work.

Another interesting detail which may throw some light on the origin of the ancient civilization of Ife is the clasp in the centre of the crown of the piece illustrated on Pl. 10(*a*). It is very similar to the phallic forehead-ornament worn by the ruler and the warriors of the ancient Kafficho empire in Kaffa, Abyssinia, which was subdued by the Amhars only little more than half a century ago. Meanwhile, the Yorubas have a tradition that they came from the east, from Upper Egypt, and it has been suggested that they were originally not Negroes at all, but became intermingled with the Negroes later.[60]

FIG. 24. Wooden Pillow (Neck-rest). Height 6.6 in.
Makalanga, Mashonaland. British Museum.

On the other hand, objects of ancient Egyptian origin have been found all over Africa. The curved ceremonial knives of the modern Azande in the borderlands of the Sudan and the Northern Congo are derived from the ancient Egyptian sickle. Head-rests, musical instruments, and even certain customs and beliefs show the signs of Egyptian influence. 'It is not plausible,' says Wilfred D. Hambly, 'that a civilization like that of Egypt existed as a selfcontained unit. Egyptian caravans penetrated far into the Sudan; Egyptian ships sailed to the land of Punt, a region generally identified with the Somali coast.' [61] G. A. Wainwright has demonstrated that the design of an unusual West African ornament, a breastplate, is of ancient Egyptian origin.

In an interesting paper on the king-god Shango and his temple at Ibadan, in Southern Nigeria, Mrs Eva L. R. Meyerowitz has shown recently that Shango was probably derived from Amun and the meteorite gods of Egypt and Nubia. The god Amun 'was brought into Yoruba and Nupe by refugee tribes from Nubia, now generally called Blemy-Zaghawa. The bulk of these tribes was forced to leave Nubia after A.D. 629, when a Sassanid Persian army in occupation of Egypt was beaten, and, retreating into Nubia, exerted such a pressure on the many tribes and peoples there that the great Kisra migration set in to the various parts of the western Sudan.' Mrs Meyerowitz then sets out in full detail that the two deities, Amun and Shango, have essentially the same functions and symbols, and that their sacred animal is the ram. I have already mentioned that in Ife there exists an almost life-size ram's head in granite (I am indebted to Mr R. L. V. Wilkes, District Officer, for this information). Ram's heads are also among the astonishing bronzes excavated at Igbo, Awka Division, Southern Nigeria, about seven or eight years ago, which have been published by Mr J. O. Field, Assistant District Officer, in *Man* (London), No. 1, 1940. These objects, including beautiful bowls and a magnificent urn, or brazier, a human head, and various pieces of obscure character and purpose, are overloaded with filigree ornaments. They are covered with a rich green patina, and their style has no parallel in Africa. Although the human head has unmistakable African features, the decorative forms can only be compared with Indian metalwork. Nothing is known so far about the origin and antiquity of these finds, which represent another addition to the various unsolved problems of African archaeology. Very interesting clay figurines, mostly human statuettes, excavated by Jean-Paul Lebeuf and A. Masson-Detourbet south of Lake Chad (Pl. 1(b)), are spontaneous and vigorous pieces of sculpture, of African originality, and devoid of any features suggestive of foreign influence. These clay figurines are definitely pre-Islamic, but precisely how old they are we are as yet unable to tell. The most interesting question whether this primitive sculpture of the Lake Chad area is older than, or a derivative from, West African sculpture in wood is also still obscure.

Further detailed research is necessary, and especially in order to prove that all the various elements pointing towards Egyptian origin have actually been derived from that source. Meanwhile, all that we know about the chronology of Ife and Benin bronzes suggests a much more recent date for the highest development of Ife portraiture in bronze. It may be that Egyptian influence came through terra-cotta rather than through bronze. More excavations in Nigeria might throw new light on this interesting problem.[62]

There are other examples of ancient African art in harder and more durable materials than wood. In some parts stone carvings have been found which are of typically African forms, and thus entirely different from Ife sculpture. In 1934 no fewer than seven hundred and sixty-five figures and heads were discovered in a clearing among oil palms, one and a half miles from Esie, in Ilorin province, Nigeria.[63] Some of these are reproduced on Pl. 11(a). They show a great variety of types, physiognomies, and tribal marks. A number of the tribal marks are still in use to-day. In the majority of these carvings the features are sufficiently individualized for them to be considered as portraits; their naturalism, however, is naïve and typically African. It is primitive art at its best.

About twenty or thirty years ago, interesting finds were made in the neighbourhood of the Uele river, in the northern Congo. These finds consisted, firstly, of ruins of stone structures, which, however, were entirely destroyed because no archaeologist or other competent person was in the area at that time, and the stones were wanted for road construction. Secondly, a stone sculpture of brownish-grey volcanic tuff, with traces of black paint, representing a human head (measurements 20 by 12 by 13.5 cm.) was excavated by a Belgian missionary. The head is sculptured in bold spaces, and its character may be described as vigorous. This sculpture is in the collection of Baron Eduard v. d. Heydt (Ascona), and is at present on exhibition in the Rietberg Museum in Zürich.* For the student of the history of primitive art styles, the importance of this remarkable piece would be greatly enhanced if the circumstances of its excavation were not for ever lost.

In the meantime, more archaeological finds have fortunately been made in Nigeria. At Abiri, a small village some ten miles from Ife, a series of human heads in terra-cotta, a beautiful terra-cotta ram's head, and fragments of other pieces, including a finely modelled human hand, also a coiled snake, were excavated. The first finds were made accidentally, but the rest was unearthed in a scientific manner by Mr Bernard Fagg, Government Archaeologist. These finds have been published in *Man* (London), No. 79, 1949.

Of at least equally great archaeological significance are the finds at Nok, a Jaba village in Zaria Province, where five pottery heads were found twenty-five feet deep in the alluvial deposit at a tin-mine. Two of these human heads were found as early as 1931, and the three others early in 1944. Together with these heads were found well-modelled representations of a human lower leg and foot and a few other objects, including a complete cooking-pot with incised decoration around the neck. Then a fine human head, just under natural size, was found at Jemaa, about twenty-four miles from Nok, and inside Plateau Province. Mr Bernard Fagg, to whom again we are indebted for the description of these finds (*Man*, No. 48, 1946), regards the head from Jemaa (see our text fig. No. 25) as culturally related to those from Nok. As the heads of Nok were found in a distinct geological stratum, their chronological classification is probably safer than

---

* I am indebted to Dr Baron v. d. Heydt for this information. I hope to publish some photographs of the head in *Arts of Primitive Peoples* ('Pelican History of Art') shortly. But Dr v. d. Heydt reminds me that the piece has been illustrated before, viz., by the late Dr Eckart v. Sydow in his catalogue of the collection of Baron v. d. Heydt under the title *Kunst der Naturvölker*, Berlin (Bruno Cassirer, 1932), and, still earlier, with a note by Alfred Salmony, in *Cicerone* (Leipzig), Vol. XV (1923).

that of many other African finds. The Nok culture is attributed to the late first millennium B.C.†

The art of the Nok culture certainly proves that, in this area, there existed a representative sculpture which may be classified as partly, but not entirely, naturalistic. There is manifest, in the

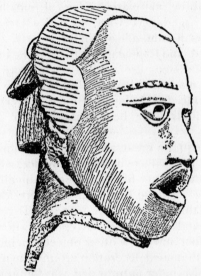

FIG. 25. The terra-cotta head of Jemaa (*c.*24 miles from Nok, Plateau Province, Northern Nigeria). Height of face *c.* 20 cm. The Nok culture is attributed to the late first millennium B.C. Drawn after a photograph by Mr Bernard Fagg, Government Archaeologist, Nigeria.

head of Jemaa (Fig. 25), a certain pathos, restrained by rigid forms already revealing the effect of conventionalization. However, this plastic art differs from the style of Ife and cannot be regarded as a preliminary stage of either Ife or Benin sculpture. In the first place, Nok sculpture does not possess the classical

† *Man*, No. 144, 1952, p. 108.

associations which are so conspicuous in the art of Ife. On the other hand, the art of Nok may well be one of the sources of certain recent styles of Negro sculpture. For instance, the traditional history of some Congo tribes points to the north as their original homeland. A comparison of the hair-style on the back of the head of Jemaa with that of the wooden Baluba figure on Pl. 7(b) reveals a striking similarity which is hardly accidental.

Of general theories which may throw some light upon the origins of African, especially West African, art, some of the most important contributions are two articles by A. J. Arkell, 'Archaeological Research in West Africa' (*Antiquity*, No. 71, 1944, pp. 147–150) and 'Gold Coast Copies of 5th–7th Century Bronze Lamps' (*ibid.*, No. 93, 1950). In the former article Arkell points out that Meroe, that famous ancient town on the upper Nile, excavated by Garstang and Reisner, was an important cultural centre during the long period from 650 B.C. till A.D. 350, when it was destroyed by the people of Aksum. It was 'replaced in northern Sudan by a strange blend of Meroitic–Byzantine civilization, known at present to archaeologists as the "X-group"'. 'There is some evidence,' Mr Arkell continues, 'that after the destruction of their capital by the invaders from the east, the royal family of Meroe may (naturally) have migrated westward', and the author considers that they might have eventually arrived in West Africa. On the strength of so many other indications, this theory sounds quite acceptable. One of the most beautiful works of African art, and certainly 'the finest of all extant Ashanti antiquities', the golden mask of King Kofi of Ashanti in the Wallace Collection in London (published for the first time, in natural colour, as frontispiece to the Golden Jubilee issue of *Man*, January 1951), a piece about two-thirds life-size, weighing 3 lb. 6 oz., is certainly strongly reminiscent of ancient Egyptian sculpture.

CHAPTER XIII

Asia

1. Prehistory (Java, China, Japan)

THE vast continent, stretching from the Bosporus to the Far East and from Novaya Zemlya to Singapore, and the innumerable islands and archipelagoes of Asia represent, from the anthropological point of view, a whole world of the greatest variety of races, peoples, and cultures, from the most primitive to the highest forms. As in Europe, however, the beginnings of art appear only at a relatively late stage.

The scanty but important relics of *Pithecanthropus erectus*, the 'ape-man' of Java, so far the most primitive type established by human palaeontology – perhaps still a pre-human form – seem to support the old theory that 'the cradle of mankind' is Asia. But no artefacts have been found in association with the few fragments of *Pithecanthropus*; obviously this very early race had not yet developed any material culture. In terms of geological stratigraphy, *Pithecanthropus* belongs to the mid-diluvial period. Other fossil remains found in Java are the *Ngandong* skulls and the *Wadjak* skulls; both are more developed types than *Pithecanthropus*, and the Wadjak race has been regarded by Dr Eugen Dubois (the discoverer of both the first *Pithecanthropus* finds and the Wadjak skulls) as the prototype of the modern Australian aborigines.

In China the fossil bones of about forty individuals of another primitive human race, *Sinanthropus pekinensis*, have been unearthed in the limestone caves at Chou Kou Tien, near Peking, and the archaeological importance of these finds lies in their association with artefacts – namely, stone implements made from various rock materials, especially quartzite and greenstone.[64] In an upper cave at the same locality the skeletal remains of seven individuals belonging to a different, more highly developed race have been discovered, and these are supposed to be more recent, viz., of the late palaeolithic period, whereas *Sinanthropus* might have been contemporaneous with, or at least not very much younger than, *Pithecanthropus*. However, none of these very early races can be credited with even the slightest attempt at drawing or carving. Still, the workmanship of the stone implements found with *Sinanthropus* is not bad; we may compare them with certain primitive types produced by Australian aborigines, and, as tools are a *sine qua non* of any art, it stands to reason that whoever made those stone implements was at least a potential artist – that is to say, if he had the talent. So far, however, no graphic or plastic art belonging to the Old Stone Age has been found in China. The palaeolithic period, as we have seen, is represented by stone implements only. From the neolithic period there is an abundance of pottery, frequently decorated with geometric designs in brown or black paint, especially from Kansu Province (Northwest China). There are beautiful types, gracefully shaped and ornamented, but the style has nothing to do with the typically Chinese forms as we know them from the Hsia dynasty (about 2205 ff. B.C.) and the Shang dynasty (1766 B.C.) onwards, but is rather reminiscent of neolithic wares of south-eastern Europe and the eastern Mediterranean. In the province of Honan, however, large numbers of a three-legged type of pottery urn, belonging to the so-called Period II, Yang Chao ware, have been found, and this form is evidently the prototype of one of the classical sacrificial bronze vessels of the historical periods – namely, a tripod, called *ting*. It is so typical that the Chinese character for it has been incorporated in the list of the 214 *radicals* – i.e., the composing elements of the Chinese script. Here, then, we have a link between prehistoric and historic forms. It is impossible here to give a summary of all the archaeological work done in China in recent years with regard to later prehistoric periods and the early dynastic epochs. So far excavations have been carried out only sporadically, and in some cases even accidentally, as during road or railway constructions. More systematic excavations have been conducted in North China and Manchuria by the eminent Swedish geologist, Mr J. G. Andersson. Of special interest to the student of primitive art are the finds made by P. Teilhard de Chardin and P. Licent in the Ordos country, in the North-west. The Ordos bronzes, which are now well represented in the principal

PRIMITIVE ART

museums of Europe and the United States, are related to Scythian art, and are probably a local variety of it. More discoveries of neolithic sites would be welcome, and maybe one day even palaeolithic art may come to light. Fresh discoveries in China may be expected at any time, and these may differ widely in the various provinces, for there can be no question of a single Chinese race, and it seems likely that the various ethnic stocks had their own separate cultures, just as, in more recent times, we can distinguish between regional art styles and local special techniques within the vast area of China.

In Japan no conclusive evidence of palaeolithic man has come to light. The oldest prehistoric finds indicate a New Stone Age which may have persisted longer than in other areas. It has left a great variety of vases, urns, and crude figurines in pottery. The latter are almost entirely female, with the sex characteristics strongly accentuated. They are very primitive, and cruder than the palaeolithic statuettes in Europe, but they show a striking resemblance to the clay idols of the New Stone Age in South-east Europe and the eastern Mediterranean.[65]

2. *Prehistoric Art in Siberia and Central Asia*

One would have thought that in Siberia, where bodies of mammoths have been found in an almost perfect state of preservation, there must be ample evidence of palaeolithic cultures. However, while an Upper Palaeolithic culture in Siberia had been established for a long time, no work of art which could with certainty be ascribed to the Old Stone Age had been discovered until recently. Primitive fish idols carved in slate or sandstone belong to the New Stone Age. Rock pictures are comparatively common, but archaeologists used to be sceptical with regard to their great antiquity, and were inclined to believe that not one rock picture could be dated back with any certainty even to the neolithic, let alone the palaeolithic period. As in other areas, rock art in Siberia consists partly of engravings or pecked drawings and partly of paintings. One rock drawing, discovered near Abansk, in the Minusinsk district, shows hunters with bows and arrows, and two naked men, one with a spear. In themselves these details

116

might suggest a very early date, as there is every reason to assume that as far back as the Bronze Age all the peoples of Siberia habitually wore thick gowns; and yet even in this case prehistorians were not sure whether the picture is even neolithic, because no accompanying stone implements have been found which could serve as a chronological guide. Other pictures definitely belong to a much later period – roughly speaking, the first millennium A.D. – and some are of Turkish, Kirghiz, and Sasanian origin, and have been identified on account of their style, and in some cases from inscriptions. Now, in recent years more finds have been made by Russian archaeologists, with the result that there is no longer any doubt that palaeolithic art existed in the Asiatic countries of the Soviet Union, notably in Siberia. For example, female statuettes like those of the Aurignacian period of Europe, some of which had been excavated at Kostienki and other sites in the Russian plains previously, have since been found at Maltá, near Irkutsk.[66] Quite recently news has come through of further discoveries in two widely distant areas – viz., first, in Yakutsk in Eastern Siberia, and, secondly, in Uzbekistan (north of Afghanistan).[67]

(1) *Yakutsk*. Expeditions under Professor Okladnikov have investigated about eighty prehistoric sites and groups of rock pictures in the middle and upper Lena valley. Numerous works of primitive art were discovered, and the members of the expeditions are satisfied that these belong not only to the Bronze and Iron Ages (which, as we have seen, is nothing new), but partly to the neolithic and even the palaeolithic periods. If the latter date is correct, it must be the Upper Palaeolithic, as far as rock art is concerned. Miss Tatyana Passek, secretary of the Institute of History of Material Culture of the Academy of Sciences in Moscow, describes the cliffs near the village of Shishkino, on the Lena River, as a 'museum of primitive art'; 'Majestic cliffs rise from the river shore in three tiers. In many places, over a stretch of a kilometre and a half the cliffs are completely covered with drawings.' Miss Passek thinks the most interesting piece is a life-size drawing of a wild horse in red paint, resembling similar drawings in palaeolithic caves in western Europe. Another site of rock art is the Suruktaakh Khaya cliff on the River Markha,

a northern tributary of the River Vilyui, which, in its turn, is a tributary of the Lena. This locality is situated between 110° and 120° E. long., and in about 65° N. lat. Here, too, the cliff is covered with drawings. They represent 'witch doctors, reindeer, cupola-like structures and various symbols', and there are some of the already mentioned inscriptions in ancient Turkish.

Fig. 26. Rock drawing from the Suruktaakh Khaya cliff, Yakutsk Lena area. From *Moscow News*, 27 January, 1945.

(2) *Uzbekistan.* These rock drawings are on the limestone cliffs of Zaraut-Saya Gorge, and were discovered accidentally by a local hunter. They are said to represent hunting scenes, the hunters carrying bows and arrows. The principal animal is the aurochs. Professor Mikhail Voyevodsky of the University of Moscow explains that this is the first primitive 'art gallery' of its kind to be found in Central Asia, and he is of the opinion that the pictures belong to several periods, beginning with the Mesolithic. There are Arabic inscriptions under some pictures, and these inscriptions belong to the eleventh to thirteenth centuries A.D. According to Professor Voyevodsky, they do not indicate the date of the rock pictures, but only prove that the pictures had been discovered earlier by the authors of the inscriptions. It is understood that bones of a youth of the Neanderthal race have been

found in a cave in the mountains of Uzbekistan, also that there are other caves in Zaraut-Saya Gorge which so far have not been investigated.

As this is only a preliminary report, a full appreciation and archaeological classification of all those finds in Eastern Siberia and, on the other hand, Uzbekistan will be possible for us only when the forthcoming scientific publication, with adequate illustrations, is available. An example of the rock drawings in the Lena region is reproduced in Fig. 26, but this should be regarded as only a rough sketch which is probably not quite accurate. Still, it is obvious that this is not palaeolithic or even neolithic art; these drawings apparently belong to the Bronze Age. However incomplete the section illustrated here may be, at least one typically primitive feature is quite distinct – viz., 'X-ray' vision; that is to say, the representation of inner parts of a body, as it has been described in Chapter II. This is one of the several characteristics which ancient Siberian art has in common with North-west American art and other American art styles, and these parallels have been specially studied by Professor Carl Hentze of Antwerp.

The Bronze Age in Siberia is largely associated with Scythian art, which flourished early in the first millennium B.C., and covered the immense area from Hungary, through Southern Russia and Persia, to Northern China.[68] Scythian art has survived in a large number of ornaments and utilitarian objects of bronze and of gold, consisting of decorative trimmings, of garments and harnesses, horse-bits, axe blades, club heads, short swords; animal and human figures, often connected with technical adjustments, such as tubes, the function of which is still obscure. As the chief objects represented are animals, both real and fabulous, this style is usually called 'animal style', which is not a good term, because it would fit certain other art styles as well; besides, it does not really characterize the style, but only the principal motif of this type of art. The Scythian style may be described as a combination of primitive vision and technical perfection – a strange mixture of decorative stylization with naturalism. In almost every instance the artists show an admirable observation of nature, but they adapted the designs with perfect freedom to the shape of the decorative field. Parts of the animal are distorted and discon-

nected to serve as decorative details. The result is that in many
of the pieces, which are cast in the *cire-perdue* process and
almost always in open work, the animal, or group of several animals, is not at first sight recognizable. Similar decorative principles
are typical of North-west American art, and they also occur
in the decoration of early Chinese bronzes. These similarities do
not necessarily indicate any historical connexions, and as far as
the earliest known Chinese bronzes of the Shang dynasty are concerned, any affinity with Scythian art is ruled out by other stylistic
peculiarities, chronological reasons, and entirely different types of
objects. However, many bronzes of a later period, that of the Han
dynasties (206 B.C.–A.D. 220), have so many features in common
with Scythian art that in my opinion a direct connexion must be
responsible for them, although even this has been called in question.

3. *Primitive features in Classical Chinese Art*

We have already mentioned that the decoration of early Chinese
bronze vessels – those of the Shang, Yin, Chou, and Ts'in dynasties, roughly speaking from the second millennium to the middle
of the third century B.C. – reveals certain primitive characteristics.
Parallels are not confined to Siberian and North-west American
art, but also occur in the ornamentation of the marble vessels excavated on the banks of the River Ulua in Honduras, and ascribed
to the second great period of Maya civilization (eleventh to twelfth
centuries A.D.) (Pl. 38 (*b*)). In all these areas decorative designs
are composed of conventionalized animal patterns, and an animal
may be represented by two symmetrical profiles, while the various
parts of the body are disconnected and arbitrarily arranged to fit
into a decorative field. This primitive device can be identified on
many, but not all, early Chinese bronze vessels. It is not at first
sight recognizable, but often has to be disentangled from a complicated intertwining of curved ornaments, scroll-work, etc.; in
other words, it will be realized only by analytical study, and thus
does not affect the aesthetic quality of the vessel. Actually, these
ancient Chinese bronze vessels are of supreme quality, ranking
among the greatest art treasures in the world. Workmanship,
shape, and arrangement of decorative patterns are perfect. In

striking contrast with them is the real primitiveness of naturalistic representations. Pictographs of the Shang period are illustrated in Fig. 6, showing the preliminary stages of some Chinese characters. It will be seen that some of those early characters are real pictographs, representing a whole animal, while others are symbols, showing one characteristic detail only, as, for example, the horns of a bull or a ram. There are no plastic representations of human figures, except on two or three famous ritual bronze vessels of a type called *kuang*, where a human figure is represented in the jaws of a monster, obviously a mythical scene. It would lead us too far from our subject to discuss at length the significance of those strange pieces and their parallels in ancient American art; suffice it to say that they probably belong to lunar mythology. The important point for us here is that those human figures are definitely of a primitive type. This is also the case with another Chinese bronze figure, illustrated on Pl. 12 (*a*). It is a statuette of a man, carrying a tray, 15 cm. high, covered with green patina. The head shows an unmistakable resemblance to those of the human figures on the *kuangs*, but these are ascribed to the Chou dynasty, whereas the statuette here illustrated is supposed to be a work of a later period, the Ts'in dynasty (255–206 B.C.). It has, incidentally, a certain similarity to Aztec stone sculptures, but this is accidental. In any case, the piece is a good example of the marked primitiveness of the rare human figures in early Chinese art, even at historical periods. More highly developed representations of human figures and horses, animated scenes carved in low reliefs on stone, appear only during the period between about 100 B.C. and A.D. 200–that is to say, the Han epoch. It may be mentioned that religious sculptures – i.e., sculptures in the round – did not exist in China before the introduction of Buddhism in the first century A.D., and that as late as the third century A.D. Buddha statues were obtained from India and other Buddhist countries.

4. *Prehistoric Art in India*

In India prehistoric archaeology has been making steady progress since 1863, when the first prehistoric stone artefacs was found in the neighbourhood of Madras by Robert Bruce Foote. The first archaic rock painting was discovered near Mirzapur by Archibald Carlleyle and J. Cockburn in 1880, and described by Cockburn in the *Journal of the Asiatic Society of Bengal* in 1883. It represents a rhinoceros attacked by six men, some of whom are wearing feather head-dresses.

Since then many more rock pictures have been found. The most important are those discovered by Anderson near Singhanpur in the Raigarh district. These are paintings in burgundy red, mauve, and pale yellow, of various figures, including men, birds, and a pig, together with geometric designs of uncertain significance. The details of primitive implements and garments, etc., depicted in some of the wall paintings in Central India bear a close resemblance to similar objects in stone sculptures of comparatively recent date. But this does not necessarily mean that the paintings belong to the same period as the sculptures. Throughout the Asiatic continent we find tools, weapons, and clothes which have survived unchanged since time immemorial. On the other hand, although some of the earliest rock paintings (at Adam Garh) are strongly reminiscent of the Upper Palaeolithic wall pictures of Spain, this cannot be taken as a proof that they are of equal antiquity. The fact is that the chronological classification of the Indian rock paintings is still an unsolved problem. The different types of figures and objects, and the fact that in some cases paintings have been superimposed on older paintings or pecked drawings, suggest that the works belong to various periods; but there is an amazing difference of opinion about the probable age of the earliest.[69] Some archaelogists place them in the Upper Palaeolithic period, while others suggest a date as late as the first millennium B.C.

The latter theory, however, is difficult to maintain beside the well-established chronology of Mohenjo-Daro and Harappa, which reaches back to the fourth millennium B.C. Even this Indus civilization is not a pure Stone Age culture, but chalcolitic – that is, distinguished by the use of both stone and copper. Some eighty miles north of Mohenjo-Daro prehistoric sites were recently discovered which appear to belong to the Old (or at least the Middle) Stone Age, and are therefore thousands of years older than Mohenjo-Daro.[70] It is true that they are a long way from the nearest rock pictures, and the creators of these pictures may have been of totally different races. But the mere existence of these early sites in the north-west adds weight to any evidence of Stone Age culture in other parts of India.

The excavations at Mohenjo-Daro and Harappa in the Indus valley, under Sir John Marshall and Dr Ernest Mackay,[71] have enormously enriched our knowledge of the prehistory and, implicitly, the earliest art of India. For a full appreciation of the importance of the archaeological discoveries in the Indus valley we must remember that until recently ancient Indian dated history began only with the sixth century B.C., and the earliest known Indian sculpture and architecture with the Maurya dynasty (from 321 B.C. onwards), especially the reign of Aśoka (274–237 B.C.). The art of the Aśoka period, however, represents a high development, and nothing was known about its earlier stages, let alone primitive beginnings. Now we have learned that as early as the third, and probably even the fourth, millennium B.C., a civilization of amazingly high development flourished in the Indus valley – that is to say, many centuries before the arrival of the invaders from the north, who, on account of their language, are known as 'Aryans'. The people of Mohenjo-Daro and Harappa belonged to a different race, or rather represented a racial mixture, because the anthropological examination of excavated skulls revealed the presence of two main races, described as the 'Proto-Australoid' and the 'Mediterranean' – both rather indefinite terms. In addition, one skull with Mongolian features and one ascribed to the so-called Alpine race have been unearthed, but such sporadic finds naturally cannot furnish any conclusive evidence. Dr Mackay explains that the majority of skulls agree in many ways with those found by him at Kish, and by Sir Leonard Woolley at Al 'Ubaid in Mesopotamia, and here it may be mentioned that according to one theory the ancient population of Mesopotamia included three different racial stocks – namely, the 'Proto-Elamites', the Sumerians, and the (Semitic) Akkadians, of which the latter two were not autochthonous, but immigrants. As a working hypothesis it has been suggested that perhaps the Proto-Elamites, the people of the Indus civilization, and possibly also the Sumerians, were the descendants of a common ancestry (Mackay, *The*

Indus Civilization, p. 12). The date of the youngest stratum at Mohenjo-Daro has been established by the fact that seals from Mohenjo-Daro have been found in both Babylonia and Elam, and there is also other archaeological evidence of cultural contact between the two areas. The Proto-Australoid element in the Indus valley suggests a relation to the ancestors of the modern Dravidians, the Proto-Dravidians, and thus it was probably a dark-skinned population which must be credited with the construction of the brick-built cities, with their baths, tanks, and well-planned drainage systems, fine pottery, jewellery, most interesting types of sculpture, and – last but not least – the invention of a script which has not yet been deciphered. Compared with these highly cultured people, the Aryan invaders of a much later period may well be regarded as barbarians.

For the study of primitive art, the plastic art of Mohenjo-Daro and Harappa is of the greatest importance. Three principal materials were used: clay, steatite, and copper. The *cire-perdue* process was employed for the copper statuettes. At least three different styles may be distinguished – viz., a very primitive naturalistic style, represented by clay figures; a more highly developed naturalistic style of great aesthetic quality, represented by human statuettes cast in copper and by animal figures of both copper and steatite; and, thirdly, highly stylized or even conventionalized naturalistic art – namely, stone statues of men and, on the other hand, the so-called seal-amulets carved in steatite, showing reliefs of animals, monsters, trees, accompanied by the already mentioned characters, or pictographs, likewise in relief. These mysterious signs, or characters, are apparently not related to any known alphabet or pictographic or symbolic script.

The fascinating theory of G. de Hévésy that many of the Indus signs were identical with the hieroglyphs of Easter Island in far-away easternmost Polynesia has been called in question by Alfred Métraux, and the opinions of anthropologists are divided.[72] I myself am unable to recognize more than a very slight similarity of a few signs on either side, which is probably accidental. Otherwise the appearance of the two scripts is, in my opinion, totally different. For the rest, the chronological distance between the high civilization of the Indus valley and the primitive culture of the

Polynesians of Easter Island is, roughly speaking, four thousand years, let alone that types and art styles in both areas are also entirely different. If the mystery of the Indus script should ever be solved, it will be by systematic comparison with the ancient characters of India, Mesopotamia, and adjacent areas. So far the only resemblance (not identity) of a few Indus signs, or symbols, seems to me to exist with some mint-marks on Bactrian coins – for example, those of Demetrius I (about 190 B.C.) and of Kanishka (Kanerkes) (end of the first century A.D.) – but this may be a coincidence, and in any case would not help us to solve the problem. I have mentioned Hévésy's theory because, if it were borne out by the facts, it would show that two totally different types of primitive art developed in spite of cultural relations. Actually, the primitive clay idols of Mohenjo-Daro may rather be compared with certain figurines of ancient Mexico, but here, too, the similarity is superficial, obviously being due to the same material and technique. Generally speaking, comparisons of this kind are useless.

Much more important is the relation between the art of the Indus valley and the historical periods of Hindu art. It is true that there is still a wide gap of two millennia or more between the Indus civilization and the Maurya empire, and yet it would appear that the plastic art of the Indus valley may be regarded as the preliminary stage of Hindu religious art. A large number of small figures of bulls, of stone or bronze, shows that the people of Mohenjo-Daro must have been very interested in these animals, and possibly treated them with the same respect as we find in Brahmanism, where the bull is the sacred animal, or 'vehicle', of Shiva. Then there are bronze, or copper, figurines, especially that of a dancing-girl, quite distinctly foreshadowing certain well-known types of mediaeval Indian sculpture. The most primitive clay figures, evidently belonging to an early stratum, represent a woman wearing a large head-dress and a superabundance of jewellery. This type has been tentatively interpreted as a goddess of motherhood and fertility, but as deities of this character are found almost everywhere in agricultural civilizations it is not necessarily the prototype of the Hindu goddess Parvati-Durga-Kali, or that of the earth-goddess Bhumi. Still, the ornaments and the head-dress of those crude figures definitely appear, naturally in more finely elaborate forms, on stone and bronze statues of deities, both Brahmanic and Buddhist, in later centuries.

These brief observations may suffice to show the great importance of the plastic art of the Indus civilization, not only for the history of Indian art, but also for the study of primitive art generally. Needless to say that the actual development of Indian art from the third millennium B.C. to the Maurya period can be cleared up only by further systematic archaeological research in other parts of the country.

5. *Primitive Art in the Middle East*

In the vast area which is usually known under the somewhat vague name 'Middle East', the arts of the ancient high civilizations can be traced back to their early stages, which in many places may be classified as 'primitive'. The following brief observations are confined to three selected art provinces – viz., Syria, Mesopotamia, and Luristan.

(1) From Syria we have to mention a primitive type of sculpture excavated at Tell Brak by M. E. L. Mallowan in 1938. At this site three strata have been established, covering the very long period from 3100 B.C., or even earlier, down to 1500 B.C. Contacts with Mesopotamia have also been discovered. Of particular interest for the art student is a number of strange, long-necked human heads of alabaster, found in one of the older strata.[73] They are very primitive, with long, straight noses, protruding eyebrows meeting in the centre, and large, almond-shaped eyes with small holes to represent the pupils. The technique employed by the carvers seems to suggest clay sculpture as the preliminary stage of this style. In contrast with those stiff and expressionless human heads, there are small stone carvings of animals, distinguished by a naïve but animated naturalism.

A different type of primitive art has come to light at Tell Halaf, excavated by Dr Max Baron von Oppenheim in 1911–13 and 1929.[74] Shrines, reliefs, and huge figures of deities, or demons, of Tell Halaf have no relation to any other style in adjacent or more remote areas, while the iconography of the reliefs links up with

Assyria (Gilgamesh scenes). These relics are of considerable antiquity (3400–2600 B.C., according to Professor Herzfeld). As Tell
Halaf was associated with a kingdom called *Subartu* in Babylonian records, the culture of Tell Halaf has been named *Subaraean*.
The stone figures, some of which are of very large dimensions, are
certainly interesting as unique examples of a queer, primitive way
of expressing the demonic nature of an imaginary supernatural
world; but from our aesthetic point of view they are anything but
attractive. Painted clay figurines have also been found at Tell
Halaf, and these are still more primitive than the larger sculptures.
They have small heads with hardly recognizable human
features, and thick, cylindrical limbs. The character of these crude
clay figures is neolithic. On the other hand, beautiful pottery
bowls of graceful shapes and with tasteful painted decoration
have been excavated at the same site.

(2) In Mesopotamia the ancient culture of Ur, popular through
H. R. Hall's and Sir Leonard Woolley's excavations, and now
beautifully represented at the University of Pennsylvania Museum,
Philadelphia, the British Museum, and – last but not least – the
Museum at Baghdad, had reached a high stage of technical and
artistic development already at the time of the first dynasty
(end of the fourth millennium B.C.).

As a whole, then, the Sumerian art of Ur cannot be classified
as 'primitive' – i.e., of undeveloped vision, design, or technique.
However, if we remember that primitiveness has also a chronological significance and that, for example, the earliest known art –
the cave-paintings of the Upper Palaeolithic of Europe – is of
the highest aesthetic quality, we may describe some of the plastic
works of the ancient Sumerians as primitive in this appreciative
sense of the term.[75] Indeed, some of the small figures of lions,
bulls, and other animals carved in carnelian, greenstone, and
other types of stone are distinguished by a remarkable truth to
nature reminiscent of the finest naturalistic wall-paintings in the
caves of Southern France, although both the media and the
dimensions are totally different.

(3) Luristan, a province in Western Iran, began to attract
archaeologists only some thirty years ago, when a large number
of heavily patinated bronze objects had been accidentally dug up

by peasants, and eventually found their way into European and American museums and private collections. The prehistoric inhabitants of Luristan must have been principally horse-breeders, as a large proportion of the finds consists of horse-bits, harness, etc. In addition, there are axe blades, club heads, short swords, bowls, and jars, all of bronze. Especially the decorations of horse-bits and harness show a characteristic style distinguished by the predominance of stylized animal forms, open work, and rigid symmetry. All this clearly indicates a relation to Scythian art – in fact, Luristan may be regarded as the country of the southern-most extension of Scythian culture. However, the art style of Luristan is not purely Scythian, but has also distinct Assyrian, Babylonian, and ancient Persian features amalgamated with the northern animal style. This is not surprising, as all those ancient cultural centres are in close proximity. Luristan art has been studied by A. Godard, R. W. Hutchinson, M. I. Rostovtsev, and other archaeologists, and a valuable analysis of the style has been contributed by G. D. Hornblower.[76] Mr Hornblower has made a special study of one particular representation, which occurs in various forms in the Luristan bronzes – viz., a group composed of a central human figure surrounded by two symmetrical and highly stylized animals in upright position, explained as a Gilgamesh hero subduing two lions. It is the human figure in the centre which is often of a striking primitiveness, its crude, rudimentary naturalism contrasting with the perfect harmony of the framework of rigidly stylized animal forms.

6. Recent Primitive Art in Asia

In modern Asia primitive tribes still survive in four principal areas: in certain parts of India, in Further India, in Indonesia, and in North Asia.

(1) Most of the primitive tribes of India have long been infiltrated by Hindu civilization, and offer little material for the student of primitive art, but in some districts there are still examples of genuine primitive art, as for instance in Orissa. Another area is West Bihar, where W. G. Archer discovered anthropomorphic pole-sculptures in wood and stone, 'images of brutal dignity', as

(a) Bushman rock engraving in the pecking (intaglio) technique, representing an eland antelope. Length (nose to tail) 28.5 cm. Klipfontein (Style II). *South African Museum.*

(b) West African pre-Islamic pottery figure of a man. Height 25 cm. Excavated at Tago (Lake Chad) by Jean-Paul Lebeuf & Mme. A. Masson- Detourbet. *By courtesy of M. Sougez, Paris.*

(a) Ivory figure of a horseman. Height 14.3 in. Yoruba, Nigeria. *British Museum.*

(b) Female ancestor figure. Wood. Bangwa, Cameroons. Height 82 cm. *Formerly in the Museum f. Völkerkunde, Berlin.*

Two chief's stools, combined with over life-size statues. From Bekom, Bamenda district, Cameroons. Height (left): 185 cm.; (right): 194 cm. *Museum f. Völkerkunde, Berlin.*

Carved door-frame. Wood. From Bamum, Cameroons. Width of architrave:
2 metres. *Museum f. Völkerkunde, Berlin.*

(a) Wooden mask, painted black and white. Mpongwe, Gabun, French Equatorial Africa. Height *c.* 10 in.

(b) Wooden mask wearing lip-plug. Makonde, Port. East Africa. Height 9 in. *British Museum.*

5

Wooden stool, the seat supported by an ancestral couple. A Baluba sculpture of the eastern Congo, illustrating the 'long-faced style of Buli' (F. Olbrechts). Height 53.5 cm.; upper diameter 45.5 cm. *Museum f. Völkerkunde, Berlin,* III C. 14966.

(a) Wooden vase. Bakongo, Congo. Height 8 in. *British Museum.*

(b) Wooden figure. Baluba, Congo. Height *c.* 5 in. *British Museum.*

(c) Ivory statuette. Bapende, Congo. Height 13 cm.

(d) Bronze plaque, Benin. Height *c.* 6 in. *British Museum.*

(a) Ivory armlet from Benin, but carved in the Yoruba style, probably of Owo. Height *c.* 6 in. *British Museum.*

(b) Bronze head representing a king wearing coral ornaments. Benin. Height *c.* 12 in.

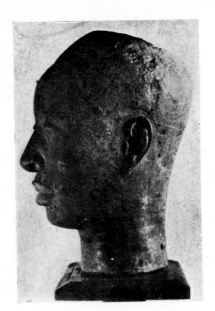

Two bronze heads excavated at Ife, Nigeria in 1938. (a) Height *c.* 12 in. (b) Height *c.* 12 in.

9

(a) Bronze head wearing crown. Ife, Nigeria. Height *c.* 15 in.

(b) Ashanti gold weights. Height *c.* 2–3 cm. each.

(a) Stone figures discovered at Esie, Ilorin Province, Nigeria, in 1934.

(b) Clay figures made by Tallensi children, Gold Coast.

(a) Chinese bronze statuette. Ts'in dynasty (255–207 B.C.). Height *c.* 15 cm.

(b) Clay figures from ancient tombs. Nilgiri Hills, S. India. Height 6.9 and 3.8 in. *British Museum.*

(a) (*left*) Amulet box of horn, with carved wooden lid. Height 27 cm. Batak. Collected in Deli (Sumatra), 1868–69. *Museum f. Völkerkunde, Basel.*

(b) (*right*) Dagger from Balige, a Toba-Batak village, Sumatra. Haft and sheath of wood. The eyes and armlets of the squatted human figure carved on the haft are of metal. The sheath is set with bands of sheet copper. Length 24.5 cm. *Museum f. Völkerkunde, Basel.*

(c) Ancestor post, *batugur*, from the Siang district, upper Barito river, S.E. Borneo. Carving in black wood, height 2 m. Coll. by Dr P. Wirz, 1926. *Museum f. Völkerkunde, Basel.*

(a) Three ancestor figures from Nias, west of Sumatra. Wood. Height 26 cm.; 30.5 cm.; 22.5 cm.

(b) Wooden statuette of 'Bolli Atap,' a magical figure. Sarawak, Borneo. Height 14.8 in. *British Museum.*

A 'cubistic' male statuette from the Philippine Islands. Height 65 cm.
Municipal Museum, Brunswick.

(a) Calabash. Massim, New Guinea. Height 9.7 in. *British Museum.*

(b) Skull of an ancestor, the soft parts modelled in clay and painted red and white. Sepik River, New Quinea.

Stool with image of an ancestor. Carved in
one piece, painted red and white. Height *c.*
3 ft. 2 in. Sepik River, New Guinea. *National
Museum of Victoria, Melbourne.*

(a) Wooden mask. Height
31 cm. Lower Sepik River,
New Guinea. *National Museum of Victoria, Melbourne.*

(b) Pottery urn with plastic
decoration and red and white
paint, Ramu Valley, New
Guinea. Height 60 cm.; diameter 50 cm. *Ethnological Museum, Bremen.*

(a) Front view

(b) Back view
Stone relief found near Anna-
berg, Ramu Valley, New
Guinea. Height 44 cm.; width
22 cm.; thickness 8 cm.
Australian Museum, Sydney.

(a) Statuette carved from a slab of chalk in memory of a deceased relative. Southern New Ireland. Height 69 cm. *National Museum of Victoria, Melbourne.*

(b) Wood carving in open-work, illustrating the *malanggan*-style. Represented are spirits and mythical beings. Red, black, and white decoration. Northern New Ireland. Height *c.* 4 ft. *British Museum.*

(a) Ancestor figures, carved from a fern tree trunk. Ambrym Island, New Hebrides. Height 7 ft 8 in. *National Museum, Melbourne.*

(b) Carved board flanking the entrance to a chief's hut. New Caledonia. Height 7 ft 6 in. *British Museum.*

(a) Wooden statuette. Height 64 cm. Buka, northern Solomon Isles. Yellowish wood stained black, head-gear and stand (all in one piece) are painted dark red. Incised lines represent armlets. The face with protruding jaw shows the prognathous physiognomy typical of the archipelago. The tip of the nose is chipped. *University of Melbourne Collection (loan).*

(b) Detail showing the treatment (unusual for Melanesia) of the hands and legs.

(a) Wooden bowl representing a bird, inlaid with shell. The wood is stained a dark reddish brown. Palau Islands, Micronesia. *British Museum.*

(b) Bird-shaped wooden bowl. Admiralty Islands, Western Melanesia. The wood is stained black. Length *c.* 30 cm. *Museum f. Völkerkunde, Berlin.*

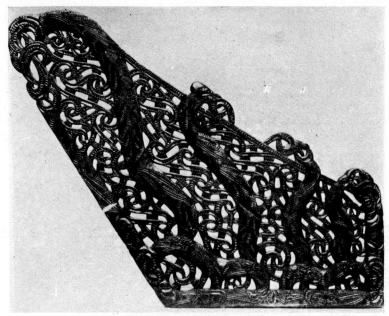

(a) Prow of a canoe. Maori, New Zealand. Height *c.* 3 ft. *British Museum.*

(b) Feather box. New Zealand. Length 21 in. *University Museum of Archeology and Ethnology, Cambridge.*

24

Wooden door-frame of a decorated store-house. Maori. The high relief carvings represent mythological figures. The protruding tongues are symbols of energy and fierceness. The eyes were originally inlaid with green *paua* (haliotis) shell. Height *c.* 1.50 m. *Museum f. Völkerkunde, Berlin.*

(a) Wooden spittoon. Hawai. Height 8. in. *British Museum.*

(b) Wood carving. Tahiti. *British Museum.*

a) Feather cloak of King Kamehameha II of Hawaii
(1827). Length *c*. 1.50 m. *Museum f.Völkerkunde, Berlin.*

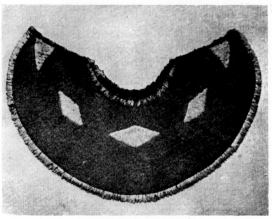

(b) Hawaiian cape of feather mosaic in scarlet, yellow,
and black. Width *c*. 89 cm. *Royal Scottish Museum,
Edinburgh.*

(a) Hoa-Haka-Nana-Ia, sandstone sculpture from Easter Island. Height *c.* 8 ft; width *c.* 3 ft. Brought to England by H.M.S. *Topaze* in 1869 and now in the British Museum. *By courtesy of the Trustees.*

(b) Part of the rock engravings at Ko Te Kari, S.W. end of the village Orongo, Easter Island. *By courtesy of Professor H. Lavachery.* (The engravings have been chalked for photography.)

28

(a) (*left*) Statuette of toromiro wood. Easter Island. Height *c.* 48 cm. *British Museum.*

(b) (*right*) An example of wooden pole-sculpture with polychrome painted designs from Yirrkalla, N.E. coast of Arnhem Land, Northern Territory of Australia. Height *c.* 91.4 cm. *Department of Anthropology, University of Sydney.*

(a) Wall painting in a rock shelter in the Kimberleys, north-western Australia, representing Wund'udu-modingari, i.e. Wund'udu, or Walanganda, the celestial hero of the Ungarinyin tribe, visible as the Milky Way. Height approximately 1.80 m. The hero is accompanied by two Wondjina half-figures. Colours: mainly yellow ochre, faces white; the eyes, breast shields, and the inner contours of face and breast are black. *By courtesy of the Frobenius Institute, Frankfurt-am-Main. Photograph by Fox.*

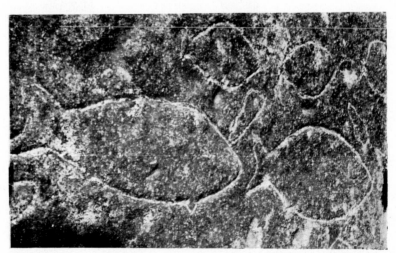

(b) Rock engravings representing a shoal of fish, on the horizontal rock surface of a site in the Kuringai Chase, Sydney District, New South Wales. Length of illustrated section *c.* 1.20 cm. *Photograph by J. Mary Adam.*

Bark painting from Groote Eylandt, Gulf of Carpentaria, Australia, illustrating the finding of a prehistoric axe-head. Subsequently, this axe-head was hafted and is here reproduced taken out of the haft to show its shape. Dimensions of picture approx. 3 ft by 15 in. White, yelow, and red ochre on black ground. *University of Melbourne Collection.*

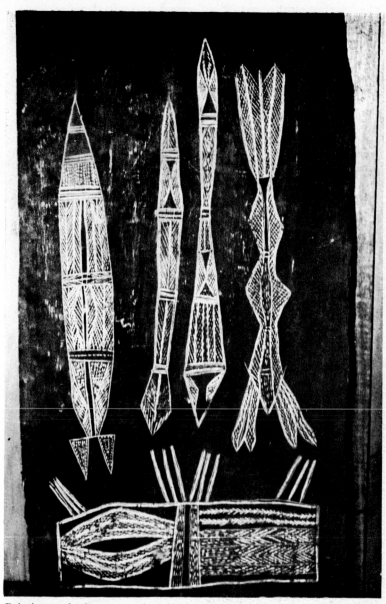

Painting on bark, representing ritual implements (top) and a pond ('billabong') with reeds and lily nuts (bottom). Groote Eylandt, Gulf of Carpentaria. Size approx. 3 ft by 16 in. *University of Melbourne Collection.*

(a) Pipe, carved in walrus-ivory.
Alaska Eskimos. Length 33.6 cm.

(b) Totem pole. Haida Indians, Queen Charlotte Islands.
Height 39 ft. *British Museum.*

33

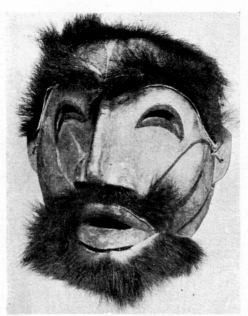

(a) Mask of the Haida Indians, Queen Charlotte Islands, British Columbia. Height 29 cm. Cedar wood, painted red and blue. The hair, eybrows, and beard consist of pieces of animal fur. Ears carved separately and joined with string. *Collected between* 1881 *and* 1883 *by Capt. Adrian Jacobsen. Museum f. Völkerkunde, Berlin.*

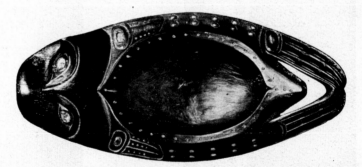

(b) Dish of cedar wood in the shape of a seal. The eyes and eye-ornaments (joint marks) inlaid with *haliotis* shell. Other inlaid ornaments are opercula of sea-snails and glass beads. Length 41 cm. Haida Indians. *Museum f. Völkerkunde, Berlin.*

(a) Mask, representing the thunder-bird. Length 21 in. Bilxula Indians, Brit. Cllumbia. *Museum f. Völkerkunde, Berlin.*

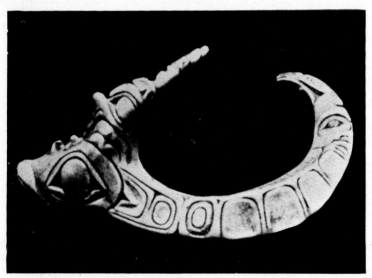

(b) Antler pendant representing a killer-whale. British Columbia. Height 2.2 in; length 6.3 in. *British Museum.*

35

(a) Upper part of a statuette of cedar wood, polychrome. Haida Indians. British Columbia. Total height of the statuette 12 in. *British Museum.*

(b) Wooden mask of the Iroquois, representing a spirit. Dark red paint. Real human hair. *British Museum.*

(a) Sandstone pipe-bowl in the shape of a frog. Length *c.* 5 in. From a mound in Kentucky. *British Museum.*

(b) A *kachina* doll, representing a rain-god. Wood, painted in bright colours. Hopi Indians. Height 8.3 in. *British Museum.*

37

(a) Archaic greenstone figure.
Chimaltenango, Guatemala.
Height 8.7 in. *British Museum.*

(b) Two marble vessels. Late Maya period. Rio Uluá, Honduras. Height
c. 4 in (left); 6 in (right). *Museum f. Völkerkunde, Berlin.*

38

(a) A *nuchu*, statuette of a European dressed in the style of the early nineteenth century, used by medicine-men. Wood, the coat painted blue. Cuna Indians, Panama. Height 12.5 in. *British Museum*. (For full description, see list of plates.)

(b) Clay figure with golden nose-ring. Cauca Valley, Colombia. Height 7.6 in. *British Museum*.

39

(a) A modern Negro sculpture in wood, Nigeria. Height 18.5 in.

(b) Art students at Achimota College. Gold Coast.
Copyright by K & M Lubinski, London.

40

he aptly describes them. These images – most of them simple rounded posts with a head carved in the round and the arms in relief – are offered 'at times of a major crisis'.[76a] One remarkable example of real primitiveness exist among the well-known pastoral tribe of the Todas in the Nilgiri hills, south of Mysore. Their culture has been admirably studied by W. H. R. Rivers. The religion is a cattle-cult, which is reflected in the plastic art of the people. The tribe is now very small, and is bound to die out in the future; but, fortunately, their material culture has been preserved to some extent, through archaeological research. Excavations of tombs in the Toda district have brought to light clay vessels and human and animal figures which are obviously the work of the ancestors of the modern Todas. Figures of cattle, which probably had some ritual function, are predominant (Pl. 12 (b)).

There is also in India a great deal of peasant art or 'derivative primitive art'.[77] We must remember that a large number of more or less primitive autochthonous tribes have been absorbed by, or incorporated in, the Hindu caste system. They live on as low-ranking local castes, often as artisans. Correspondingly, local varieties of Brahmanic cult and ritual sometimes include survivals of ancient, more primitive, forms of religion, and this amalgamation may be reflected by religious art. Through the entire system of cults and sects which usually goes under the name of Hinduism we find pictures, wood-carvings, and brass figures of village deities. These are either derived from more finely elaborated models in the centres of Hindu culture, or can be traced back to old local demons. Delightful examples of primitive plastic art are the so-called 'marriage toys' made by the hill-tribe of Kutiya Kondhs, chiefly at Belugunta (Ganjam). These figures representing animals, riders, carts, etc., reveal a refreshing simple naturalism, and serve as presents to the boy-bridegroom. A collection is in the Indian Museum at South Kensington.

In Ceylon the innumerable devil masks of the Singhalese deserve special mention. They are carved in wood, coated with a white slip, then decorated in bright oil-colours and, finally, varnished. Some of these masks embody good or evil spirits, such as the demons of deafness, malaria, and other diseases, while others represent legendary figures. Certain types are of Indian origin,

while others may be derived from the autochthonous pre-Buddh-
ist heathenism of Ceylon. A third category is probably of European origin, introduced by the Portuguese a few centuries ago.

FIG. 27. Sinhalese mask from Ceylon, representing the demon Riri-Yäka.
Wood, the lateral pieces carved separate and joined with pegs. Yellow, red,
white, and black paint, and lacquer.

(2) We now turn to the north-eastern border of India. In the
hills of Assam, between the upper Brahmaputra valley and
Upper Burma, we find the head-hunting Naga tribes. The Nagas
are typically primitive people, but they have long passed the stage
of mere hunters and are agriculturists. They believe – or at any
rate did so until quite recently – that a year cannot be successful
unless at least one human head has been taken. They have attained a remarkable standard in wood-carving, both in the round

and in relief, and human heads are among the principal models. Another favourite model is the head of the *mithan* – a large breed of cattle which represents the greater part of their wealth and is actually kept for prestige rather than for practical purposes.[78] Among the several tribes, the Angami Nagas stand supreme in artistic achievement. The life-size human figures which the Nagas erect over the tombs of their relatives – representing partly portraits of the deceased and partly mourners – have a parallel in similar statues which are found among the tribes in the interior of French Indo-China. Another parallel, but of smaller dimensions, are the ancestor statuettes of Nias, an island west of Sumatra. The Nagas are of Indonesian origin, and both their ornamental style and their plastic art resemble the work of primitive tribes in the Malayan archipelago. However, there exist still more interesting cultural parallels, or rather indications of ancient connexions, between the Naga hills and even the Pacific area, more particularly Melanesia. The late Dr Henry Balfour, of the Pitt Rivers Museum, Oxford, has shown that, for example, the beautiful breast- or forehead-ornaments of Melanesia, consisting of thin discs of turtle-shell carved in open work (see Fig. 37), have a more primitive parallel in the ear-pendants of the Konyak tribe of Assam.

(3) Indonesia is a melting-pot of altogether different races, from the light-skinned Malays and Javanese, with straight hair, to the dark negritos. Accordingly, we find a variety of cultures, from really primitive types up to highly developed Oriental civilizations. In the sphere of art the contrast between the Buddhist sculpture of medieval Java, the grotesque Hindu statues and masks of Bali, and the entirely different decorative and plastic arts of the primitive tribes of Sumatra, Nias, Borneo, the Philippines, and a large number of other islands reflects the history and the widely different artistic talents and achievements of all those peoples. In Sumatra the plastic art of the Bataks, consisting of carvings in wood or horn, as well as brass work cast in the *cire-perdue* technique, often shows an arrangement of human and animal figures squatting on top of one another, reminiscent of typical pole-sculptures as we find them in North-west America and elsewhere. The already mentioned ancestor statuettes of Nias are wood carv-

FIG. 28. Part of a Painting on Wood (*Henta-Koi*). Nicobar Islands. Colours: blue, scarlet, and yellow. Height 9 in., length 27.2 in. Paintings consisting of two or more parallel sections are made in case of an illness according to the directions of a shaman. This type of art was probably influenced by European pictures introduced by missionaries who arrived in the seventeenth century. But a typically primitive arrangement is obvious. British Museum.

ings, but without any individual features, let alone an attempt at portraiture (Pl. 14 (*a*)). Sometimes – but not always – the mouth is not represented at all, a peculiarity which occurs also in other primitive art styles (e.g., neolithic figures of the eastern Mediterranean; wooden statuettes from Nukuor in Micronesia; the *wondjina* figures in rock paintings in the Kimberleys, North-west Australia). As these typical ancestor figures from Nias are rigidly conventionalized, they display, at their best, good craftsmanship, but cannot really be classified as works of art. In striking contrast with them is an unusual piece from Sarawak (Pl. 14 (*b*)), representing a demon. It is called 'Bolli Atap', and is supposed to provide magic protection against sickness. This figure is distinguished by its naturalism and its rhythmic movement, and it certainly reveals imagination. The quality of the statuette is manifest, although it is a torso. A wooden statue from the Philippine Islands (Pl. 15) shows a totally different style, which can only be described as cubism. This, however, is a naïve variety of cubism which probably developed spontaneously from the technique. 'Cubism' occurs sporadically also in other areas, especially in Western Africa, though not quite in the same extreme form. I wish to refer, however, to the paragraph on p. 44. As far as I can see, cubism in primitive art is confined to wood sculpture. Evidently the structure of certain kinds of wood invites working in large, plain – rather than curved – surfaces.

For a full appreciation of Indonesian art we ought to include the beautiful architecture, especially that of the Bataks of Sumatra, with its gabled houses and almost Gothic roofs, but there is no space for adequate illustrations in this brief survey.[78a]

The decorative art of Indonesia – i.e., the ornamentation of tools, weapons, vessels, and containers of any description, also patterns used in tattooing (for example, in Borneo, some of the Philippine Islands, and the Mentawei Islands) – is distinguished by curved lines and arrangements as the predominant and most conspicuous patterns. Thus we here find a great variety of scrolls, coils, and concentric circles. These curvilinear patterns are typical of Indonesia. It has been suggested that these curved designs were developed from metal-work, especially spiral ornaments made of bronze wire, and that therefore the decorative art of

Indonesia might have been influenced by the Bronze Age of South-east Asia. This may be so, yet it would not suffice for a full analysis, because a good many forms, in particular those found among the Kenyah-Kayan tribes of Borneo, are decidedly either floral designs or zoomorphous. These questions are of importance also for the study of Papuan and Melanesian decorative art.

FIG. 29. Incised Figure on a Wooden Shield from Borneo. Burgundy red paint and set with lead. British Museum, No. 7291.

(4) North Asia. Similar conditions in the arctic and sub-arctic regions have produced a similar mode of life and, correspondingly, similar primitive cultures in northern Asia as well as North America, so the term 'arctic culture' has been introduced in anthropology. It means that the influence of environment has brought about a specific type of material culture, but also a peculiar mental outlook of the populations. We have to take into account also that in both continents the peoples of the extreme

134

north belong to the Mongolian race, or at least may be classified as Mongoloid. The northern Mongolians, however, were probably not the aborigines of their present territories, but immi-

FIG. 30. Part of a Painting in Red and Green on a Shaman's Drum. From Siberia, probably Ostiak. Height 9 in. Total diameter of drum: *c.* 27 in. British Museum.

grated from the south in prehistoric times, driving an older population into the easternmost parts of the Asiatic continent – namely the Chukotski and Kamchatka peninsulas. These older peoples, called *Paloeoasiatics*, are the Chukchi, the Koryak, and the

Kamchadal. They are all fishermen and hunters, while the tribes of the sub-arctic regions also depend on animal husbandry (the reindeer in the Old World, and the related caribou in America; Siberian reindeer have been imported into Alaska in recent years, to replace large numbers of caribou which had been lost through an epidemic). For transport, all the northern peoples use sledges drawn by dogs in arctic America, and by either dogs or reindeer in the Old World. Raw materials are: bone, walrus ivory, animal skin, sinews, wood, and birch bark. In the extreme north wood is naturally very scarce, mostly drift-wood. This list shows, implicitly, the art materials. There is both graphic and plastic art.

FIG. 31. Reindeer Group Engraved on the Sheath of a Dagger. Bone. Lapland. Height of bone: 0.7 in. Length of group: 4.2 in. Coll. Miss Marion G. Anderson, London.

The Chukchi and, on the other hand, the Ostiaks in the central region of the north have wooden idols of a very simple type of 'pole-sculpture'. The Koryak excel in walrus ivory and bone carvings, similar to the naturalistic figures of the Alaska Eskimos.[79] Koryak culture is, indeed, closely related to, if not identical with, that of the western Eskimos, and their linguistic affinities lie on the American, and not on the Asiatic, side of Bering Strait.

A different type of primitive culture is that of the Gilyak and neighbouring tribes in the Amur region, with fish-skin and birchbark as principal raw materials, and game, fresh and dried fish, and fish-oil as staple foodstuffs.[80] Native materials have been replaced by Chinese goods for quite a long time, especially cotton goods have been introduced from China, and with the cloth came Chinese decorative patterns, with the result that the original Gilyak style – coils and spirals carved in relief on bark containers, etc. – now shows marked Chinese features. The aborigines of the Kurile Islands, Hokkaido, and the southern part of Sakhalin are the Ainu, a palaeo-Asiatic people known for their small stature, long beards, the tattooings on the faces of their women (with a pattern resembling a moustache), and their religion centring in a bear-cult, resembling that of the Gilyak. It is possible that the Ainus once inhabited the whole, or the greater part, of the Japanese islands, and that they were driven north by the invading Japanese. Their artistic talent is quite remarkable. Carved grave-posts preserve the primitive Ainu style, but decorative patterns carved in low relief on wooden implements and especially ornamental designs on garments reveal Japanese influence, which, of course, is not surprising.

The westernmost exponent of arctic culture is in Europe – that of the Lapps of northern Scandinavia. Their existence rests entirely upon the reindeer. They have a peculiar type of dagger, with an iron blade and a haft and sheath of bone. These sheaths are always decorated with engravings, in which scenes of Lappish life, but especially reindeer, are depicted. Material, technique, and models are all very similar to Eskimo work (compare Figs. 31 and 42).

CHAPTER XIV

Oceania

OCEANIA is enthnographically divided into three principal areas: Polynesia, Melanesia, and Micronesia. The Melanesians are supposed to have migrated many thousands of years ago from south-eastern Asia. The Polynesians arrived at a later date, and probably came from India across the Malayan archipelago. The Micronesians are a racial mixture in which the Polynesian element is uppermost. In various parts of Oceania these three principal racial stocks were preceded by earlier, now extinct, populations, and in some islands now inhabited by Melanesians there are still surviving non-Melanesian aborigines, as, for example, the Baining in the interior of the Gazelle peninsula of New Britain. New Guinea has so many characteristic features, and is itself subdivided into so many entirely different anthropological and ethnographical areas, that it ought to be regarded as a separate ethnological province. It is largely inhabited by Papuans, but there is a Melanesian population in the south-east, and certain regions in the interior are inhabited by Pygmies.

The arts of this vast Pacific area are as manifold as its races, and the variety of styles is even greater than in Africa. It is impossible in a few pages to cover the whole field, and we must limit ourselves to a few details illustrative of the styles and techniques of some of the principal regions.

The prehistoric art of Oceania may be the work of the ancestors of the modern natives, or else of older populations now extinct. It consists largely of rock pictures such as have been discovered in Melanesia, in New Guinea and in various parts of Polynesia as far east as Easter Island.[81] On the north coast of Dutch New Guinea no fewer than four stylistic groups of rock paintings have been found. The latest are fairly modern; the oldest show stencilled hands, arms, and feet, very similar to those found on the Australian continent (comp. Fig. 8). Rock drawings, engravings, and paintings are a universal feature, and do not in themselves indicate any historical connexion between the areas in which they occur. But it is worth noting that rock engravings which are almost reliefs have been found in Sarawak,[82] so that at least a geographical link exists between the rock pictures of the South Seas and those of the Old World. Prehistoric stone sculptures of New Guinea and Western Melanesia will be mentioned in the next paragraph.

But even the 'modern' art styles in the South Seas reveal very old traditions, which must have developed in the course of millennia. Moreover, most Oceanian arts are not exactly primitive: on the contrary, they are very often quite sophisticated.[83]

1. *New Guinea*

In New Guinea, as we find it to-day, or as it was in the recent past, several areas with different art techniques and styles may be distinguished. As Professor Raymond Firth puts it, 'One may talk of New Guinea art as distinct from Maori or Australian aboriginal art, but the aesthetic idiom varies so greatly from district to district that any generalization must always be translated into terms of objects of some specific area before it has much meaning.' New Guinea has been described as one of the three most prolific centres of primitive sculpture in wood, the other areas being Negro Africa and North-west America. Actually, however, sculpture in the round is not practised everywhere in New Guinea, but is confined to certain regions. On the other hand, wood is used as a raw material for practical purposes everywhere, and ornamentation of utilitarian objects, with engraved patterns, often filled in with colour pigments, or, in many parts, decorative designs carved in open work, is more common than in any other part of the world. In fact, throughout the vast island there is hardly any implement, ritual or profane, without a plastic or linear decoration of some kind. But even utilitarian objects are mostly adorned with motifs derived from the mythology, religious beliefs, ancestor-cult, or magic of the tribes.

Some principal art provinces are: the western half of the island – i.e., Dutch New Guinea; the Sepik and Ramu river valleys; the Purari delta; the Massim area in the south-east. But if the art styles of the numerous islands and archipelagoes off New Guinea are included, the list is longer. For example, Tami Island (Hüon Gulf) has its own conspicuous art style, although it is related to that of the opposite mainland. On the other hand, in the Trobriand Islands, part of the D'Entrecasteaux Group, we find a decorative style which is almost identical with that found in south-eastern New Guinea.

The west – Dutch New Guinea – clearly reveals Indonesian influence. We have seen in Chapter XIII (sect. 6, p. 133–4) that the

FIG. 32. Wooden Head-rest. British New Guinea.
Length 7.3 in. British Museum.

principal patterns of decorative art in Indonesia are curvilinear, consisting of scrolls, coils, spirals, concentric circles. Genetically, these Indonesian ornamental forms are of two kinds – viz., one developed from stylized animal or plant motifs, and the other at first sight purely geometric. There is, however, the possibility that the latter category is actually of technical origin – namely, derived from metal-work, especially coiled wire, open-work (such as filigree), or curvilinear designs engraved in bronze, as we find it in the Bronze Age of South-east Asia. As a matter of fact, it is the theory put forward by Dr Robert Baron Heine-Geldern, and accepted by other scholars, that the decorative art not only of Indonesia and New Guinea, but largely also that of the Melanesian islands, and even New Zealand, may be ultimately traced back to that period and locality. This is certainly a fascinating theory. It would mean that the early migrations of both Melanesians and Polynesians might give us a clue to the history of decorative art in the western Pacific, perhaps even in the Pacific area generally. However, it would be incorrect to interpret every single decorative pattern of Indonesia and the western Pacific in this way. For example, concentric circles and concentric spirals are an almost universal feature, and occur in the Upper Palaeolithic of Europe, in Eskimo engravings, in ancient Peru, on painted pottery among modern tribes of the Rio Negro basin (North-west Brazil), and elsewhere. Still, if we apply the theory with the necessary reserve, it will be very helpful.

A ritual object typical of Dutch New Guinea is the *korwar* – i.e., a wooden casket, or shrine, for the skull of an ancestor. A *korwar* has the shape of a squatting human figure surrounded by decorative scrolls, all carved in one piece. Smaller specimens which do not hold a skull, are replicas of the larger original type. All *korwars* are supposed to be an abode of the spirit of an ancestor. The type of the decoration is so characteristic that the term '*korwar* style' has been introduced.

The Sepik and Ramu valleys, with a Papuan population, are distinguished by the highest development of sculpture in the round, but there is also a wealth of beautifully shaped bowls and implements decorated with carved reliefs, or supported by human or animal figures. In the Ramu area we also find highly developed pottery, often of large dimensions, with ornamental designs in relief and painted in bright colours (Pl. 18 (*b*)). Sepik and Ramu sculptures are predominantly representations of ancestors, men and women, from small statuettes of only a few inches in length to over life-size figures. In the religious belief of the Papuans the 'soul-bird' plays an important part, and carved figures of birds, both separate sculptures and additions to human statuettes and masks, are typical of the Sepik and Ramu art provinces. As far as the representation of the human face is concerned, the style of this area reveals two genetic elements. There is on the one hand an astonishing naturalism, often rising to true portraiture (Pl. 17), while we find on the other hand rigidly stylized figures and masks (Pl. 18 (*a*)), characterized by conventional forms of

FIG. 33. Central part of a wooden board carved in open-work, with an ancestor's face at the top. Decorative designs consist of two pairs of interlocking horn-bills, surrounded by conventionalized human skulls. Tambunum, Sepik River, New Guinea. National Museum, Melbourne. Dimensions of illustrated section: Height 90 cm. Width 47 cm.

eyes, nose, mouth, and forehead, carved in strict symmetry. The naturalistic component is probably the result of the treatment of the skulls of ancestors (Pl. 16 (b)). The skull is regarded as the abode of the still-existent vital power of the ancestor. It is therefore necessary to restore the appearance of the head as it was during the person's lifetime. The soft parts are modelled in clay, and the face is painted in white and red, showing the same patterns with which the ancestor used to adorn himself for ceremonies. Finally, real human hair is fastened to this semi-sculpture. The examination of a number of these modelled skulls shows an amazing variety of individual physiognomies, which is in conformity with the racial types as they actually occur among the Papuans. One type is distinguished by narrow faces and slim, curved, sometimes aquiline noses, while another category has more rounded features and short noses. It is the former variety which is represented in most of the wooden masks, but the conventionalized forms often show prolonged noses, turned into beaks. The idea of the soul-bird probably accounts for this peculiarity. In other specimens the lower jaw of the mask assumes the shape of a beak, and there are real bird figures as well. On many statues and statuettes we find concentric circles, or spirals, carved in relief on the shoulder-blades and buttocks. This is strongly reminiscent of a characteristic feature of North-west American Indian art, where the joints, or the whole shoulder-blades and buttocks, are usually represented by two or more concentric oval designs – the so-called 'eye-ornament'. The majority of the Sepik and Ramu statues of ancestors and demons are connected with some utilitarian device. We find them as supports of bowls, as decorations of head-rests, and especially as hooks, whereby the outstretched legs of the figure serve to hang up foodstuffs or baskets. These hooks are a unique feature of the country, and have evidently been invented to protect food from the rats, but also to save space. They occur in all sizes, from 10 in. to life-size, and even larger. There is a great variety of forms, and sometimes the spirit, or ancestor, is standing on a crescent-shaped base, with the ends turned upwards. The most interesting combination of an ancestor figure with a practical object, however, is the figure-stools, which are made only in the region between the villages of Angraman and Jambon in the Sepik

River valley. They are always carved in one piece from a cylindrical section of a tree-trunk. One type retains the cylindrical outline when it is finished: it consists of a flat seat supported by carved ancestor figures, or masks, or crocodiles, connecting the upper part with the flat bottom. A second type has the same flat seat and base linked together by simple legs, while an ancestor figure is seated on the edge, or leaning against the seat (Pl. 17). The underlying idea is to bring the person who is sitting on, or leaning-against, the stool into close contact with the spirit of the ancestor, so as to ensure the still beneficent influence of his *mana*.[84]

All Sepik and Ramu sculptures are painted a dark red ('Indian red'), sometimes white and red.

The graphic art of this area consists of linear patterns painted on the surface of sculptures or on bark cloth, or carved in relief on wooden objects, such as drums, etc. Curvilinear designs are obviously prevalent, but the same holds good for almost every art province of New Guinea. Professor Felix Speiser, of the Ethnographical Museum of Basel (Switzerland), considers that the originally Indonesian *korwar* style of Western New Guinea spread along the coast of New Quinea in the ninth century A.D., but he distinguishes between this style and the 'Papuan curve-style', which is typical of the Sepik region, and is supposed to be older than the *korwar* style.

A most interesting feature of the Ramu art province is stone sculpture. Smaller objects, such as bowls, mortars, and birds, modelled in bold outlines, have been recorded from various parts of New Guinea, especially the Watut and Bulolo river valleys, south of the Finisterre Ranges, by C. A. W. Monckton, R. Neuhaus, E. W. P. Chinnery, V. H. Sherwin, and others in previous years. Other stone sculptures have been found in the Bismarck Archipelago. Important discoveries have been made in the Ramu valley recently – namely, in the Annaberg–Atemble district. All these finds may be classified as 'prehistoric' because the modern natives do not produce any stone sculpture of this kind; nor do they know who made them, so that it is uncertain whether they are the work of the ancestors of the recent tribes or of an older, now extinct, population. Two huge bowls of granite have been found on the surface, half-buried in the ground, and one of these has recently been illustrated and described by Rev. Fr. Alois Kasprusch. This bowl is 2 ft high and has, on the outer surface, a crude relief of a head, arms, and a frieze of bosses. Still more interesting to the student of primitive art is the stone sculpture illustrated on Pl. 19. Lieutenant P. R. N. England was fortunate to collect this remarkable piece some years ago, and gave a detailed description of it in *Mankind* (Sydney), vol. 3, No. 8 (1946). The piece is 44 cm. long, 22 cm. wide, and 8 cm. thick, and consists of a hard, igneous rock, probably andesite. These dimensions, in connexion with the photographs of both surfaces, show that this is not a sculpture in the round, but, as I have described it, 'a stone plaque worked in relief on both surfaces'. It is a linear relief, all the principal features being represented, as Lieutenant England puts it, in 'convex ridges'. As the shoulder-blades and buttocks are marked by spiral designs, it is probable, in my opinion, that the piece *is* Papuan, and the work of the forefathers of the modern Ramu tribes.

Although the modern natives do not claim all those stone artefacts as part of their own culture, they regard them with awe, ascribing to them magical power. Thus Lieutenant England tells us about the sculpture illustrated on Pl. 19: 'Tradition credits it with the power of locomotion, and it is reported on at least one occasion to have used physical violence on a native who failed to treat it with proper respect. It was also regarded as a charm to bring success in the chase.'

These stone sculptures are prehistoric, because they do not belong to the recent primitive culture recorded by ethnographical field-workers, and there is so far no authentic information about their origin and function. This does not mean that they must be of great antiquity in terms of prehistoric archaeology. From the ethnological point of view a 'prehistoric' piece may be only a few centuries old.

Coming back to the more recent primitive art of New Guinea, we must add a few words about the style of the Massim area and the Trobriand Islands. One conspicuous decorative element of this style is a design which may be described as 'interlocking question-marks'. Otherwise this style reveals what we may call a *horror vacui* – an aversion to empty spaces and, implicitly, an aesthetic urge to fill these spaces with ornaments. Fig. 35 shows an example; it also illustrates the decorative method of accentuating the outlines of an object by deeply incised lines running parallel to the edge, or still more strongly by several parallel lines, sometimes separated by meandering lines, or else by coils or spirals. The ob-

FIG. 34. Carved Handle of a Lime-spatula. Ebony. Trobriand Islands. Length of carved section $5\frac{1}{2}$ in. National Museum, Melbourne.

jects are therefore frequently over-decorated, and may perhaps be characterized as baroque, if not rococo. It is possible that a good many designs of this style are not derived from naturalistic forms and have no mythological or magic significance. However, it is advisable to be very cautious in our own interpretation of primitive designs, which in our eyes seem to be just geometric patterns. It is in New Guinea that we find the astonishing symbolic landscapes, which look to the European eye like simple four-square frets or similar geometric forms. Ornaments of this type engraved

146

on bamboo cases were explained by the Beliao people as follows:
'Quiet deep water – rain on the sea which is rippled by a breeze –
the sea moved by the wind – rock with surf beating up against
them'.[85]

Various kinds of wood are used by carvers in the Massim art
province. Canoe ornaments and dancing-shields are, for obvious

FIG. 35. Boat Ornament, Carved in Wood with Traces
of Blue, Pink, and White Paint. Height 11.9 cm. Trobriand Islands. National Museum, Melbourne.

practical reasons, made from soft wood, but clubs and lime-
spatulas are often of ebony. In the Trobriands wood carving is
confined to Kiriwina, more particularly to one village of the island.
Its inhabitants are regarded as outcasts by the other tribesmen of
Kiriwina, notwithstanding their artistic talent. They eat shell-fish
and use the shells for scraping the wood; they also eat sting-rays,
using the rough skin as a sand-paper after the scraping. This accounts for the astonishingly smooth sourface of all the ebony carvings. The other natives of the island do not eat either shell-fish or
sting-rays, believing that the latter are the spirits of their ancestors, and therefore sacred. The ebony is obtained from a small
island called Nubiam, west of Kiriwina. This material does not

originally show the deep black colour for which it is so highly appreciated, but is rather of a dull grey, sometimes greenish. To darken it, the natives bury the rough wood in mud for some time before working.[86]

2. *Melanesia*

The plastic art of the natives of the Bismarck Archipelago is outstanding, and the principal art province is New Ireland, or, as we can still find it on older maps under its beautiful native name, the island of *Tombara*. The aesthetic quality of the sculptures of Tombara is relatively low in the south, higher in the central parts of the island, and exquisite in the north.

The sculptures of the south are memorial statues of deceased men, women, or children, carved from large slabs of chalk, and thus of a shining white colour, but scantily decorated with red, and sometimes black lines (Pl. 20(*a*)). These figures were made either by one of the nearest relatives or by special sculptors. They were kept in a separate house, where only men were admitted, but were exhibited outside from time to time to give the mourning relatives the opportunity of expressing their grief. After a certain period, however, the statues were removed and broken. Some of these chalk figures are life-size, but the majority, including the images of adults, are smaller. The style may be described as a crude naturalism. In this case the shortcomings of primitive vision and technical imperfection outweigh the merits – namely, the boldness and naïvety of the carvings. Apparently no attempt at real portraiture has been made. The great variety of forms and attitudes is all the more surprising, and one single piece, such as Pl. 20(*a*), is not sufficient to provide an adequate illustration of the style. To the European eye the impression remains grotesque even when we have learned that the statues have their function in a mourning custom. Let us not overlook, however, that the natives themselves do not regard these brittle carvings as lasting monuments, and that they treat them accordingly.

Central New Ireland is the home of the famous *uli*, commemorative images of famous chiefs, often life-size or even larger. They are wood sculptures, without the individual features of real portraits. The style is conventional, the head-dress, reminiscent of the crest of a helmet, represents – according to Dr H. Nevermann – an old-fashioned mourning-gear which has been out of date for a long time. The *ulis* are always painted in bright colours – red, white, and black, sometimes with a little blue; there is another type decorated in darker shades, such as brown and purple, but always interrupted by white lines and spaces.

FIG. 36. A Wooden Bowl with Four Legs and Handles in Open Work. Admiralty Islands. Diameter *c.* 4 ft. After a photograph in *Cahiers d'Art*, 1929.

The eyes are represented by the *opercula* of a certain sea-snail, small convex discs of a pale yellow, with a large dark-green spot in the centre. Inlaid in the eye-sockets of a statue, or a mask, these discs produce the amazing effect of real eyes with a somewhat demonic expression. The *ulis* are displayed during the mourning ceremonies at regular intervals, and are carefully wrapped up when not in use.

Northern New Ireland is distinguished by large wood-carvings characterized by an abundance of open-work, red, white, black, and blue* decoration, and rhythmic compositions of conventional motifs derived from human forms, fishes, and especially birds. These are the celebrated *malanggans*, of which there are two types, one horizontal, consisting of huge boards, from 2 ft. to 3 yd. long, sometimes even larger; and the other vertical, typical pole-sculp-

* The blue pigment is relatively recent and of European origin.

ture (Pl. 20(*b*)). Here again the variety of forms is so overwhelming that it would be necessary to illustrate a larger number of pieces to give a real impression of this magnificent art style. Professor Augustin Kraemer has presented us with a monograph (*Die Malanggane von Tombara*, Munich, 1925), wherein he describes New Ireland as 'one of the first-rate and most important art provinces of the world'. The function of the *malanggans* is connected with the cult of the dead. Actually, *malanggane* is the name of a festival devoted to the memory and honour of the dead, which is held from May to July every year, when the carved boards are exhibited and masks of the same style are worn at the ceremonies. Other *malanggans* are used in the sun- and moon-cult, fishes and hornbills representing moon phases. All these carvings are exhibited in special exhibition huts, or courtyards, when the time comes, but before the ritual season they are kept secret, and the women especially must not see them. This sounds as if the *malanggans* were regarded as sacred, yet this is not the case. Professor Kraemer found that the principal reason for so much secrecy is rather the artists' ambition not to disclose their professional secrets inopportunely, to be able to take the public by surprise at the official opening.

In New Britain, or *Birara*, we find stone sculptures, carved from a soft grey rock, sometimes decorated with painted designs. Human figures and animals are represented in rough outlines and simple planes, the brittle material making it impossible to bring out details. These sculptures are made by the members of a secret society, called *ingiet*, and are used for magical purposes. Dr Nevermann tells us that each figure has two names, one profane and the other ritual, and that all the sculptures are supposed to be related to each other. In New Britain there is also a peculiar type of mask similar to the remodelled skulls of New Guinea; they are made from the front part of a skull and jaw, the soft parts modelled in resin, and the face then painted a deep reddish-brown, decorated with lines in bright shades. A wooden stick, fastened on the back of the mask, is held between the teeth. These masks are now completely conventionalized, and have no individual features. They cannot compare with the Sepik skulls, and are not works of art.

Turning to the Solomon Islands, we find wood sculpture every-

where, but their style is different in the two contrasting art provinces. The northern islands – Buka, Bougainville, and Choiseul-
are distinguished by polychrome decoration of carvings. Statuettes and dancing-clubs, made from light wood, with conventionalized human figures, triangular and circular patterns carved
in relief, are painted in red, white, and black, which is probably
due to influence from the Bismarck Archipelago. In the southern
islands sculptures are invariably blackened and inlaid with nautilus mother-of-pearl. The small pieces of shell are first carefully
fashioned into tiny angular ornaments before they are fitted into
the incisions and fastened with resin. Wooden objects of all sizes,
from small prow-ornaments (usually shaped as human heads of
a striking prognathic type) to whole canoes, are decorated in this
way, and the fine older pieces, which are not overloaded with too
much mother-of-pearl, reveal good taste, and are often quite exquisite. A large war-canoe in the National Museum in Melbourne
is the largest piece I have so far seen, and is a magnificent sight.
Modern pieces, however, are not so very pleasing; the workmanship of the carving is poor, and the soft wood is now mostly over-
decorated with crudely shaped pieces of mother-of-pearl. In the
past human statues were decorated in the same style. Some of the
older life-size statues, with eyes of nautilus pearl-shell and real
human hair dyed white, in the fashion of the people, are evidently
true portraits; they are more lively than the stiff pole-sculptures
of other primitive tribes, as the limbs are carved separately and
joined to the trunk, which allows the sculptor full freedom of
expression.

The variety of plastic art styles in Melanesia is astonishing. It is
only in the neighbourhood of New Guinea that we find obvious
resemblances and affinities. Otherwise the sculptures in the
various groups of islands are all widely different; in some cases
there are differences even between neighbouring islands.

In Pl. 21(a), we see a typical pole-sculpture, representing two
ancestor figures, carved from the trunk of a fern-tree, a soft and
perishable material. This style and material is typical of Ambrym,
one of the New Hebrides. West of Ambrym, in Malekula, we find
an entirely different kind of ancestor figures. Here the skull of the
ancestor is treated in the same way as in the Sepik area of New

Guinea, the soft parts of the face being modelled in clay and resin. But in Malekula the people are not content with the skull alone; they mount it on a life-size doll modelled in clay over a frame-

FIG. 37. Forehead Ornament of Turtle Shell, Carved in Open Work all in One Piece. Mounted on a White Disc of Shell. Solomon Islands. Diameter of carving 4 in. National Museum, Melbourne.

work of bamboo and fibre. According to Nevermann, these astonishingly realistic statues – actually only semi-sculptures – are older than the carvings in wood and fern-tree, which were probably developed as a substitute.

The most interesting examples of the now extinct art of New Caledonia are large boards flanking the entrance to the huts of the chiefs (Pl. 21(*b*)). These boards are carved in relief. The upper part shows a stylized human face, while the rest of the surface is occupied by angular or zigzag patterns. There is a variety of these patterns, and the faces, too, are not always identical. The rigid symmetry of these decorative boards is remarkable. It is probable that they represent the final stage of a long development and that the space now filled by the geometric designs was originally occupied by a representation of the body. It has been suggested that the patterns themselves might have been derived from conventionalized human forms, but this theory is certainly not borne out by the designs as we find them to-day.

Generally speaking, then, the prominent feature of primitive art in Melanesia is sculpture. It is impossible in this brief survey to deal with the decorative arts of this area, but at least one attractive form of ornament must be mentioned, not only on account of its technical and aesthetic merits, but also because of its wide distribution from New Guinea as far as the Marquesas Islands in Eastern Polynesia. This ornament, known as *kapkap*, consists of a thin disc of turtle-shell, carved in open-work and mounted, both for protection and coloristic contrast, on a white disc of *tridacna* shell (Fig. 37). Ornaments of this type are used as breast ornaments, for example in the Bismarck Archipelago, or as forehead ornaments (Southern Solomon Islands; Marquesas Islands); sporadically as ear-pendants (Ulawa, Solomon Islands). The finest pieces were made by the Marquesas Islanders, but the example illustrated here from the Solomon Islands is not inferior to them. The delicate beauty of these carvings is all the more admirable as they were made without metal tools. The late Dr Henry Balfour considered that the original home of the prototype, and the centre from which it was gradually spread over the Pacific by seafaring natives, was Melanesia. With regard to the antiquity of this type of ornament, Dr Balfour stated that in the Marquesas it was 'firmly established long, probably, before the group was discovered by Mendaña, in 1595'.[87]

3. Micronesia

There are three principal art centres in Micronesia – Yap, Nukuoro, and the Palau Islands – all belonging to the Caroline group, and all very different in character. The sculpture of Yap is notable for its admirably naturalistic wood-carvings of animals and groups of animals. Formerly human figures of equal quality were carved, and one artist, Giltemag of Toru, made statues so life-like that even a European captain was under the illusion that they were living people.[88]

The wooden statuettes of Nukuoro, in the south-east of the Caroline Islands, are of precisely the opposite character. They are so highly stylized that they have no faces at all, but merely egg-shaped heads with completely even surfaces. Arms and legs are represented, but without hands or feet; the figures are thus reduced to an almost abstract form. Similar carvings occur in the Philippine Islands and in Nias, but they are not quite so simplified. The most striking parallel is to be found in the prehistoric idols of the Cyclades.[89]

The natives of the Palau Islands in the extreme west of Micronesia excel in two types of decorative art: polychrome carvings of mythical and other scenes in low relief which decorate the gables of their bachelors' houses, and wooden bowls of either abstract or representational forms, dyed with red earth pigment, varnished with vegetable lacquer, and frequently inlaid with shell (Pl. 23(a)).

4. Polynesia

Throughout the whole of Polynesia a marked sense of beauty is revealed in the geometric designs printed on the native bark-cloth, or *tapa*. But apart from this there is a sharp distinction between central Polynesia – Samoa, Tonga, and Fiji (which is partly Melanesian) – and the peripheral groups. The central islands have very little sculpture, but it is well represented in Tahiti, the Hervey Islands, the Marquesas, Hawaii, New Zealand, and Rapa Nui (Easter Island). Even the central Polynesians, however, have attained perfection in the shaping of their instruments and in the noble curves of the *kava* bowls of Samoa and Fiji.

The Polynesians are on a higher cultural level than most of the other peoples in the Pacific, and with few exceptions, such as the grotesque idols of the Hawaiians, their arts are of a more refined type. It has been suggested that Polynesian art might be called 'aristocratic' in contrast to the 'peasant art' of the Melanesians and Papuans.[90] In their decorative arts, at least, the Maori and the Marquesans have a more finely elaborated technique. Their patterns reveal a longer and more complicated development, and the use of them is closely associated with the social activities of the ruling classes.

An outstanding element in Polynesian sculpture is an ornamental figure known as the *tiki*, carved in nephrite or whale-bone, and usually worn as a neck pendant. The *hei-tiki* of the Maori resembles an embryo, but is either an ancestor figure or a mythical being. It is noteworthy that each *hei-tiki* bore an individual name.

Another figure typical of Maori carvings is the *manaia*, a bird-headed animal or demon. Usually two of them are symmetrically attached to an ancestor figure, while others appear on door lintels, etc. Combined with spiral patterns, the *manaias* are reminiscent of the *garuda*, the fabulous eagle of the Hindu pantheon, who is always represented holding two snakes in his claws. As a very similar composition frequently occurs in the horizontal *malanggans* of northern New Ireland, it is not impossible that all these arrangements indicate a historical connexion. However, some specialists in Maori art still think that the *manaia* motif was developed in New Zealand.

Spirals and scrolls in open-work are the principal patterns of Maori decorative art (Pl. 24). Much has been written about their origin. It has been suggested that they come from an Asiatic source, because spirals are common in the decorative arts of South-east Asia. But actually spiral patterns occur in many parts of the world, and are not in themselves a satisfactory argument for a historical connexion between two different areas (compare Pls. 7(*a*) and 38(*b*)).

On Mangaia (Hervey Islands), the surfaces of wooden objects, especially graceful ceremonial paddles, were completely covered with a network of geometrical designs, partly engraved and partly worked in relief, derived from minute squares and triangles, or simple zigzag bands and concentric circles. The delicacy and rhythmic accuracy of these beautiful patterns produce a lace-like effect.

Hawaii has developed a specific kind of grotesque sculpture which still preserves distinct naturalistic features (Pl. 26(a)). The carvings of Tahiti may be recognized by a certain stiffness and a preference for symmetrical arrangements (Pl. 26(b)). The Marquesas Islanders have a peculiar technique of rigorously stylized and almost geometric ornaments in relief, of which the principal design is derived from the human skull.

Two entirely different kinds of sculpture were practised by the ancestors of the Easter Islanders. There are first the huge stone figures of human beings, with exceptionally large heads and faces, which every Londoner knows from the two – by no means the largest in existence – which stand in the front portico of the British Museum. Some of these figures might have been connected with the cult of a sea-bird god, but the majority are believed to be memorials of important men. Most of them are made from porous material, and their state of preservation in the Easter Island climate proves that they cannot be of very great antiquity – that is to say, the date should be estimated in terms of centuries rather than millennia. Moreover, even as late as the eighties the older men in the island knew their individual names. As an exception, the statue Hoa-Haka-Nana-Ia, now in the British Museum (Pl. 28(a)), consists of hard stone. It is recognized as 'the masterpiece of Easter Island sculpture' (Alfred Métraux). The name means 'Breaking-waves'. The piece was taken from a stone house at a locality known as Orongo. It once stood on a stone slab, with the back turned towards the sea. When found, the statue was painted red and white, but the pigment was washed off during its transport to H.M.S. *Topaze*. The back of the statue is carved in relief, showing several figures, including a bird-man. Professor Métraux also points out that this statue is the only one positively known to have been connected with a cult.[90a]

Easter Island has also a peculiar type of wooden statuettes. These had individual names, too, and represented deceased persons. The material is *toromiro* wood, and it is this material which conditioned their curious shape (Pl. 29(a)).

CHAPTER XV

Australia

THE native tribes of the Australian continent seem at first sight to be at the lowest cultural stage of any living people. They are not, however, as primitive as they appear. Their languages, of which there are several different categories, are as melodious as they are complicated. Most of them have a well-developed grammar and syntax, providing a wide range of expression. The tribal organizations, too, with their moieties, totem clans, and very complicated marriage laws, show that the culture of the Australian aborigines is the product of a long development. The tribes must have immigrated from the north at a very early period. It is probable, for various reasons, that their original home was southern India. The immigration took place in intervals extending over a long time, and partly in the north-western corner of the continent, partly via the Cape York Peninsula. The oldest tribes were those in the south-east – i.e., southern New South Wales and Victoria – and are now practically extinct.

The art of the Australian aborigines is a true reflection of their culture.[91] The study of their intellectual capacity, compared with their material culture, reveals a striking contrast. The Australian aborigines possess a remarkable intelligence and learning ability. It is true that their mental outlook differs widely from our own, but this is due to the influences of environment, tribal tradition, mode of life as primitive nomads, and lack of education in the modern sense of the term. During the immeasurable period before the arrival of the Whites, when the aborigines were the masters of their own country, their progress was handicapped by the deficiency of natural resources. There were neither any cereals nor domesticable animals, except the dingo, and consequently no encouragement to settle down to a sedentary life. Hunters and collectors of scanty wild fruit, etc., are bound to roam the country in small groups, which makes social and technical co-operation of larger numbers impossible, though periodic gatherings may be held for ceremonial purposes. Nomads on foot cannot carry bulky and heavy things from camp to camp, so it would not occur to them to make pottery, although suitable clay is available. Instead, they use bowls and trays of a lighter material, wood, hollowed out and fashioned in simple forms; bags are knitted from vegetable fibre, and twisted human hair serves as strings and cords.

Australian art is predominantly graphic. The most important type of graphic art is rock engravings and rock paintings. They occur in various parts of the continent, from the Kimberleys to Victoria, and belong to altogether different periods. Some of them, perhaps the majority, are prehistoric, but it is as yet impossible to suggest even approximate dates. It is certain, on the other hand, that some of the rock paintings have been made since the arrival of the Europeans, and those in the rock shelters of the western part of North Kimberley are still the object of religious practice among the natives. Everywhere the style of Australian rock art is principally naturalistic, and the best examples of realistic engravings representing the outlines of human beings and animals, such as kangaroos, whales, birds, fishes, etc., are in the Sydney district. Frederick D. McCarthy, the distinguished ethnologist of the Australian Museum in Sydney, assisted by a team of other experts, has been engaged for several years in making systematic records of all the engravings in the Sydney area. So far thirty-seven groups have been studied, measured, and published with illustrations of the outlines. These engravings are mostly found on the ground, and many are of very large dimensions. For example, at Kuring-gai Chase, Lambert Peninsula, there is, among many other engravings, a figure with a bird-like head, interpreted as a culture-hero, which is no less than 19 ft. long, the width of the body being 4 ft. 6 in., and this is not the largest specimen. A technical detail may be interesting: the engraved lines representing the contours of this figure are 1 in. wide, and $\frac{1}{4}-\frac{3}{8}$ in. deep, and have been produced by 'large conjoined punctures, smoothed both by rubbing and weathering'. McCarthy points out that in many cases the engravings are not separate representations, but parts of whole compositions. Out of a large number of examples we may mention the paintings in the rock shelter at Glen Isla, Victoria, where emu and kangaroo hunts are depicted in animated figures, proving the primitive artist's gift of observation and remarkable skill. This and other Australian pictures are to some extent reminiscent of Bushman art, but generally speaking Bushman pictures are of superior quality. The draughtsmanship is better, the treatment of colour pigments more refined, and other superior features have been described in Chapter XI. On the other hand, there are no rock pictures in South Africa of the huge dimensions of the ground engravings in the Sydney district or the wall paintings in the Kimberleys. It stands to reason that a very large space is much more difficult to survey than a small one, and still more so if the artist has to deal with the ground, instead of a more or less vertical wall; at least, these difficulties existed for primitive draughtsmen. It is the same problem which has been so miraculously solved, on a much larger scale, by the Bronze Age men who constructed the hill figures in England as well as by the moundbuilders of North America. If we realize this, we can only say that at least those primitive Australians who were responsible for the gigantic naturalistic rock engravings in New South Wales deserve our admiration.

Of the various 'aboriginal art galleries' in other parts of Australia, the paintings in the rock shelters of Northern Kimberley are famous for the mysterious *wondjina* figures, paintings in bright white, red, and black of strange beings, evidently derived from human forms, but by no means naturalistic. The *wondjinas* have no mouths, a peculiarity which is not so unusual in primitive art, as we find it in the ancestor figures of Nias, the statuettes of Nukuoro, and in prehistoric (neolithic) figures in the Eastern Mediterranean. Otherwise the faces of the *wondjinas*, with large black, oval designs instead of eyes, and another black spot underneath where we should expect the nose, seem to be conventionalized representations of human skulls. The limbs, sometimes only rudimentary, sometimes with only four, or even only three fingers, in other cases not represented at all, a large design below the face, which may be a breast-ornament – all these and other details indicate that the figures are expressionistic, namely, a reflection of belief, fear, and hope. Their meaning had been

a puzzle for a long time since they had first been discovered by
Sir George Grey in 1837, until they were eventually studied and
satisfactorily explained by Professor A. P. Elkin of the University
of Sydney. The *wondjinas* are supposed to embody the power
which makes the rain. Very Rev. Fr Ernest Worms, P.S.M., told
me that the natives of the Kimberleys attribute a great significance to the fact that the *wondjina* figures have no mouth. If they
had a mouth, or if they were ever to get one, they explained, it
would rain incessantly, and all human beings would perish. The
wondjinas are often associated with representations of snakes, and
the rainbow-snake plays an important rôle in the mythology of
all the tribes in the north and in the centre of Australia. There
are many other designs connected with the *wondjinas*, and among
these are certain round forms, about an inch in diameter. At
first sight these simple designs may not suggest any particular
significance, but with the help of native informants Professor
Elkin discovered that they are, in the eyes of the aborigines, most
important. They represent a green plum-like fruit, called *nalge*.
'The regular supply of this fruit is maintained by painting or
re-painting representations of it on a *wondjina* gallery during the
wet season.' This example shows that designs which might easily
be interpreted as purely geometric, symbolic, or pictographic,
may in fact be meant as naturalistic representations; it is also
another proof that Australian aboriginal art, like many other
primitive arts, cannot be properly understood without studying
its religious background. The style of the rock paintings in the
Kimberleys indicates foreign influence, either from Indonesia or
from New Guinea, or both. There are other proofs of culture
contact with both areas, some of them of more recent date, and
some quite modern. These rock pictures, then, are important not
only for the study of the history of art, but also from the point of
view of anthropology and for the early history of Australia. What
is needed is a comprehensive survey of Australian rock paintings
and engravings, not merely a scientific catalogue, but a well-
illustrated publication with adequate photographs and colour
plates, like Helen Tongue's publication of Bushman paintings,
or Frobenius' and Obermaier's *Hadschra Maktuba*. As a matter
of fact, a number of rock pictures in the Kimberleys have already

been admirably copied by an expedition sent out by the Frobenius Institute at Frankfurt-am-Main shortly before the outbreak of the Second World War. These copies were subsequently exhibited in London, and it is understood that they will be published. This is an important contribution which will be appreciated by students all over the world; but much more remains to be done.

Another type of representative art is the paintings on bark which were first collected and published by Sir Baldwin Spencer (Figs. 7, 8, 38). Spencer obtained a large collection of sheets of bark, painted in red, white, and black, from the Kakadu tribe, Northern Territory. The natives adorn their primitive huts or shelters with these decorated sheets, but the majority of those collected by Spencer were specially painted for him. These and other collections from the same area are now in the National Museum of Victoria, Melbourne. A scene like that reproduced in Fig. 7 rivals the prehistoric pictures of Eastern Spain (cf. Fig. 15), or some of the scenic Bushman paintings, in its realism and animation. Fig. 8 shows a pair of stencilled hands produced by exactly the same technique as those on palaeolithic wall pictures in Europe. Stencilled hands are also a frequent feature in Australian rock paintings all over the continent. Figs. 8 and 38 illustrate the 'X-ray' vision described in Chapter II. Related to this method is the frequent combination of two different views at the time; for example, we find a picture of a crocodile seen from above, because this is the best way to show the characteristic armour on its back, but, nevertheless, the tail is drawn in profile to show the characteristic serrated ridge. As the 'X-ray' style is confined to a limited coastal area in the north, and as it is also practised in Melanesia (Fig. 3, No. 1), the Australian examples may be due to Melanesian influence. Bark paintings are made also by other tribes of Northern Australia – e.g., in Arnhem Land and Groote Eylandt, in the Gulf of Carpentaria. The pictures from Groote Eylandt are particularly interesting because of their variety of colour pigments and several styles, which may be due to a number of individual artists who are personally well known to the few missionaries and students. It is not so difficult to tell that a bark painting is probably by Timundu, Papatama,

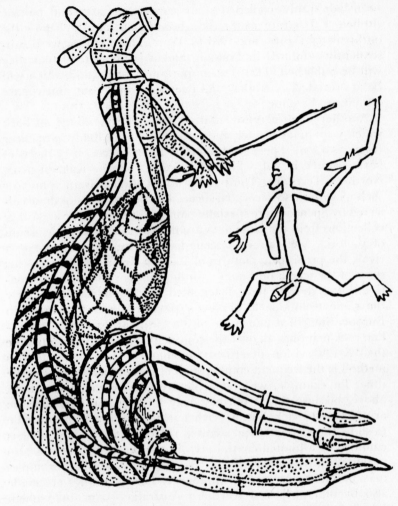

FIG. 38. Bark Drawing of a Native Spearing a Large Black Rock Kangaroo. 'X-ray' drawing showing spine, ribs, and inner organs of the kangaroo. The native is supposed to have been searching for Mormo, or sugar bag, with which he has filled the dilly-bag that hangs from his neck. He is represented running along with his spear-thrower, from which he has just hurled his spear. Kakadu tribe. After B. Spencer, *Native Tribes of the Northern Territory* (Fig. 86 and p. 437). By courtesy of Messrs Macmillan & Co. Ltd, London.

or Mini-Mini, which are the names of the principal painters to-day. Painting on bark, then, is still practised, and the artists of Groote Eylandt, far from reiterating old designs, seem to be experimenting with new colour effects. In contrast with the style of the Kakadu tribe on the mainland, where pictures are always painted either on plain bark or on a ground of red ochre, those of Groote Eylandt are done either on a black ground, which seems to be the earliest type, or on a bright yellow or a red ground. As I am writing this chapter I have in front of me a bark painting, 23 in. long and 10 in. high, which is divided in two sections. On the left are three turtles on red ground, on the right two crocodiles on white ground, all the animals being painted in yellow, white, and red. However, one can see that originally the whole ground had been painted black, and the figures still have a narrow black frame, as it were, bringing out the bright contours still more clearly. Evidently, however, the painter did not like the dull black ground, so he tried both red and white; the latter is quite unusual. The Groote Eylandt paintings were first described by Norman B. Tindale of the South Australian Museum, Adelaide, who noted, among other details, that pigments are mixed with a starchy liquid obtained by rubbing the fleshy stems of various tree-orchids (*dendrobium*), which gives adhesive qualities to the colour. All the colours are mineral pigments. So far the largest and finest collection of Groote Eylandt bark paintings has recently been brought together by Mr Frederick H. Gray, a resident of the island, and the greater part of it now belongs to the University of Melbourne. Two of these pictures are illustrated in Pls. 31 and 32. Both paintings are by Mini-Mini. I have selected these examples because Pl. 31 illustrates a scenic representation, while Pl. 32 shows typical patterns used in the painted decoration of wooden implements. In Pl. 31 we see a stone axe with a painted wooden handle lying in front of the picture. No less than eighteen axe-heads of stone, with ground cutting-edges, had been found during an excavation of a sandhill, when the sand was needed for a dam across a creek at the Umba-Kumba gardens. The gardens are represented by the rows at each end of the picture. The four lines across the centre represent the dam, from which the creek runs into a pond ('billabong') marked by the concentric circles

on the left. On the other side of the dam the finding of some of the
axe-heads is depicted, the men, painted yellow, standing in
a circle. In the centre, however, we see ten human figures, which
are painted white. These 'represent the dead men of long ago
who camped at this spot'. Pl. 32 shows four vertical designs,
representing the carved and painted sacred sticks used at
ceremonial dances. 'The painting at the bottom represents
a billabong down at Talimbo, the markings being the lily-nuts
found there, and the long markings outside the edge are reeds.'
It is fortunate that we possess these accurate and authentic
interpretations given by Mr Gray. An 'analysis' of primitive
pictographs, without the help of native informants, is only too
often merely guesswork, and in the case of prehistoric rock drawings, unless they are naturalistic or otherwise unmistakable, we
have to leave it at that. Many designs in the cave paintings, but
also in the bark pictures, of Groote Eylandt are representations
of totems, and have been identified as such by Mr Frederick
Rose. One of these, which is shaped like two fish-tails joined
together, is the south-east-wind totem, called *mamariga*. That
was all Mr Rose could get out of his native informants, but why
a wind totem should have this particular shape they could not –
or, in any case, did not – tell. Subsequently Mr Rose found that
this totem is undoubtedly the characteristic sail of a Malay craft,
as it is frequently depicted on bark.[91a] There are also other
examples of totems identical with, or derived from, naturalistic
forms. It is interesting that, according to one of my informants,
Mr H. L. Perriman (of the Church of England Missionary
Society, Melbourne), the Groote Islanders often paint 'simply
for the enjoyment of doing it', while the paintings are 'sometimes used to instruct children in the recognition of animals
and objects, such as the frequently illustrated Macassar boats'.

An entirely different type of art is found in Central Australia.
The Aranda and Luridja groups of tribes disclaim any authorship
of the rock engravings in their country; nor do they ascribe them
to their forefathers, but rather to the mythical beings of the
'dream-time'. This attitude is in agreement with the fact that,
according to linguistic evidence, these tribes must have been relatively late arrivals in prehistoric times, although their immigra-

tion took place thousands of years ago. Their art consists principally of linear designs engraved on their most sacred objects, the *tjuringas* (*churingas*). Technologically, a *tjuringa* is either a flat slab of slate, or of a micaceous stone, or a wooden board. The sizes vary considerably; there are small specimens which are only about 3 cm. long, while large stone *tjuringas* may be up to 3 ft. long, and wooden ones even up to 6 ft. The shape is oval, but that of the larger specimens is more like a willow-leaf. Those of wood (and very few of stone) have a small perforation at one end. Only wooden *tjuringas* are used as bullroarers, in which case a string made from human hair is attached to them. *Tjuringas* are usually buried in the sand at secret places, and periodically used for ritual purposes. There are various categories and functions of *tjuringas*. I have seen a few wooden ones, of small size, showing incised realistic drawings of female figures. These specimens came from the Kimberleys in the far north-west, and were described to me by my informant as instruments for love-magic. But this is an exceptional type, which does not seem to occur in Central Australia. The principal type of *tjuringa* is connected with the ancestor-cult and totemism. Every totem clan is supposed to be related to a species of animals or plants, and has a legend or several legends concerning the origin of this imaginary relationship. It is these legends which are usually recorded on the *tjuringas*, recorded but not represented, because there is no representation of any individual features. The records consist invariably of a limited number of conventional patterns, spirals, concentric circles, square or oblong designs, sometimes a spiral zigzag line. Although there exists a large number of clan legends, the small number of patterns was sufficient to record altogether different texts, but they can be 'read' only by the initiated. C. Strehlow and, many years later independently, C. P. Mountford, have established that a pattern – for example concentric circles – may have altogether different meanings, even when it occurs on the same *tjuringa*. Such an arrangement of concentric circles may mean, for example, a water-hole, fruit of some kind, a 'damper' made from ground fruit, a gum-tree, or a fig-tree, or a spot where some mythical ancestors disappeared underground or, conversely, the spot where they emerged from the ground, etc.,

etc. Moreover, the significance of the same patterns varies from tribe to tribe. In other words, all these designs are not ideograms, but simply mnemotechnic marks. They will help the man who knows the legend to recite it correctly, but they mean nothing to other people. A *tjuringa* of this type is therefore in the first line a document, at least potentially. The piece illustrated in Fig. 39 belongs to a different category for both style and meaning. The curves here form a rhythmic pattern contrasting with the quiet symmetry of the ordinary *tjuringas*. This is a bull-roarer of a type called *nankara*. The designs are meant to represent an *ara* – that is, a red kangaroo – and this bullroarer is therefore an *ara-nankara*. It is given after his circumcision to a youth whose totem is the red kangaroo. According to the late C. Strehlow, the ornament at the bottom represents 'the sitting

FIG. 39. A large Bullroarer with Incised Ornaments symbolizing a Red Kangaroo in various Attitudes. Central Australia. After Carl Strehlow, *Die Aranda- und Loritja-Stämme*, Frankfurt-am-Main, 1908, vol. i, part ii, Fig. 2.

kangaroo', while the others indicate 'the kangaroo turning round as it eats'.[92] It is difficult to recognize the sitting kangaroo, but the other drawings may be accepted as pictographic sketches of the movement of the animal. However, here too one has to be initiated to be able to tell that it is a red kangaroo. Apart from their cryptic meaning, many *tjuringas* are undoubtedly aesthetically attractive, and it is an established fact that the natives themselves enjoy the symmetry, or the rhythm, of the patterns and appreciate the fine workmanship of the parallel curves of the engravings, all done with opossum teeth. These ritual objects, then, are also works of decorative art, and this particular type of decoration is virtually the national art style of the Central Australian tribes. The conclusion is that, if these aborigines should ever be given the opportunity of developing their artistic talent in a changed world where there is no room for primitive rituals, they should be encouraged to turn those ancient patterns into a modernized decorative style in connexion with useful arts and crafts. That this is not impossible is proved by the modern development of American Indian art in the United States.

FIG. 40. Detail of the Decoration, Carved in Relief, of a Wooden Shield from Victoria, Australia. National Museum, Melbourne.

It was formerly believed that the Australian aborigines did not produce any sculpture in the round, although it had always been evident that they were interested in three-dimensional forms. The beautiful incised decorations of the fighting-shields of the Kimberleys and, on the other hand, of Victoria and New South Wales are actually sculptures in relief. Fig. 40 illustrates an example, a detail from an old Victorian shield, with striking effects of light and shadow and alternating diamond and square patterns showing up as the shield is held at different angles. A variety of similar effects, but of larger dimensions, occurs on the carved trees ('den-

droglyphs') in the burial-grounds of the now extinct Kamilaroi
and Wiradjuri nations of New South Wales. A large proportion
of the bark was removed on one side of the tree, and reliefs of
geometric designs, mostly diamond patterns and meandering
lines, were sculptured out of the living wood. But we have even
two modern examples of real sculpture in the round, and it is
significant that these exceptional cases occurred in two widely
distant areas of the Australian continent – viz., in the extreme

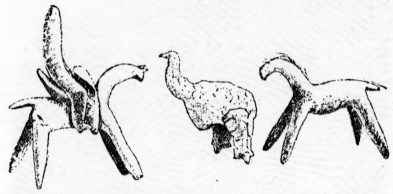

FIG. 41. Three Clay Figures, modelled by Djaro tribesmen, Kimberley
Division, N.W. Australia, in 1937. (I) Rider on horse-back (note the saddle);
(II) Emu; (III) Horse with mane and tail of real horse-hair. Average length
of these and other pieces: 4 to 5 in. Courtesy of the Rector of the Pallottine
Missionary College, Kew, Melbourne.

west and in the east. It is also of particular interest that in one
of these cases the artist is a woman. The sculptress, Kalboori
Youngi, a member of the Pitta Pitta tribe in Central Western
Queensland, works in soapstone and clay. Her human figures and
groups have a naïve, almost early Gothic simplicity. They were
illustrated in 1939 by G. H. Goddard,[92a] who pointed out that
Kalboori Youngi has never left the district of her tribe and that
she had not seen any sculptures when she started her work quite
spontaneously. Some of the western examples are illustrated in
Fig. 41. They were obtained by the distinguished ethnologist,
Very Rev. Fr Ernest Worms, when he was camping at Rockhole
Station, 20 miles west of Halls Creek, in the interior of the

Kimberley Division, Western Australia, in 1937. As it happened, suitable clay was brought to the surface during the boring of a well, and two young men of the Djaro tribe, aged twenty-three and seventeen, quite spontaneously began to model figures, representing an emu, a lizard, but especially horses. The emu (Fig. 41, No. II) shows a distinct contrast between the head, neck, and body, which are astonishingly true to nature for such a first attempt; and, on the other hand, the clumsy legs. This is probably due to the fact that the body was made by one man and the legs by the other. The horses – one with the mane and tail of real horse-hair – may be regarded as prototypes of veritable primitive art, and are reminiscent of very early figures from the Mediterranean, even of archaic Greek statuettes. The rider (No. I) is still more primitive, as no attempt has been made to delineate the head and the trunk, while the saddle obviously specially attracted the men. The horse, rider, and saddle were first made separately and then fitted together. Being completely ignorant of the technique, the men could do nothing to harden these figures by baking, so they will probably fall to pieces sooner or later.

In 1946, Ronald and Catherine Berndt of the Department of Anthropology, University of Sydney, discovered that at Yirrkalla, in north-eastern Arnhem Land, a whole pantheon of anthropomorphous statuettes, real sculptures in the round, though of the primitive pole-sculpture type, exists among the aborigines, who carve and paint these figures and use them, partly, as sacred objects, representing spirits and other supernatural beings, in religious rituals, whereas another category play a rôle in a certain secular ceremony. Some of these profane statuettes are actually conventional portraits. In addition to statuettes, there are carved solid wooden heads, likewise decorated with polychrome paintings. Sacred and profane statuettes are distinguished only by different symbols painted on them, while the plastic treatment of both categories is identical. Pl. 29(b) shows one of the statuettes; it is supposed to represent the 'Elder Wauwelak Sister'. She 'gave birth to a child through an incestuous union with a clansman'. The treatment of the face of this particular figure is peculiar to the craftsmen of a certain moiety of the tribe and is used only for the Wauwelak sister and one other type. Every detail, every little stroke of the painted decoration has its symbolic significance, and Mr and Mrs Berndt took great care to record them all.*

* A. P. Elkin, Catherine and Ronald Berndt, *Art in Arnhem Land*, Melbourne and London, 1950, p. 50.

CHAPTER XVI

America

It is generally recognized to-day that the American tribes immigrated from Asia over Bering Strait, that they came over in several waves and that the first immigration must have taken place many thousand years ago, when the mastodon and other now extinct animals were still in existence. The various contingents of immigrants were of different racial stocks and arrived at different periods. This may be concluded from the diversity of racial types – Mongoloid and others – and the great variety of languages and cultural standards among the American peoples from Alaska to Cape Horn.[93] The very early date of those immigrations suggests that the oldest American civilizations were of a very primitive type and that the development of the characteristics of American Indian cultures took place in America. It would appear, then, that Asiatic parallels in American civilizations,[94] such as occur on the north-west coast, in Mexico, Central and South America, emerged largely from racial affinity, similar mental outlook and intellectual capacity, rather than from direct cultural influence. Sporadic contacts of cultures, of later dates, both over Bering Strait and across the Pacific, may account for some more distinctly marked Asiatic, Polynesian, and even Melanesian features. But taken as a whole, the American civilizations are no doubt autochthonous. This is particularly true of the American art styles, both ancient and modern.

These art styles show an overwhelming variety throughout the American continent. Some tribes excelled in sculpture, while others specialized in graphic arts or in coiled, twined, or plaited basket-work; in artistic weaving or in pottery, plain or painted; or in metal-work, etc., etc. Apart from material and technique, all stages are represented, from real primitiveness to the highest perfection. Generally speaking, it appears that in America – just as in other continents – graphic as well as plastic arts started with an experimental stage of crude beginnings, then sometimes reached an early ('archaic') stage of relative perfection, distinguished by a naïve and refreshing truth to nature, and eventually lost their spontaneity through the paralysing effect of conventional devices. In other cases, however, remarkable artistic developments apparently came to an end before they ever reached a stage of exhaustion or degeneration. Such seems to have been the case of the plastic art of the so-called 'mound-builders' in the eastern half of the United States. Examples of the former development, on the other hand, are the art of the coastal tribes of North-west America and to some extent the plastic art of ancient Mexico. The great diversity of American art forms corresponds to the different stages of cultural development as they were reached by the various Indian nations and tribes before the arrival of the Whites. Again, these stages were the product of both abilities and opportunities; of different environments and actual happenings, or historical events, as everywhere in the world.

Until about twenty years ago it was generally assumed that even the oldest traceable cultures of America could not rival the palaeolithic age of the Old World in antiquity. Sporadic finds made in various parts of the United States had been repeatedly interpreted as palaeolithic, but all those earlier finds were soon recognized by experts as neolithic, or even more recent. Therefore, as an Austrian anthropologist, the late Dr Victor Lebzelter, put it, it became 'a fashionable dogma of prehistory' that the human race in America must have been of a recent type. However, during the last two decades or so more systematic palaeontological and archaeological field work has been carried out in several States, with the result that the former theory has had to be revised. While, on the one hand, the first enthusiastic claims that in Nebraska human artefacts belonging to the Pliocene – i.e., the uppermost stratum of the Tertiary period – had been discovered and that the skeleton of a young woman, accompanied by a dagger of antler and a shell pendant, which was excavated in Minnesota was of Pleistocene age have not been accepted by competent critics, it is now recognized, on the other hand, that pre-neolithic men did exist in America. Thus William

D. Strong and other students have come to the conclusion that the earliest men in Nebraska lived during the Upper Palaeolithic period, and that a later cultural statum in the same state may be classified as Mesolithic; and, as far as the skeleton of Minnesota is concerned, even a very cautious critic like G. M. Morant, who does not accept Professor Albert E. Jenks' theory of the antiquity of the find, yet admits that 'the individual apparently has an excellent claim to be considered the earliest known American'.[95] As the radio-carbon dating method has been invented and developed by American scholars, most of the dates so far worked out with the help of this method belong to American antiquities. The oldest-known finds associated with the Folsom point were found to be roughly ten thousand years old, but the Folsom arrow-point occurs over a very large area and in localities of different antiquity. Accordingly, a Folsom site in New Mexico turned out to be comparatively younger, viz., 'only' between 4,033 and 4,533 years old.[95a] All these recent discoveries are invaluable from the point of view of human palaeontology and prehistoric archaeology; but for the study of primitive art they are so far only of theoretical importance. Moreover, for the analysis of primitive art as such we are interested in quality rather than antiquity. American Indian arts provide ample evidence of the fact that typically primitive features may still survive when purely technical devices have already reached a high stage of perfection.

If we describe the characteristics of the New Stone Age as those of a predominantly sedentary mode of life, with agriculture, pottery, basket-making, and more finely elaborated stone implements, then many American Indian cultures may be classified as neolithic.[96] A good many American nations, however, had developed a certain amount of metal-working (especially copper, gold, and silver) and these more highly advanced civilizations should rather be compared to the *chalcolithic* stage in the Old World, when stone implements were still used side by side with metals, in particular bronze. In ancient Mexico and Peru the political structure of the community, law and order, the organization of trade and commerce; on the technical side stone architecture, road construction, pottery, weaving, etc., were so highly develo-

ped that these communities, at least at the time of the Spanish conquest, cannot be regarded as primitive. The arithmetical and
astronomical knowledge of the Mayas, as it is recorded on their
stone monuments, was unique in the ancient world. The graceful
forms and painted decoration of Mexican, Maya, and Peruvian
pottery rival Greek vases of the best periods for aesthetic quality;
Mexican carvings in hard stones and crystal have their equal only
in China; and the textile art of ancient Peru surpassed that of the
Copts, to which, at first glance, it is so similar. Taken as a whole,
then, the arts of the ancient higher civilizations of America are
fine arts in the best sense of this term, and thus not primitive,
while to our eyes they have the charm of the exotic. Yet those
civilizations emerged from primitive beginnings, some of which
are still manifest in belief and ritual, mythology and customs of
the advanced period. This primitive background of the higher
civilizations has also left a reflection on both decorative and representative art. On the other hand, in both hemispheres of the
American continent certain art forms developed in the centres of
higher civilization can be recognized in the arts of primitive tribes
not only in the vicinity, but also sometimes at considerable distances, as we shall shortly see. This must be due to culture contact
of some kind (either migrations or trade routes, peaceful or
war-like expeditions, etc.), in any case to historical events and
developments.

Some primitive arts of America have survived to the present
day, while most of them have been extinct for a long time, and the
best are prehistoric. The following brief survey is confined to the
principal types of primitive art, arranged in the geographical
order – i.e., beginning with the northernmost tribes – and with
only occasional references to the ancient high civilizations.

A. *Primitive Arts of North America*

1. *Eskimos*

Although the Eskimos are not – and probably never have been –
very numerous, they occupy a vast territory stretching from
north-western Alaska to Greenland and Labrador. In terms of

ethnology, their area is even larger, since Eskimo culture is characterized as 'arctic culture', and as such includes peoples inhabiting the arctic regions of the Asiatic continent. However, in this
chapter we are concerned with the art of the Eskimos of arctic
America. This art has reached its highest development in Alaska,
and this holds good for both ancient and recent art. They have
two more or less durable media for small plastic work in common: walrus ivory and bone. The most important works of art
from the aesthetic point of view belong to the so-called Old Bering
Sea culture, and have been published by Henry B. Collins, Jr.
(1930).[96a] A female ivory statuette, unfortunately a torso, found
in Punuk Island (Collins, Pl. 16), is outstanding. Another remarkable feature of the Old Bering Sea culture are certain flat carvings
resembling a large moth, or butterfly, with outstretched wings
which are decorated with incised circles and concentric circles.
These carvings have not yet been satisfactorily explained, but we
are told that they have nothing to do with the so-called 'banner-
stones' of the mound cultures of the United States. According to
F. Rainey, the Old Bering Sea culture was preceded by a phase
which he has called the 'Okvik'. Collins himself regards the
Punuk culture (and art style) as the final, mature phase of the Old
Bering Sea culture and the art of the modern Eskimo as a de-
generated development. Frederica de Laguna has recently pointed
out that the Punuk culture emerged from the Old Bering Sea culture 'because of cultural enrichments from Siberia', but she also
observes that we do not know a great deal about the Old Bering
Sea culture, as no skeletal remains have been found and the burial
customs of those people are practically unknown. In recent years
the most important archaeological finds in Alaska have come to
light through the excavations at Point Hope and Ipiutak by Froelich Rainey, Louis Giddings, and Helge Larsen. These excavations began in 1939, the latest was carried out in 1949. A wealth of
peculiar art forms has been discovered at Ipiutak. Carvings in
walrus ivory and antler include, among other forms, delicate zoomorphic objects, such as long-beaked birds' heads with twisted
necks and similar forms; miniature carvings of seals, miniature
human heads, and – most peculiar of all – two composite masks
consisting of ivory pieces, every piece beautifully carved and de-

corated with engraved lines, the whole set of approximately the natural size of a human face. Larsen and Rainey recognize 'an undeniable resemblance with ancient Chinese art', and indeed there is a definite Chinese parallel, viz., the large composite animal masks (*fang hsiang*) found in tombs at Hsün Hsien in Honan, and published by Bishop White in his *Bone Culture of Ancient China*.[96b] These Chinese masks, representing monsters, or de-

FIG. 42. A Scene representing Eskimos Travelling with Loaded Sledges and Dogs. Eskimo engraving on a fire-drill bow of walrus ivory. Alaska. Length 170 mm.; total length of bow: 16 in. Coll. H. Longden, Shoreham-by-Sea, Sussex.

mons, were placed in the tombs to dispel evil influences. It would be hard to suggest that there exists no genetic relationship between these Chinese composite masks and their counterpart in Alaska. Still the chronological discrepancy is enormous; the Chinese pieces belong to *c*. the twelfth century B.C., whereas the Ipiutak culture in Alaska is two thousand years or more younger, as has been established by radio-carbon tests recently.[96c] But these recent dates (roughly from the middle of the eighth century A.D. to the middle of the twelfth century A.D.) do not exclude a historical connexion with the Chinese parallel. We must remember that, in some parts of the world, stone implement types of neolithic and even paleolithic character survived until the nineteenth, even the twentieth century, especially in areas far remote from the higher civilizations. If a genetic connexion between ancient Chinese art of the Shang period and Ipiutak exists it might also be responsible for certain formal parallels between ancient Chinese art and the decorative art of the North-west American coastal Indians. When Ipiutak was discovered, the first theory was that it might represent the relatively oldest phase of Palaeo-Eskimo culture. But Dr Frederica de Laguna at once expressed her doubts that Ipiutak could be ancestral to the Old Bering Sea phase, and when the comparatively recent age of Ipiutak had been established by radio-carbon dating it was proved that she was right. All theories about the relative chronological order of the various Eskimo cultures and art styles, including the latest presentation of the problem by K. Birket-Smith, will have to be revised in the light of the radio-carbon findings. Larsen himself has already recognized that another culture which was unearthed at Cape Denbigh (Alaska) by James L. Giddings recently is 'de-

finitely pre-Ipiutak'. A radio-carbon test of a Denbigh specimen resulted in the figure 2016 ±250, which means the period between 314 B.C. and A.D. 186 (Libby, p. 90, test No. 563, submitted by Rainey). Other sites in Alaska and in the Aleutian Island were found to be much more ancient.

Although, generally speaking, recent Eskimo art, i.e., the modern development of the Neo-Eskimo phase, differs from the art of their ancestors – or perhaps we should more cautiously speak of their predecessors – yet there are a few features which they have in common. The nature of the hard raw material for small carvings – ivory and bone – is responsible for the technique of engraving by thin incised lines. At least one decorative element, the circle, or a group of concentric circles, with a dot in the centre, has survived from the Old Bering style up to modern times. But modern Eskimo art in Alaska is distinguished by realistic engravings depicting Eskimo life, especially hunting scenes, which are not found on ancient pieces. By 'modern' we mean principally the nineteenth century; it seems that, in the twentieth century, this delightful miniature form of graphic art has been on the decline. This art is essentially utilitarian and decorative; the majority of objects adorned in this way are fire-drill bows, tobacco pipes, and needle cases. Some pieces, such as the tobacco pipe illustrated on Pl. 33(a), are decorated with both linear engravings and plastic art, and the latter may even be represented in two forms, viz., high relief and miniature sculpture in the round. The drawings are often so extraordinarily animated that they are considered by many as ranking with the palaeolithic art of Eastern Spain or with Bushman paintings (compare, for example, text Figs. 15 and 52). Engraving on ivory is an extremely difficult technique – much harder than chipping on a more or less crumbling rock wall. The Eskimos, however, are so familiar with it that they prefer it to any other medium in which they have had no practice. Thus, when Kaj Birket-Smith of Copenhagen asked an Eskimo to draw a walrus hunt with pencil on paper, the native made several serious attempts, then gave it up, and, taking a walrus tusk, engraved the scene on ivory.[97] Similarly, Eskimo women and girls like to illustrate the telling of stories by scratching drawings on the ground with a bone knife.[98]

The modern Eskimos possess a highly developed talent for dramatic performances. The personification of mythical beings and spirits and the ritual dramatization of myths require the use of a variety of wooden masks, sometimes decorated with feathers. In this way the people have developed a plastic art which is religious in the widest sense of the term. Both ceremonial masks and others of a burlesque type, worn by players in comic performances, are often ingenious works of art, grotesque effects, sometimes of amazing vigour, being produced with very simple means. The face, usually painted plain white, or perhaps with some sparse pink spots, may have one large round eye and just a narrow slit for the other eye; the mouth may be a wide, gaping hole or a curved slit, expressing laughter or pain, a grin or cynicism, threat or fear. Mask carving still flourishes.

2. North-west America

The coast and islands of Southern Alaska and British Columbia form one of the most important centres of primitive art and the most conspicuous type of North-west American Indian art, the so-called totem pole, is now so popular all over the world that it can be regarded as a symbol of the country.

Apart from a number of more or less highly developed crafts, such as weaving and basket-making (no pottery), North-west American art consists of both sculpture and graphic art (drawing and painting), and both fall into two groups, one realistic, the other highly stylized and conventional.

Realistic graphic art in this area is prehistoric. It is represented by rock engravings, for example, a group of masterly naturalistic animal figures – halibut and some quadrupeds – engraved on a rock at Nanaimo (Vancouver Island). The date of these engravings

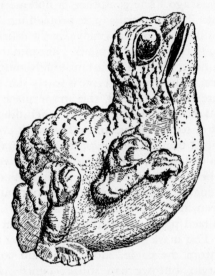

FIG. 43. Naturalistic Wood Sculpture of a Toad. Hollow. Found in a tomb on the upper Fraser River, British Columbia. Length 22 cm. Collected by Mr William Charles (Hudson Bay Company). Berlin, Museum f. Völkerkunde. After L. Adam, *Nordwestamerikanische Indianerkunst* (1923).

is so far unknown, and it is not even certain that they were made by the ancestors of recent Indian tribes (i.e., for Vancouver Island, Nootka and Kwakiutl); they may be the work of other tribes of prehistoric times.

But as far as sculpture is concerned, there can be no doubt that the peculiar conventional style, which is typical of the eighteenth and nineteenth centuries, and has survived up to the present day, was preceded by a highly developed naturalistic style, sculpture in wood, distinguished by an admirable truth to nature. It is obvious that the perishable material could not last very long in a damp climate; consequently very few examples have survived, and this early naturalistic art of British Columbia is not so well known, not even to all the students of the more recent art of the Northwest. The wood carving of a toad illustrated here (Fig. 43) was unearthed from a burial-place on the banks of the upper Fraser river many years ago. The sculpture is hollow, and shows no traces of paint. The eye-balls are protruding, almost semi-globular, with a shallow circular groove, in the centre of the upper part, suggesting that it had been inlaid. The animal is represented as it is just about to jump. The astonishingly naturalistic treatment of the surface showing the typical warty skin of the amphibian is also noteworthy. Indeed, this masterpiece can compare with any animal sculpture of high quality, including the excellent representations of toads, crabs, and other small creatures which we find in some of the Japanese *netsukes*. Of human images, the portrait statues of famous chiefs made by the Kwakiutl Indians have already been mentioned in a previous chapter. A good example of the high standard of naturalistic portraiture in recent times can be seen in Pl. 36 (*a*).

Conventionalized plastic art is illustrated in our plates 33(*b*), 34(*b*), and 35. The mask (Pl. 35(*a*)), representing the 'thunderbird' derived from the eagle, shows the rigid contours of the conventional style, but we can still recognize its naturalistic origin. Masks carved from cedar wood, mostly painted in black, red, blue, white, or – among the northern tribes, especially Tlingit and Haida – a pale sea-green, are one of the characteristic features of the north-west coast. They are used for ceremonial dances during the great winter ceremonies. One peculiar type is a double mask with an ingenious adjustment consisting of two or four sections, together representing a second mask mounted on the edge of the other. These masks are used to represent transformations which not infrequently occur in the mythology of the tribes. The performer operates them by pulling some strings connected with the sections of the superimposed mask, in this way displaying the inner mask, and thus illustrating the transformation into another being. However, the classical examples of conventionalized sculpture are the carved poles showing a series of figures seated on top of one another. The name 'totem poles' is inaccurate; the figures are not normally totems, but in the majority of cases either characters in clan legends or the crests of the inhabitants of the house.

The larger of the two poles now in the British Museum illustrates two different legends.[99] The hero of the first is Yetl (Yelch),

F<small>IG</small>. 44. Monumental Painting on the Wall of a House of the Tsimshian Indians, British Columbia. (After F. Boas, *Primitive Art*, p. 225.)

the raven, the mythical creator of all things, whose innumerable adventures are the main theme of myths among the Tlingit Indians of Southern Alaska, and the Haida of the Queen Charlotte Islands. Once upon a time, when he was hungry, he dived into the sea and swam to a large village, where the inhabitants were fishing for halibut. Keeping himself invisible, Yetl helped himself to the fish on the hooks as fast as they were caught until eventually he was caught himself. But the fishermen were unable to pull in the line because Yetl, with his supernatural strength, was holding tight to the sea-bed with his claws. Suddenly the line slackened and the men fell back. The Raven's beak had been broken. The fishermen found its upper part on the hook, and took it away, not knowing what it was. Later on Yetl appeared in human form, got hold of the fragment, and replaced it, flying away through the smoke-hole in the roof. When he became hungry again he once more took the shape of a chief, sat down among the men and ate with them, holding a chief's staff in his hand. The figure on the summit of the pole shows him disguised as a chief, with a chief's hat and staff, while the second figure represents him with his broken beak (Pl. 33(*b*)).

The principal feature of conventional sculpture is its rigid symmetry. For the rest, both plastic and graphic conventional art is governed by the same strict principles. The first to recognize and define these unwritten rules of North-west American art was the late Professor Franz Boas of Columbia University.[100]

Designs are almost always derived from the animal kingdom. The animals are represented by a kind of symbolism, using one or more of the characteristic features of each. A bear, for example, is distinguished by many teeth, a protruding tongue, an abrupt angle between snout and forehead, and large paws (Fig. 44); a beaver by large incisors, a big round nose, scaly tail, and a stick held between elevated fore-paws. There are no front views in the proper sense of the term. Instead, we find two symmetrical profiles (Figs. 11 and 44). In Fig. 44 the animal is cut from back to front, so that only the front part of the head coheres, while the two halves of the lower jaw do not touch each other. The Indians call such a design 'bears meeting', as if two bears had been represented. Fig. 11, representing a dog-fish, is based on the same principle, except that the head might pass for a real front view.

The various symbols, and other details such as eyebrows, have standardized forms. The Indian can tell from the shape of a highly stylized ornamental detail whether it represents the wing of an eagle, a raven, an owl, etc., and the same holds good for conventional forms of tails, fins, and the like. Joints are represented by 'eye ornaments' which have nothing to do with actual eyes. Naturally, the question arises: *why* are joints drawn in this way?

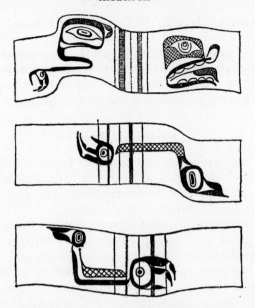

FIG. 45. Designs Engraved on Gambling-sticks of Bone or Wood.
Haida Indians, Queen Charlotte Islands.

(I) Sea-bear; left: leg with hip-joint and claw-joint
indicated by eye-ornaments. The fin at the
right-hand side of the hip-joint indicating sea-
animal. Right: the head with protruding
tongue and teeth.

(II) A raven symbolized by a claw (left) and a wing
(right). The eye-ornaments are the joints.

(III) Another raven; left: wing; right: claw. The
ornament linking the two indicates the body
and feathers.

After John R. Swanton, *Contributions to the Ethnology
of the Haida.*

The answer to this question is not so difficult to find if we remember that one important feature of North-west American graphic
art is the so-called 'X-ray' vision described in the second chapter
of this book. In other words, the 'eye ornament' is actually a
representation of a cross-section of a joint, and hence its rounded,
oval, or kidney shape. These eye ornaments drawn on claws often

look like birds' heads (e.g., the four paws in Fig. 44). Sometimes they are even filled in with faces, which have no significance, but are purely decorative additions (Fig. 11). The various parts of the body are often disconnected, and fitted symmetrically into a decorative field. The most sophisticated method reduces the drawing to a minimum by representing one or two symbolic details only (Fig. 45).

3. *Iroquois and Algonkins*

The two antagonistic groups of tribes, the Iroquois and the Algonkins, have both developed a decorative art of remarkable quality, the most important technique being porcupine-quill embroidery on hide – replaced in later times by bead work or embroidery with dyed grass, sometimes on fabric of European origin. Motifs are partly geometric, partly derived from vegetable forms. The decorated objects are garments, belts, bags, and the like. Especially in the older pieces we admire a marked sense of rhythm and of colour. These Indians were masters at the decoration of a given space with pleasing, unobtrusive designs, avoiding overloading it with too many details, and using only a few, quiet colours at a time. The natural shade of porcupine quills is white, sometimes a dark brown, but this material was sometimes dyed orange, which gives a pretty effect in combination with white. Technically still more difficult is the bead-work which we admire in the famous *wampum* belts, which often had a pictographic or symbolic significance, and in this case actually had the function of a document. The beads were made from shells by the Indians themselves, and thus are not to be confused with the imported glass beads of European origin. The natural colours of the wampum beads are white and a deep mauve. A wampum belt would show, for example, a group of several white conventionalized human figures on a mauve ground; but the technique employed in these belts was not embroidery. The beads were joined together with fine leather strings, so that when held against the light the gaps between the beads could be distinguished. The technique is therefore a kind of mosaic.

The Iroquois have also evolved a type of sculpture which deserves special mention – namely, wooden masks for use in religious ceremonies. Representing demons or spirits, these masks are of a grotesque character. Some of them have real human hair inserted in small holes, a technique which was also employed in North-west America, Japan, and China. F. H. Douglas and R. D'Harnoncourt tell us that among the modern Iroquois these masks are still made and used by ritual societies, and the same authors make the interesting observation that 'the preliminary carving of Iroquois masks is done on living trees because the Indians wish the masks to be alive also.'[101]

4. *The Mound-Builders*

Indian art in North America undoubtedly culminated in the sculptures of the so-called 'mound-builders' who inhabited the entire east of the United States, including the Ohio valley and the lower Mississippi valley. The mounds, which must be regarded as the most important archaeological monuments of eastern North America, are of very different shapes and dimensions. Some of them are very large – several hundred feet long – and in some cases over 30 ft. high. It has been established by excavations that the various types of mounds had different functions; in particular, some are tombs, whereas others were associated with the religious life of the tribes, and again others served merely as platforms for dwellings. A curious type – the 'effigy mounds' – so called because their lay-out represents the outlines of gigantic figures, e.g., animals, such as snakes – has a parallel in the 'hill-figures' of England. As far as the mounds themselves are concerned, their importance lies on the technical rather than the artistic side. They provide a clue to the understanding of the mode of life of the prehistoric population of the country. Those ancient tribes of North America were sedentary, and had reached a cultural stage which was certainly superior to that of the nomadic or semi-nomadic Indians of the plains as it survived up to the nineteenth century. They were capable of well-organized team-work and, on the other hand, evidently had sufficient leisure to develop arts and crafts. For the history of art the objects buried in the mounds are of outstanding importance, because they include a large number of stone sculptures, mostly of small dimensions, which must be regarded as some of the finest works of art ever made in America, and may well compare with the plastic art of the best periods of ancient Mexico, and even of the Mayas. These sculptures are of various kinds; there are, first of all, human figures sculptured in the round, usually represented in a squatting position. The material is sandstone, porphyry, or other types of rock. Some figures have the indefinable air of portraiture, as for example a statuette of $21\frac{1}{2}$ in. height, found near Stilesboro, Bartow County, Georgia (A. J. Powers collection, Mt Vernon, Iowa; illustrated in *Prehistoric Art*, by Thomas Wilson, Annual Report, Smithsonian Institute for 1896, Washington, 1898, pl. 44), but there are several others of equal aesthetic merits. Then we find a large number of stone pipes or pipe-heads, often representing animals or even groups of animals. At least one modest example is reproduced in Pl. 37 (*a*). A third category may be described as discs of either stone or shell, with engraved designs, sometimes carved in open work. Many of these may be ornaments (gorgets), but the function of others is not clear. Again, another type is definitely 'utilitarian'; bowls, shaped as animals – e.g., birds similar to, but in our own eyes more beautiful than, the bird-shaped wooden bowls of the Admiralty Islands, the bird-shapes or fish-shaped bowls of the southern Solomon Islands, or the seal-shaped bowls of the Northwest Coast of America; but comparable to certain zoomorphic pottery vessels of ancient Peru. There are, however, pieces of other materials, too; in the first line, pottery. Some pottery jars of human form are again strongly reminiscent of Peruvian ware – e.g., the portrait vases from Chimbote, etc. There are also pieces of sheet copper, engraved or decorated in chased work.

The finest plastic works have been found in Ohio, Arkansas, Georgia, Tennessee, Alabama, and Kentucky, but remarkable finds have also been made in other states. Animal figures, or rather heads of animals excavated at Key Marco, Florida, reveal an astonishing gift of observation and truth to nature. There is the head of a deer in the University of Pennsylvania Museum (illustrated in F. H. Douglas' and D'Harnoncourt's book, p. 96), which is of exquisite beauty. The latter sculptures belong to a relatively late period, being ascribed to the fifteenth century A.D.

The art of the mound-builders can be properly studied only in

American museums. The most prominent collections are in the U.S. National Museum; the Museum of the American Indian (Heye Foundation), New York; the University of Pennsylvania Museum, Philadelphia; the Peabody Museum, Harvard University, Cambridge, Mass.; and the Ohio State Museum, Columbus. Other remarkable examples belong to the Tennessee Historical Society collection (first published in General Thruston's book *Antiquities of Tennessee*), and to various university, municipal, and private museums. Outside America this art type is not adequately represented, not even in some of the great European museums with otherwise rich American collections. Apparently there has always been a tendency to keep these antiquities in America, probably because the people of the United States have long been aware that the relics of the indigenous population are the invaluable monuments of the prehistory of their own country. This leads us to the famous problem: who were the mound-builders? The fact that the mounds cover such a vast area, and, on the other hand, that there exists a variety of distinct styles, makes it obvious that what is usually described as 'mound-builders' art' cannot be the work of one nation, but that probably several more or less different peoples must have been responsible for those different styles. A large proportion of the stone sculptures, but especially the engravings on shell, are distinguished by their marked Mexican features; in fact, some of them are typically Mexican in both motif and style. This has been generally recognized for a long time and the conclusion is that Mexican Indians must have lived in the country, who introduced more highly developed arts and crafts, together, no doubt, with religious beliefs and rituals. It is also probable that these were the immigrants from the south who imported the cultivation of the principal Mexican cereal, the maize. However, we must remember that 'Mexican culture' and 'Mexican art' are very general terms, and that the ancient civilizations of Mexico and Central America actually comprised a great variety of cultures, ranging from really primitive types to relatively very high developments; also that they were the result of a history of many centuries. Some of the figures and engraved designs of the mound-builders reveal the style of the Aztec period – i.e., the style which flourished on the plateau of Anahuac, roughly speaking, from the thirteenth to the end of the fifteenth century A.D. Other pieces, however, have the features of an earlier Mexican style which preceded the Aztec epoch. Certain vases in the shape of a short-legged dog are similar to a well-known type of dark-red pottery found in the district of Colima, near the Pacific coast of Mexico. We may therefore assume that the prehistoric cultural relations between the eastern United States and the southern civilizations extended over a long period. The Mexican immigrants probably arrived in small numbers, and as time went on were gradually absorbed by the various tribes of the indigenous population. It is now generally recognized that at least some of those native tribes were the ancestors of some of the Indian tribes of more recent times, while the identity of other mound-builders is still uncertain. It must be emphasized that the high development of plastic art was only partly due to Mexican influence, and that many other works are distinguished by their obvious originality and typically primitive simplicity. Until recently, the chronology of the older strata of mound culture had been obscure. With the help of the radio-carbon dating method, a number of important dates have already been ascertained.* In the Hopewell Mound Group, Ross County, Ohio, Hopewell I was found to be between 1794 and 2294 years old, i.e., it belongs to the period between 342 B.C. and A.D. 158; Hopewell III lies between 199 B.C. and A.D. 200, while Hopewell II from Illinois is even older than Hopewell I of Ohio, viz., between 634 and 134 B.C. In comparison, the Adena cultures of Ohio and Kentucky were found to be considerably more recent; the upper margin of a Kentucky site is as recent as the first half of the tenth century A.D.

5. Plains Indians

We now turn to a more recent development – the art of the Indians of the plains. The history of numerous tribes, belonging to different ethnic and linguistic stocks, accounts for the character of their artistic activities. Before the introduction of the horse, the forefathers of these tribes were sedentary in settlements along the

* Willard F. Libby, *Radiocarbon Dating* (University of Chicago Press, 1952), p. 78.

border of the prairies, so their nomadic mode of life was only a few centuries old before it came to an end through the white man's extermination campaigns against both the Indians themselves and their principal source of food and raw materials (hide, sinews, etc.), the bison. Perhaps some of the ancestors of the modern plains Indians belonged to the mound-builders, who, as we have seen in the preceding chapter, excelled in plastic art. And, indeed, this talent apparently did not entirely become extinct in the modern hunters of the plains, since we find now and then a war club, comb, or pipe-head, carved in some naturalistic form, still reflecting something of the plastic quality of those prehistoric works of art. But these are exceptions, and generally speaking the unsettled life of nomads is not favourable to the development of sculpture. Everything must be practical, there is no room in a tent for things other than the strictly utilitarian; but even indispensable requisites may be given pleasing forms or decorated with ornaments or designs. The Indians of the plains had a marked talent for graphic art, which is manifest in their polychrome paintings on buffalo hides used for tents ('tipis'), garments, and a few other articles. The complicated technique of these paintings has been recorded by John Cansfield Ewers, and a summary has been given above (Chapter II, Sect. 1). Purely geometric patterns were the work of the women, while the representative forms were painted by the men. They specialized in often extraordinarily animated fighting and hunting scenes. An example is shown in Fig. 2 – one out of many scenes and figures painted on a large buffalo hide which is in the British Museum. It gives a vivid impression of a horse-hunt, and the tracks of the thundering hoofs have been carefully marked by the artist. The oldest specimen of Plains Indian painting still in existence is a buffalo robe done by a Mandan artist about 1800, and now in the Peabody Museum at Harvard.[102]

The sad story of the North American Indians during the nineteenth century is well known. The buffalo herds, the economic basis of their former life as nomadic hunters, are no more. The great majority of the tribes have lost their original territories, and their remnants survive under changed conditions, while other tribes are entirely extinct. Still, the surviving tribes are not dying out, and their future looks much more hopeful under the so-called New Deal for the American Indian. It is a new legislation, distinguished by fairness and humanity, and operated by the Indian Bureau in Washington. In this way the clash of cultures, which had resulted in open conflict in the past, has now made way for a systematic process of acculturation. A most interesting periodic illustration of this modern development is an official magazine entitled *Indians at Work*, which shows, among other features, that the old arts and crafts are still being practised, although the raw materials have naturally changed. The Indians still retain the memories of the hunting life of their forefathers, and occasionally still depict scenes similar to those which used to be represented, perhaps in a slightly different style and with more leisure and care, on buffalo hides in the olden days. Moreover, modern art media and utensils have been made available for Indian artists, so that some of them have been able to develop the ancient style in an easier technique. In recent years Indians have been enjoying European–American art education, with astonishing results, as we shall see in Chapter XVIII.

6. *The Ancient Art of Texas*

The vast area of Texas is rich in archaeological treasures, both human remains and artefacts, and the University of Texas, in particular its laboratory of archaeology, is the centre of archaeological and anthropological research in this state. Two features deserve special mention – viz., pottery and rock art. The pottery bowls and bottles found in the Caddo territory, Camp County, Texas, are distinguished by simple, graceful forms; bowls decorated with little animal figures mounted on the rim have been excavated in Anderson County. Some pieces from other sites are fashioned in the shape of fruit, such as melons, etc., a device which has a well-known parallel in Peruvian pottery.

A tripartite bottle, unearthed from a burial site on the Red River, Lamar County, Texas, has a striking similarity to an almost identical type of Fiji pottery – a true parallel, and certainly not due to culture contact. But the most important monuments of primitive art are the rock paintings and engravings scattered over a wide area of the state. Some of these are of colossal dimensions, such as the gigantic paintings of a fabulous snake or dragon which plays an important part in the mythology of the tribes in many American countries. It would appear that, at least in dry regions, it is always the mythical rain-snake which is represented. Similar 'rain-snakes' occur in the mythology of the Australian aborigines

FIG. 46. Detail of a Fret showing Interlocking Coils. From a Pueblo Pot of the Black and White Tularosa Type. *c.* A.D. 1290. After H. P. Mera, The 'Rain Bird'.

and in rock paintings in northern and north-western Australia. The rock paintings of Texas show a great variety of figures and scenes, and there are various styles and different degrees of perfection. The oldest pictures may go back more than fifteen hundred years, but most of them appear to be less than five hundred years old, and some even less than one hundred.[103] In many cases the tribal dress of Indians represented, or the fact that horses are depicted, give us a clue. As everywhere in the world where rock paintings exist, we find more recent designs, often superimposed on older works. Needless to say that, as in Australia and elsewhere, some of these precious historical relics have been damaged by white vandals.

It must be mentioned that rock paintings and engravings are found also in other parts of the United States, for example in California and in Utah. Some of them are probably pictographs.

7. *The Pueblo Indians*

The art of the Pueblo Indians of New Mexico and Arizona is noted for its variety and antiquity. Its beginnings have been traced back to far remote prehistoric times, and the chronological strati-

FIG. 47. Designs from Six Different Early Pueblo Pottery Fragments illustrating various Stages of Development. After H. P. Mera, The 'Rain Bird'.

fication of its stages has been established by archaeologists. The most celebrated branch of Pueblo art is painted pottery, and if we consider that it began in the fourth century A.D. and is still being practised, we have to regard it as the second oldest living ceramic industry in the world, Chinese ceramics being the oldest. But there is a difference with regard to style: while Chinese ceramic art still turns to older periods for its inspiration, deriving forms and designs from those developed largely during the Ming dynasty and the Ch'ing dynasty up to the close of the reign of Kien Lung

(1796), the evolution of Pueblo pottery so far has not come to a standstill, but is evidently still in progress. In fact, some very attractive decorative patterns have been developed in quite recent times. This is certainly a remarkable proof of the vitality and creative power of the Pueblo Indians. Some Pueblos are still inhabited, but others are now in ruins. Each Pueblo had its own style, and the gradual development of these can be traced almost up to the present day, except of course those local industries which are extinct or prehistoric. The evolution of designs from simple patterns to complicated coils and frets is shown in Figs. 46 and 47. Other designs are derived from vegetable and animal forms. Birds are the commonest, and the representations of quadrupeds are of later origin. The principal types of Pueblo pottery are bowls and jars. Handles we find only in a few cases, for example on the 'sacred meal bowls' of Santo Domingo Pueblo. As in other parts of America, pottery is a monopoly of the women. A detailed account of the technique has been given by Kenneth M. Chapman. The potter's wheel is unknown, and the vessel is gradually built up with rolls of clay pressed on top of one another and then scraped and smoothed outside and inside. So far the method is identical with that followed by other primitive peoples in America, Africa, and the South Seas, but it is followed by some more elaborate technical devices – namely, 'slipping' and polishing. Next comes the painting, and, finally, firing. The slipping deserves special mention because it is responsible for the attractive cream-coloured surface of many Pueblo wares, which has only one parallel in America – viz., the beautiful pottery of Nazca in Peru. The clay itself is red, or of a reddish grey, but several coatings of bentonite dissolved in water provide the cream slip, which is subsequently finished by polishing with a smooth stone. Next comes the application of a red slip, consisting of dark red ochre, to the lower portion of the vessel, sometimes also to the inner surface of the opening or neck, and there are types with red slip all over the exterior or interior surface (here, too, we find a striking parallel in Nazca pottery). It is impossible in this brief survey to quote any more technical details, and readers interested in this fascinating subject are referred to the works by A. V. Kidder and C. A. Amsden; P. E. Goddard; Charles F. Saunders; K. M. Chapman and H. P. Mera, to mention only a few prominent authors out of a voluminous special literature.[104] The attractions of Pueblo pottery lie not only in its forms, but also in its painted decoration. Pueblo Indian art at its best is graphic rather than plastic. Large polychrome wall paintings have been discovered in the ruins of prehistoric Pueblos, where the walls of the shrines or ceremonial rooms, the *kivas*, are covered with mythological designs of a very striking decorative effect, revealing a marked sense of rhythm and symmetry. In their ritual performances the Pueblo Indians, like other primitive peoples, use wooden masks of grotesque forms, decorated in bright colours, representing a whole pantheon of deities or spirits. Small models of these mask dancers – the so-called '*kachina* dolls' – are made as toys for children, implicitly an easy way of introducing them to the religious beliefs of the tribe (Pl. 37(*b*)). There is a sharp contrast between the grotesque primitiveness of these figures and the matchless beauty of the greater part of the pottery, but wood carvings are the work of the men, whereas, as already mentioned, the women are the potters and painters of the pottery. One type of sculpture in wood is particularly interesting because it belongs to the most primitive plastic art styles. These are the idols of the Zuñi tribe, representing war gods, which consist only of a pole with crudely carved heads and rudimentary arms, sometimes even without any limbs at all. These crude images have some resemblance to the equally primitive carvings of the Bari tribes on the upper Nile, also to the huge pole sculptures of the Azande of the Anglo-Egyptian Sudan and northern Belgian Congo.

Of other arts and crafts of the Pueblo Indians we can only briefly mention basketry and weaving. And a word must be said about the 'sand paintings' of the neighbouring Navajos – i.e., representations of religious figures and symbolic patterns produced by sprinkling sand of various colours on the ground. Actually, then, this is not 'painting', but a specific technique of its own, resembling mosaic work. It requires great skill, all the more so as the designs are often of very large dimensions. Yet after the ceremony they have to be destroyed before sunset.

B. *Primitive Art of Mexico and Central America*

As already mentioned in the introduction to this chapter, the fine arts of ancient Mexico and Central America – architecture, sculpture, and pottery – are anything but primitive, and thus, as a whole, beyond the narrower scope of our brief survey. It has been said that the higher civilizations of ancient America, in particular their art, can be traced back to primitive beginnings. The classical example with regard to the development of Mexican sculpture has been furnished by the excavations at Teotihuacan, with its famous step-pyramids. A distinct stratification could be established which is marked by different types of pottery, and especially pottery figures and heads revealing different antiquity, ethnic types, and degrees of technical and artistic perfection. There is the oldest stratum, with small human heads of a definitely primitive type, modelled in a reddish clay; this cultural stage has been associated by archaeologists with a primitive tribe, the *Otomi*. A more recent stratum, dated about the tenth to eleventh century of our era, is already highly advanced, and may be classified as archaic. A large number of small dolls of clay, with movable arms and legs, was embedded in this layer, but only a small number of complete ones were found, together with many little heads – fragments of once complete specimens. These heads, or at least a great many of them, are works of art of great quality, all the more admirable for their small dimensions (only about 3 cm. high). The human faces are modelled true to life, and they are obviously portraits of various racial types. There is one type distinguished by a narrow face with a narrow, slightly curved nose and a high forehead, and a different type with a broad face and shorter nose, and so on. This remarkable stratum is ascribed to the *Toltecs*, once a legendary people, but now recognized as a historical reality. The most recent stage at Teotihuacan is Aztec, artistically a setback compared with the aesthetic sensations of the Toltec stratum. This is, of course, only a rough outline of the archaeological situation at this particular site.

Apart from the beginnings, even the advanced phases of Mexican art always retained certain primitive traits. Thus, while representations of human physiognomies are often masterly, the Mexican sculptors were not always successful in the portrayal of the body and limbs, except in some squatting figures. The stiffness, wrong proportions, and, generally speaking, imperfect plastic elaboration of many Aztec statues and their countless small replicas in clay – all these shortcomings are not stylistic

FIG. 48. Design from a Modern Pueblo Pot. After Kenneth M. Chapman. *The Pottery of Santo Domingo Pueblo.*

peculiarities, but rather symptoms of undeveloped vision. Still, we must remember that only relatively few works of Mexican art have survived the iconoclastic ardour of the Spanish invaders – which, incidentally, was not unpardonable, if we realize that the Aztecs were in the abominable habit of sacrificing their prisoners of war to their gods – and we know nothing about the artistic quality of all that has been destroyed. Furthermore, a large proportion of Mexican art was probably peasant art (see above, Chapter VII).

Ancient American plastic art – sculpture in the round as well as in relief – reached its highest development in the two great periods of the Maya culture of Guatemala, Yucatan, and Honduras; the Old Empire, approximately from the second century B.C. to the fourth century A.D., and the end of the New

Empire from about the eleventh to the twelfth centuries. Maya reliefs and stelae of those great periods are usually covered with hieroglyphic dates and other symbolic decorations; hence the frequent criticism that Mayan art is over-elaborate.[105] This, however, is a generalization, and some archaic works are distinguished by simplicity and grandeur. The greenstone figure from Chimaltenango (Guatemala) (Pl. 38(a)) provides a glimpse of an early, though not the earliest, stage of Mayan art. It is primitive art at its best. But the outstanding sculptures of the great periods, such as the famous reliefs of Palenque, Menché, and other palaces and temples, have nothing to do with primitiveness, and the reliefs of deities, priests, and worshippers, extraordinarily animated and full of expression, are the work of accomplished artists. There exists a stone bust of the Maize-God, found at Copan in Honduras, and ascribed to the third century A.D., showing the god with his mouth open, speaking or chanting; looking downwards upon the worshipper, both hands stretched forward, the face and every single finger full of life and expression – a masterpiece which for quality can compare with classical Greek sculpture.

The more utilitarian types of Mayan art, such as the gorgeous pottery with its decorative paintings in orange, red, and white, or the already mentioned marble vases of Honduras (Rio Uluà) (the finest collection of these in the University of Pennsylvania Museum; some other examples in the British Museum and in the Ethnographical Museum at Berlin), are also not 'primitive', and some of the latter are reproduced here only for comparison (Pl. 38(b)).

It is now generally recognized that Mayan art was the dynamic agent which inspired the arts of Mexico and a large proportion of Central America. A number of local styles might have been the product of a synthesis with autochthonous primitive developments; but these interesting problems of Central American archaeology cannot be dealt with in our summary of primitive art. But I may mention at least one conspicuous detail concerning the plastic arts of southern Central America and northern South America (in particular Colombia), namely, the strange phenomenon of typically primitive forms presented in the most precious medium – gold. In Costa Rica (Nicoya Peninsula), gold figures of animals, cast in the *cire-perdue* technique – for example, eagles, monkeys, sharks, and spiders – have been excavated which are fine naturalistic sculptures without any marked primitive features. Human masks, too, made from sheet gold in the *repoussé* technique, are of high quality. Human figures, however, usually retain the characteristic shortcomings of really primitive art. Still more striking is the contrast between the splendour of the gold works of Costa Rica and certain small idols of greenstone found in large numbers in the same region and in association with the gold objects. These idols consist of flat slabs of stone of an average length of only 3 in. and a width of 1 in. or less, two engraved dots to mark the eyes, and not even always a third little groove to indicate the mouth.

C. *Primitive Arts of South America*

The principal areas of ancient art in South America are, in geographical order, Venezuela, Colombia, Ecuador, Peru, Bolivia, and Northern Argentina, and much has been done by the Governments of most of these countries during the last few decades to promote excavations and the study and preservation of archaeological relics. Ancient Peru extended far into what is now Ecuador, Bolivia, and Chile. The arts of Peru, notably architecture, pottery, and textiles, had reached a very high standard by the time of the Spanish conquest. Primitive features survived in the decorative designs of painted pottery, in the patterns of woven *ponchos*, and especially in representations of human figures, with the only exception of the admirable portrait vases of the latest period – that of the Incas. However, it is impossible to illustrate some primitive examples taken out of their context and without showing the characteristics of the various Peruvian art styles (Nazca, Tiahuanaco, Ica, Pachacamac, Cuzco, Chimu, with its distinct stratification; the strange ancient Chavín in the north, and so on). Therefore the present chapter is largely confined to one, more typically primitive art province – that of Colombia.

Ancient Colombia was inhabited by several nations, of whom the most important were the Quimbaya, in the Cauca valley, and the Chibcha, in the highland of Bogotá. These peoples are responsible for the large number of gold treasures – helmets, human and animal figures, bottles, and ornaments – which are now in the Museo Nacional in Madrid and elsewhere. Guold, silver, copper, and various kinds of alloys were worked in sothern Venezuela, Ecuador, and Colombia; the *cire-perdue* technique, chased work, a kind of filigree work (Fig. 49), gilding, and soldering, were all practised, and the study of pre-Columbian metallurgy and metalworking techniques has already resulted in a rich special literature.[106] But while the animal figures are distinguished by a certain truth to nature, and the decorative details reveal a marked sense of beauty, neither the Chibchas nor the Quimbayas were able to master the human figure. They retained throughout the characteristic shortcomings of really primitive art; but these are more obvious in clay figures (Pl. 39(*b*)) than in gold statuettes, where they are counterbalanced by the beauty of the material. In a black-and-white reproduction, where the quality of the material does not appear, the primitive character of design and technique in a piece like Fig. 49 is quite unmistakable. This group, made of solid gold in a filigree technique, is a good example of Chibcha work. It was found in the lake of Siecha, Cundina-marca (Colombia), and is of great archaeological interest because it is obviously an illustration of the famous ritual in which the ruler of the district, his body covered with gold dust, had to bathe in the holy lake, where the gold was washed off and sank to the bottom, as a sacrifice to the gold of the lake. Hence the name 'El Dorado' ('the Gilded One'), which at the time of the Spanish conquest and for a long period afterwards used to be associated, not with a person, but with the country. Although this was etymologically wrong, yet it was justified on account of the wealth of gold in that area. Fig. 49 shows the ruler, the 'Dorado', seated on a raft and surrounded by a number of smaller figures, representing Indians rowing. The figures consist of small pieces of sheet gold; the head-dress, eyes, noses, mouths, and limbs are of gold wire soldered on the flat surfaces; and the raft is a coil of wire. The height of the large figure is

7.1 cm., that of the smallest figure 3.2 cm.; the weight of the whole piece is 162 gm., or $5\frac{7}{10}$ oz. The difference in size between the chieftain, or high priest, and his attendants is noteworthy; it is the same idea as in ancient Egyptian, Indian, and other Oriental arts, where deities, kings, and other superior beings are represented larger than the ordinary people.

FIG. 49. Ancient Chibcha Sculpture, cast in gold. The group probably represents 'El Dorado', a chief, or *cacique*, surrounded by oarsmen on a raft. From the Lake of Siecha, Cundina-marca, Colombia. Height of the large figure, 7.1 cm. Ruiz-Randall Collection. Bogotá. After E. v. Sydow.

In eastern Colombia, near San Agustín on the upper River Magdalena, there are prehistoric monuments of an entirely different type of primitive art, consisting of huge sculptures in basalt and other volcanic rocks, the largest over 13 ft. high. Some of them are still standing in an upright position, others lie on the

FIG. 50.
Prehistoric Stone Pillar,
San Agustín,
Colombia.
After K. Th. Preuss.

ground, and some are still buried below the surface. Again others are in shrines built from large slabs of stone and half-embedded in the slopes of hills; in other words, 'dolmens', in terms of pre-historic archaeology – i.e., a primitive form of architecture belonging to the neolithic stage. One of these statues is shown in Fig. 50. The British Museum possesses a very fine original of smaller size, and a few other originals and a collection of casts are in the Ethnographical Museum in Berlin. There is a great variety of human figures (both male and female). Many of these have canine teeth, which suggest demons (readers familiar with the iconography of Hinduism will remember that in India, too, canine teeth indicate a demoniac character, and that the *rakshasas*, or devils, are always represented in this way). Other sculptures of San Agustín are naturalistic images of monkeys, jaguars, owls, snakes, etc. No doubt all these gigantic works, including the 'warriors' flanking the entrances of shrines, are of a religious character, and some sort of lunar mythology may be their principal subject. The significance of the peculiar smaller figure represented at the top of some of the pillars (Fig. 50) has given rise to interesting theories. The late Professor K. Th. Preuss suggested that it may symbolize the *alter ego* of the main figure,[107] but this is sheer conjecture. Walde-Waldegg, Colombian Government Archaeologist, believes the carving represents a bat, symbol of death, with human features; and indeed this explanation seems to settle the problem if we consider the position of the smaller figure and the ornament on top of it, which may well be interpreted as a bat's skinny wings. It is remarkable that the other type of figures, the demons with canine teeth, are not accompanied by a bat, probably because they were not supposed to be mortal.

The megalithic culture of ancient San Augustín was first studied by K. Th. Preuss, who from 1913 to 1919 conducted the first systematic excavations in the district. His work, published in 1929, was subsequently translated into Spanish by Hermann von Walde-Waldegg. From 1932 onwards Walde-Waldegg then made two expeditions to the region, and was able to excavate no less than 142 statues, in addition to 120 which had been known at Professor Preuss' time.[108] Walde-Waldegg was also fortunate in discovering human remains in one of the tombs, and in finding quantities of pottery and other objects. It is important that at some sites he could establish a stratification. On the strength of this discovery, and by comparison of stone axe blades, types of pottery, and art styles, he came to the conclusion that it is now possible to draw up a tentative sketch of chronological sequence, as follows: the earliest stage may have lasted from about 250 B.C. to A.D. 200; the second from A.D. 200 to A.D. 700, and the third period from A.D. 700 to A.D. 1000. Walde-Waldegg considers that 'the cause of the artistic decline of San Agustín may have been invasion by a more powerful nation or a gradual disintegration of the people from other causes'.

The prehistoric culture and art of San Agustín is certainly one of the most interesting – and most mysterious – archaeological relics of America. Some day it may be possible to link its history with that of other cultures, and Walde-Waldegg has already made a start by establishing that 'the upper level of the San Agustín culture merges with later cultures, the approximate dates of which are known'. In this connexion I should like to call attention to a strange parallel – namely, a recently excavated prehistoric stone sculpture of very large dimensions, which in my opinion shows a remarkable resemblance to the heads of the stone figures of San Agustín. I am thinking here of a colossal head of 6 ft. height, 18 ft. circumference, and over 10 tons weight, which was unearthed near Tres Zapotes, near Hueyapa, Vera Cruz, in Mexico, some years ago. This gigantic piece has been illustrated by Matthew W. Stirling in the *National Geographic Magazine* (*U.S.A.*), Vol. lxxvi, No. 2 (1939). It has so far been described as 'unique in character among aboriginal American sculptures'. Is it a relic of a very early megalithic culture, which might have extended as far as South America?

A few words must be said about the prehistoric art of a vast area, the Amazonas basin. Archaeological research here is of recent date, the earlier ethnographical studies having been confined to the living primitive tribes. The tropical rain forest is not favourable to the preservation of artefacts made from perishable materials, such as wood, while stone and pottery survive. A large number of prehistoric sites has been discovered throughout northern Brazil, from the delta of the River Amazon as far west as the upper Rio Negro, the Yapurá, and the Rio Napo. Some important archaeological localities are, among others, Marajó, Maracá, Couanany, Caviana, and Santarem. The sites so far examined near or in the Amazonas delta have been found to be post-Columbian, because European glass beads occur together with Indian pottery. Other sites, however, are older, and some may be many centuries old. Pottery is the outstanding feature. There are painted bowls or deep plates of very graceful shapes, and decorated with colourful geometric patterns. Another variety of Amazonas pottery is zoomorphous, representing the armadillo and other animals typical of the country. There are also anthropomorphous urns, a device well known from other South American areas (Peru, Colombia, Venezuela, Northern Argentina). The eminent Swedish archaeologist and anthropologist, the late Baron Erland Nordenskiöld, has pointed out that there must have been a distinct influence by the higher civilizations in the Andes, while three-legged pottery types suggest an influence even from Central America, where this particular form is very common.[109] The Indians who are responsible for the prehistoric relics in the Amazonas basin were, according to Nordenskiöld, principally the ancestors of the recent Aruacs (sometimes spelled 'Arawaks'). This ethnic group gradually occupied a vast area stretching from Central Brazil to the Antilles.

Some observations about the art of some modern tribes of South American Indians have been made on pp. 41 ff.

CHAPTER XVII

Primitive Art and the European Artist

MODERN European artists were not necessarily the first to discover the aesthetic merits of primitive art. In the seventies and eighties of last century a few anthropologists, such as J. Crevaux and G. Brough Smyth, drew attention to the excellence of primitive work in South America and in Australia, while G. Fritsch praised the Bushman paintings. But it is modern artists, art dealers, and collectors who are responsible for the new understanding of the plastic qualities of West African sculpture.

Up to the middle of the nineteenth century some European artists had illustrated the narratives of the great discoverers by reproducing works of primitive art as ethnographical specimens. A few painters like Catlin, who lived among the North American Indians, travelled and worked on their own account. Hume Nisbett, who over half a century ago was 'the only professional artist who has visited the mainland of New Guinea', already recognized the Papuans' 'true antique instinct for lines and colours'.[110]

From about the seventeenth century onwards exotic details had appeared, though only sporadically in still-life and genre painting. European expansion during the eighteenth and nineteenth centuries was to some extent reflected in the sphere of art, but the interest in exotic forms gravitated towards oriental rather than 'savage' themes.

In those days artists went to foreign countries for fresh models and motifs only; their European vision and means of expression remained unchanged. The number of French painters who thus explored the beauties of the Eastern world is astonishingly large. A whole gallery at the Musée de la France d'Outre-Mer in Paris is set apart to represent *l'orientalisme français*.

There was also Gauguin, whose work stands for an entirely different development in the history of European art. Gauguin did not belong completely to the romantic school which was content with its academic equipment, and merely sought to enrich its palette or to find new models. He approached the strange atmosphere of the West Indies and the South Seas in a humble attitude of naïve receptivity. His interest in exotic subjects and forms arose from a feeling of surfeit and weariness with the fictive representation of nature, perfected at the end of the nineteenth century, which offered no prospects of individual advance to painters who were striving after a completely new technical and visual achievement. The longing for the primitive did not mean that primitiveness was to be an end in itself. On the contrary, it was the beginning of a completely new vision.

Gauguin went first to Martinique, and later to Tahiti, where he painted his well-known South Sea pictures and wrote his book *Noa-Noa*. Here he developed his own markedly decorative style, with bold contours, broad spaces, and a symphony of subtle and often unmixed colours. In his paintings we are taken out of the noisy European world and set down among brown Polynesians in a completely new atmosphere – peaceful, serene, orderly, and apparently care-free. But we experience this through the medium of a European artist, who is far from feeling as a savage, although it often seems in his book as though he would like to do so.

The astonishing thing, however, is that Gauguin does not once mention the art of the natives, and though the artist must have seen the rigid sculptures of Tahiti (cf. Pl. 26(*b*)), there is no sign that his figures were influenced by them. When Gauguin was in Tahiti, however, genuine indigenous culture had already ceased to exist. He found a French colony with rapidly advancing 'civilized' islanders, and the best examples of primitive art had already been placed in the museum. In spite of its exotic atmosphere, Gauguin's art remained fundamentally European.

Another European painter, Max Pechstein, went to the Palau Islands in Micronesia. He, too, painted the natives and the South Sea landscape, and enriched his palette with brilliant tropical colours. Primitive art was still flourishing in the Palau Islands, and Pechstein devoted his attention to the native idols and carvings, and to the painted gables of the house. He sought to capture a primitive atmosphere by rejecting all academic technical refinements, and using vigorous brush strokes in unmixed colours. It is possible that this technique was influenced by the polychrome decoration of the native carvings, but otherwise Pechstein's art, like Gauguin's, retained its essential European character, though it cannot be compared with it for quality.

These are instances of European artists living in primitive surroundings. Oddly enough, those artists who actually produced 'primitive' works did so at home under the influence of primitive sculptures from Africa and the South Seas. As far as we know, neither Modigliani nor the Russian Archipenko had lived among primitive men. But Modigliani, as Professor Talbot Rice puts it, 'models his forms on those of Negro art, and again, adopts as his own something of the Negroes' aesthetic approach'. Archipenko's figures are sometimes of the same abstract character as the neolithic idols of the Cyclades, or the figurines from Nukuoro, though generally more animated.

One German sculptor, the late Ernst Barlach, was also greatly influenced by West African Negro sculpture. His greatness lay in his wood carvings – figures of astonishing simplicity and force. He aimed at producing as small a number as possible of large surfaces, and at expressing a strong spiritual emotion by the attitude of these characters, portrayed with the simplest technical means. His models are usually thick-set, even plump figures, taken from the people.

Barlach was impressed by a technical peculiarity of many Negro sculptures, the treatment of the surface by revealing the unplaned marks of the chopping-tool – a technique which occurs also in other areas such as North-west America, and the Sepik region of New Guinea. He actually copied a number of real Negro sculptures, not only for the purpose of technical study, but also for pleasure. Yet he did not come exclusively under primitive influence. He was still more strongly influenced by Gothic art, and his sculptures have, indeed, something of the Gothic in them.

It is the work of Pablo Picasso which is usually associated with primitivism in modern art. No doubt Picasso studied some of the many varied primitive arts, gaining inspiration from them, but he has re-fashioned these inspirations to a large extent. His work up to the present day falls into several periods, all extraordinarily different from one another. For this reason alone it is a mistake to connect his work as a whole with primitive art, and merely to say that 'he studied the significance of Negro and Polynesian sculpture for plastic form'.[111]

Picasso's primitiveness is quite definitely his own 'Picassian primitiveness'. It is obviously not spontaneous, like the productions of a South Sea Islander or an African, but the outcome of a more or less complicated intellectual process. This is made clear by his more realistic periods. It is true that many of his works, in particular the series of paintings of the first half of 1929, seem to take us into a world of unreality, populated by grotesque beings and disconnected parts of real figures. But even here it is said that he never once strays from reality: 'A aucun moment sa vision intérieure ne s'oppose aux objets, mais, au contraire, elle les accepte totalement. La réalité contemplée en solitude n'est pas moins la réalité, et si Picasso perçoit les objets, c'est qu'il les a vus' (Christian Zervos).

The attitude of some primitive artists towards their subject gives a key to the understanding of their work. There are certain details which interest them so much that their vision is concentrated on these particular features and eventually absorbed by them. The result is that they represent these features to the exclusion of the rest of the subject, which implies a considerable deviation from merely optical reality as the European understands it. An extreme example is to be found in the X-ray drawings of Melanesia and North-west America, which were described on p. 39 ff.

There is another kind of primitive art which consists in representations of fabulous monsters and demons. These are creations of the primitive imagination, although even here the 'savage' cannot entirely dispense with the natural forms with which he is familiar. Head, eyes, limbs, etc., are essential parts of any living creature, and these are adapted to the world of spirits and demons, though they may often take the most remarkable shapes.

Primitiveness in modern art, however, is by no means always associated with, or derived from, the art of primitive people. If an artist attempts to free himself from the fetters of academic tradition in the search for a new spontaneous approach to his material, he may show a neglect of real proportion or conventional arrangement, and may himself consider this neglect as symbolic. In this case the similarity to the obvious imperfections of primitive art, above all the false proportions of limbs, is merely accidental (compare, for example, Epstein's Adam).[112]

Modern art can learn from primitive plastic art, particularly from African sculpture, a refreshing naïveté, a wholesome concentration on essentials, and a spontaneous approach to both man and beast, without arbitrarily adopting its obvious imperfections. The aim should be not to introduce another kind of 'ism', but to get rid of certain modern 'isms' by recovering the spontaneity which European artists have largely lost. The artist of to-day, however, even when he captures that original naïveté, will never produce really primitive works. Art is the expression of the artist's mentality, and inseparably bound up with his whole life, surroundings, and history. Civilized man cannot unlearn all that he has learnt, or rid himself of the centuries of science and technical knowledge which have become an inherent part of his nature. Imitating the mere 'primitiveness' of primitive art is like rejecting all modern comforts and acquisitions, and going back to caves and skins. It is not only against all rules of logic, but utterly untrue to our own nature.

European Art and the Primitive Artist

In wide areas of the world industrialization has disintegrated the social and economic structure of primitive communities. The natives transferred from their home villages are no longer able to devote themselves to their traditional arts and crafts. Nor are they willing to do so; for modern education, broadcasting, cinemas, etc., have discredited the customs and beliefs in which their art was rooted. Educated natives look down on the superstitions of their ancestors, they resent being called primitive, and in fact the term no longer applies to them.

Already ethnographical dealers find it hard to procure primitive objects of real value. The best of the old works are now in museums and private collections. Most of what is available to-day is of inferior quality, made carelessly for curio-hunting globe-trotters by modern methods, and with European tools. New Zealand, where the beautiful art of the Maori once flourished, has become a centre for such pseudo-primitive production. Before long modernization will have reached the few tribes in Africa, Indonesia, New Guinea, and Australia, where genuine primitive art is still alive.

But the populations survive, and with them their innate artistic capacity. So long as primitive men passed as savages, and their works as mere curios, no one took these native talents seriously, but the discovery of the aesthetic value of primitive art, as well as its psychological and social functions, could not fail to attract the attention of educationists, missionaries, and colonial administrators. In Africa, the United States, the Dutch Indies, and in French Indo-China it is now a recognized task of native education not only to maintain and encourage the indigenous arts and crafts, but also to teach and improve them.

At the University College at Achimota, on the Gold Coast, the teaching of arts and crafts is in the hands of an Arts Supervisor who is a trained art teacher and himself a sculptor. The majority of his assistants are Africans. Instruction in wood-carving is under the direction of the Chief Wood-carver of the Asantehene of Ashanti. The College is also associated with the revival of Benin art. The chief of the Brasscasters' Guild in Benin has been sent to Achimota by the Benin Native Administration, and at the request of the Oba, to take a course in chasing and reproducing and to act as a demonstrator in brass-casting.

According to the programme of Achimota College,[113] the aims of an arts and crafts education is 'not to keep alive the last remains of a dying culture in a native society fast becoming Europeanized, but as a necessary part of its economic and social life'. Pupils are shown 'how to select what is valuable in African arts and crafts and how to adapt it to the needs of a changing African society'.

One of the principal aims, therefore, is to develop the utilitarian value of artistic production. The African's natural need of plastic and graphic ornamentation should be satisfied by African works of good craftsmanship, and not by imported European patterns, often of inferior quality. The native craftsmen and the native artist should then be able to work in the first place for the local market as a solid economic basis for his activities.

But another entirely different task of art education is the teaching of European vision, and the European techniques of drawing, painting, and sculpture. The idea is not for the African to copy European works, but to enable him to adapt the new equipment to a specifically African mentality and outlook.

As a sculptor, the African has little or nothing to learn from the European. Pl. 40a shows a modern sculpture in iroko wood by B. C. Enwonwu, then a twenty-year-old student of Onitsha and Government College, Umuahia (Nigeria), who was described as the most sophisticated of the five artists who were represented by wood carvings, terracottas, and water-colours at a Nigerian art exhibition, held at the Zwemmer Gallery in London, 1937. The artists had been trained 'on methods adapted from those made familiar by Miss Richardson of the London County Council'. We see correct proportions according to European academic-naturalistic standards; in fact, this is a work which could have been done by a European. It is true that this sculpture represents an African woman but it cannot be claimed that this is an example of genuine African art. All the spontaneity and vigour of real African art, as we perceive it on Pls. 2 to 7 and elsewhere, is gone, it is obscured by acquired European academic convention. This can hardly be called 'progress', although it is interesting as a result of the impact of European vision and technique. Another modern Nigerian artist is Felix Idubor (born as the son of an Edo farmer at Benin City in 1928). Idubor, too, has learned his European lesson; but, in addition to academic statuettes illustrating native life, he has retained, or revived, in some of his works, the true African spirit, as could be seen from carvings like his mask representing a dream, which was on exhibition at the Imperial Institute in 1957.[113a]

Indigenous graphic arts are not entirely absent in Negro Africa, though they never attained the high standard of Bushman art. Figures and scenes depicted on house walls in various parts of West Africa are interesting, though they are markedly crude and stiff. All the more astonishing is the discovery that the Africans can draw and paint excellently. In both West and East Africa art students are now taught on European lines (Pl. 40(b)), and the results are remarkable.

During the last few years experiments in the teaching of painting by modern methods have been begun by Miss Fisher at the Christian Missionary Society Girls' School, Gayaza (Uganda), and by Mrs Margaret Trowell at Makerere College, Uganda. Mrs Trowell explains that the student's home background exercises a strong influence on his work. Zanzibar has produced a painter in clear sparkling colours, while the arid brown plains of Kenya inspire dry, hard browns, reminiscent of early Flemish work. Some sixty of such pictures were shown in London at the Imperial Institute, South Kensington, in the spring of 1939.

In an interesting article entitled 'African Art – the Next Phase' (*Oversea Education*, Vol. x, No. 4), Mr G. A. Stevens says that, given the necessary freedom and encouragement, the African is able to take hold of a traditional European craft, and make it into something of his own. Mr Stevens believes in what he calls 'the vitality of the Negro aesthetic genius'. Needless to say, the outcome of this development will no longer be primitive art, though it may be African art.

In America, Indians of the Potawatomi, Kiowa, Navajo, and Apache tribes excel in mural paintings. They have been trained by O.B. Jacobson and the Swedish painter Olaf E. Nordmark, and the walls of the recreation room in the Department of the Interior Building, Washington, are covered with their works.[114] This modern development of Indian art in the United States is most satisfactory because the European art teachers are obviously familiar not only with the ancient traditional art forms, but also with the material culture and the customs of the tribes. Therefore they wisely refrained from demonstrating to their Indian pupils 'how to do it', which would inevitably imply the suggestion 'how to observe' and 'what to paint'. Instead, they strictly confined instruction to the technical side, but left it entirely to their students to choose their own subjects. The result is that modern American Indian artists do not imitate European vision and European art styles. Nor have they adopted typically European subjects, such as landscape-painting, which is something altogether alien to their own tradition. In other words, these Indians do not compete with their white colleagues, but they give us something of their own: they depict Indian life in colourful paintings of superb draughtsmanship, composition, and rhythm.

A different course has been taken in Australia. During the last ten years or so a distinguished Australian landscape-painter, Mr Rex Battarbee, has scored a triumph as art teacher of a number of natives of the Aranda tribe in Central Australia. His first pupil was Albert Namatjira, now a recognized landscape-painter, whose water-colours have been exhibited more than once in the capital cities of Australia. A beautiful illustrated book, with colour-plates, has been published about Namatjira and his work,[115] and it is understood that even a biographical film is now in preparation. Albert Namatjira, as his biographer, Mr C. P. Mountford, puts it, 'has become conversant with European methods of artistic expression'. He has a marked sense of colour, is a good draughtsman in the European sense of the term, and, thanks to his teacher, knows all about linear and colour perspective. Many of his pictures are distinguished by their excellent composition, and they have the true atmosphere of the country. But it is European art, and Namatjira's achievement is by no means a step towards an organic development of the primitive art of his people, but only a wonderful proof of the Australian aborigines' latent talent and learning ability. Mr Mountford tells us that Namatjira can still draw the symbolic designs as we know them from the *tjuringas*, and there is no connexion between those ancient patterns and his new vision. After Namatjira's first great success – his pictures fetch astonishingly high prices – several other tribesmen have begun to paint water-colours. The most prominent of them, Edwin Pareroultja, who held his first exhibition in Melbourne in 1946, works in large spaces of very bright colours, and his landscapes have something of the poster. His success was not so surprising in Australia, where the percentage of art lovers is very high and appreciation of good craftsmanship is a feature of the national character. Of course, not all these Central Australian water-colours are of the same quality; and yet, even pieces which would hardly find purchasers if they were the work of Europeans sell well. No doubt many people who may be less critical with regard to artistic quality are attracted by the fact that these paintings, or sketches, are produced by aborigines who are able to depict their homeland with European means of expression; as the well-meaning art critic of a Melbourne paper put it, 'their paintings have the double attraction of being true works of art and the works of an exceedingly rare type of artist'. Financially, thanks to the principle of clan solidarity, the success of the aboriginal painters turned out to be beneficial for a large proportion, if not the whole, of the aboriginal community of Hermansburg, although it is understood that the aborigines are not allowed to spend all the money at will.

This 'Hermansburg school of native painters', as they have been called, has grown up in an area of culture contact between black and white, and thus not from the undisturbed setting of the nomadic hunter. Unfortunately, their output is very large, and it is interesting that not only the 'stars' but also members of the younger generation are taking part in this development, since we

are told that 'many of the seventy children at school at Hermansburg, in charge of Miss Hilda Wurst, draw lively sketches of animals and landscapes, which they sell to visitors, spending the
money at the store'.[116] But there are already indications of a mass
production on the part of the more serious group of adult
painters, and Clive Turnbull, the prominent art critic of Melbourne, introduced his review of another exhibition of these
water-colours as follows: '...therefore, one might suggest, even
at the risk of being accused of an anti-social project, that the
Central Australian aboriginal painters form themselves into
a cartel with a view to restriction of production to an output
which will ensure a sellers' market'.*

Let us hope, however, that the case of the native water-colour-
ists of Central Australia will remain an exception, for it is irre-
levant for the solution of a much deeper, and more important
problem, namely, the future of *real* Australian aboriginal art
(Ch. XV, pp. 152 ff.) and the development of the aborigines'
own artistic talent rather than their imitative ability.

It does not follow that the aborigines should not use modern
art materials. Their use alone does not necessarily mean that the
native artist will become the ape of the white man. This is inevitable only if a European artist practises in the presence of talented
aborigines, even without talking to them. *Exempla docent.* But
when European art materials are made available to the aborigines
with only a minimum of simply technical European art instruction, the result may be amazing, as in the case of the pastels,
crayon drawings, and water-colours done by a group of aboriginal children of about thirteen years of age at the Carrolup
Native Settlement in the Great Southern District of Western
Australia.† Although not every single piece is good, many of
them are. There is the mystic character of form and colour in the
scenery, and especially the trees and shrubs, of the country, and
there are men and animals depicted full of life but without any
shallow photographic naturalism. The art of these black children
may perhaps be compared to a mixture between Henri Rousseau

* *The Herald*, Melbourne, 8 December 1947, p. 8.
† *Child Artists of the Australian Bush*, by Mary Durack Miller in association
with Florence Rutter. London (Harrap), 1952; with 36 plates, some in colour.

and Kubin. Unfortunately, the group no longer exists; artistic activities of the children were eventually discouraged when it was found that the young artists, when they had left school, were unable to hold their own in a different environment and in more practical jobs.

It would be good if the competent authorities would help the aborigines as a whole to develop their ancient primitive art and to adapt its attractive decorative patterns to modern require-ments, as I have already pointed out on pp. 166–7. The difficulty lies in the fact that, while the aesthetic effect of this art is decorative, the emotional background is decidedly expressionistic. This holds good even for weapons, tools, and other profane objects. It has nothing to do with the actual origin of the various geometric patterns, which has been discussed on pp. 41 ff., but only with their subsequent, though probably very old, inter-pretation by the natives themselves. A. P. Elkin has pointed out that 'the designs are usually the same as those depicted on the sacred symbols used in the secret religious life, and can only be worked by those fully initiated men who know the songs or chants connected with them, and these designs ... duly "sung", endow the instrument or weapon with a potency which comes from the world of spirits, culture-heroes, and magic. A boomerang so marked is not just beautified; but, through its artistic decora-tion, it has become a perfect, sure, and never-failing boomerang.'* These observations show that aboriginal art is esoteric; the various symbolic patterns belong to different totem groups, but their actual use for ritual purposes is the privilege of a small number of male individuals *within* that group; moreover, the right to produce those patterns is a copyright vested in a few older individuals or even one single person (compare pp. 66 ff.). It is clear that, with the inevitable gradual disappearance of primitive beliefs and rituals, there will be no room for ritual objects in the future. The point, then, is to find a way to encourage the natives to retain and develop their old designs for their *decorative* value, that is to say, *without* their original ritual or magical function. It will not be necessary to let their

* A. P. Elkin, *The Australian Aborigines*, 2nd ed., p. 16.

mythological significance fall into oblivion, as primitive religious texts may, by degrees, be reduced to simple folk-tales. Here again, the educational methods so successfully employed in British West Africa seem to suggest the course to be taken.

There are two handicrafts in which aboriginal art could be usefully employed, viz., pottery and weaving. Weaving has already been introduced, on a small scale, on some mission stations, but European designs are still principally used. I can imagine that carpets and rugs, made in an Oriental technique but decorated in purely aboriginal patterns and colours, would produce a magnificent effect and probably soon be in great demand; they might also become a high-grade article for export. The fine Australian wool may be suitable for rugs, while a coarser type of wool would have to be used for carpets.

Furthermore, aborigines could be trained as potters, and pottery of any description, crockery, bowls, vases, and tiles, could be decorated by them in their own style, painted under the glaze or on the surface of unglazed ware.

All the guidance required would be purely technical – i.e., how to handle the loom or, respectively, the potter's wheel – whereas aesthetic arrangements of the designs and shades should be entirely left to the genius of the aborigines, without any interference by white artists, whose vision is different, and whose ideas would naturally spoil the originality of aboriginal work.

We must remember, however, that a large proportion of the surviving tribes are still nomads, so that only a minority of more or less sedentary aborigines would be available for any form of art education, and probably the half-castes ('*Euralians*', as they have been aptly called recently) would play an important part.

CHAPTER XIX

Primitive Art in Museums

EXCEPT for the originals of rock engravings and paintings, primitive architecture, and certain very large sculptures in wood and stone, primitive art must be studied in ethnographical museums. There are no special museums of primitive art – with possibly one or two exceptions – because the aesthetic approach to primitive art became popular only a few decades ago, when ethnology was already a well-established discipline. Consequently, practically all the important works of primitive art will be found in the ethnographical museums, collected, catalogued, and displayed, not as works of art in the first place, but as ethnographical specimens. This situation, however, is by no means unsatisfactory for the student of art because, as we have seen in this book, it is indispensable for the real understanding of primitive art to be familiar with its significance and functions, notably its religious and social implications. Not infrequently the primitive artist has been unable to bring about ʳhe effect he wanted to produce, so that the aesthetic result of his efforts may be accidental. Moreover, primitive man often shows, or conceals, his emotions in a way totally different from our own, and this difference may be reflected in representative art. For example, a mask with its eyes and mouth wide open may give us the impression of a frightful personification of fear, whereas the legend may tell us that it is actually meant to express an entirely different attitude, maybe no emotion at all, as in the case of the memorial statues of southern New Ireland. Of many primitive works of art the true significance is still unknown, but this should all the more be taken as a warning to refrain from premature aesthetic interpretations from the European (often pseudo-psychological) angle.

It is the very character of primitive art as an integral part of primitive culture which should be regarded as sufficient reason not to separate primitive art from its general cultural background.

In primitive cultures, utilitarian art is much more generally employed than in higher civilizations with their wealth of mechanical devices and mass production of implements and practical objects of any description. Consequently, a 'museum of primitive art' would soon, and inevitably, be indistinguishable from an ethnographical museum, unless it is confined, say, to masks or statuettes, in which case it would be incomplete. There is another point to be considered: there exists only a limited number of primitive works of art of outstanding quality. On the other hand, there is also bad primitive art, pieces of mediocre workmanship, and others of no aesthetic merits at all. The bulk of the ethnographical collections consists of a comparatively large number of good typical pieces, or replicas of lost, or unknown, originals. As primitive art is not only a subdivision of the history of art but also an integral part of anthropology, it stands to reason that it would be wrong to pick out the finest works to form a museum of primitive art and to leave only pieces of medium quality in the ethnographical museum. The problem can easily be solved in two ways: first, by arranging the exhibits in an ethnographical museum not only from the scientific, but also from the aesthetic point of view; and, secondly, by temporary special exhibitions of primitive art. Both methods have been successfully employed in Europe as well as in the United States.

Apart from public museums, a few distinguished art dealers and private galleries have helped a great deal to make primitive art more popular, also to exhibit important pieces of private collections. Dr Eduard Baron v. d. Heydt (Ascona), who enriched several European museums by the presentation, or loan, of his various collections, was one of the first to collect primitive art on a large scale. He persuaded Alfred Flechtheim, a distinguished art dealer who flourished in Berlin between 1910 and 1930, to exhibit works of primitive sculpture in his gallery. Flechtheim displayed primitive art, in particular pieces from Melanesia, together with modern art (Picasso, Klee, Matisse, Archipenko, and others). A similar arrangement is in operation at the Museum of Modern Art in New York, but is, fortunately, absent in the valuable publications of primitive art from various geographic areas issued by the same museum and based on its remarkable special exhibitions (see Notes 83 and 101). As some modern artists have undoubtedly been inspired by primitive art (compare Chapter XVII, pp. 205 ff.), it is certainly instructive to see occasionally their work side by side with the art of primitive man; but I would not recommend this juxtaposition as a principle of permanent display.

Exhibitions of primitive art have a distinct educational value, not only for the European student but also for the modern descendant of primitive man, namely, in connexion with modern art education in colonial areas, in particular Africa (compare Chapter XVIII, especially p. 211). As nearly all the good old pieces are now in European or American collections, certain parts of Africa are practically stripped of their treasures, so that the present generation of natives is more or less completely ignorant of the art of their forefathers. For the revival of native arts and crafts, the presence in the country of a fair number of good originals is essential. Consequently, in British West Africa, the administration is now anxious to build up local museums, and some fine old examples of African sculpture will probably be returned to their country of origin.

CHAPTER XX

Forgeries

FROM the beginnings of prehistoric archaeology, the genuineness of excavated objects was called in question by sceptics, and this was particularly so in the case of the palaeolithic cave paintings of south-western Europe (Chapter IX). Many people would not believe that a primitive prehistoric race was responsible for the superb draughtsmanship as we find it in the wall paintings of the Upper Aurignacian and Lower Magdalenian, and it took the archaeologists some time to convince the public of the authenticity of the earliest known European art. The artistic quality of the masterpieces of Altamira, Lascaux, and other famous caves (compare p. 77 ff.) is so high that they seem to defy any attempt to fake them, whereas the cruder, earlier work of the Lower Aurignacian might not be so difficult to imitate. On the other hand, smaller and cruder 'prehistoric' carvings and especially stone implements have not infrequently been forged. Frauds inevitably occur wherever there is a demand, but the faking of prehistoric objects was, unwittingly, encouraged by the archaeologists themselves, who offered substantial rewards to their workmen for bringing to light specimens in a good state of preservation. Stanley Casson recalls the story of an old lady at Abbéville who watched a workman striking flints in front of his door and asked him what he was doing. The astonishingly frank answer was: 'I am making Celtic axes for Monsieur Boucher de Perthes!'* This anecdote may be apocryphal, but is a humorous illustration of the unfortunate experiences of that pioneer of prehistory. Modern trained archaeologists are not as easily decieved. When the late Professor Hugo Obermaier excavated a cave in Bavaria, he was personally present all the time while the digging was in progress, so as to make it impossible for the workmen to smuggle in any fakes. Yet, strangely

---

* *The Discovery of Man*, 2nd ed., London, 1940, p. 179.

enough, certain objects were unearthed at considerable depth which were at once recognized as forgeries. Obermaier then investigated and discovered that, during the night, workmen had sneaked into the cave and with long iron bars pressed the fakes deep into the ground, so that they could be excavated only after strenuous digging the next day.[117] One of the few known cases where an attempt was made to fake palaeolithic drawings happened during the excavations of the so-called 'Kesslerloch' near Taingen, in the district of Basel (Switzerland) in 1874. There, three 'prehistoric' drawings were found which turned out to be the work of a workman called Merks. It was discovered that he had copied one of the drawings, the figure of a fox, from a picture-book. Faked 'prehistoric' bone artefacts, including, among others, carvings of human figures and animals, were purchased by the local museum at Baden, near Vienna; subsequently, they were recognized as forgeries and are now in the museum of the metro-politan police of Vienna, and the forger was found out and convicted in 1902.[118] Some clever forgers use real old wood, or bones, as raw materials for their fraudulent activities, just as forgers of antique furniture use real old timber, or fragments of genuine antiques, or as forgers of old pictures superimpose their products on genuine old paintings, etc., etc. A detailed illustrated account of notorious forgeries will be found in Robert Munro's book *Archaeology and False Antiquities* (London, 1905), and a rich material of technological and chemical facts, which will help the student to recognize prehistoric fakes, is recorded in Dr Siegfried Türkel's book quoted in Note 117.

Turning to ethnographical objects, i.e., artefacts of recent primitive peoples, we find that forgeries are more frequent but almost entirely confined to imitations of sculptures. It is advisable to distinguish between forgeries and copies made without any fraudulent intention; but, unfortunately, the latter may subsequently be used for less harmless purposes. It has been suggested that we must allow even for a mass production of ethnographical imitations to satisfy a popular interest in exotic forms. Actually, however, this interest is not nearly as great as that in Oriental arts and crafts which culminated in the eighteenth century, with its *chinoiseries*. Both Oriental and certain primitive objects were

copied in European countries and large quantities exported
overseas to meet the demand of tourists.

Good copies may serve legitimate purposes, educational and
decorative. The famous old stone-cutting industry at Oberstein-
Idar, in the Rhineland, specializes in carvings in hard stones, such
as quartz crystal, rose quartz, jade, nephrite, and other beautiful
materials. Apart from European forms and a great variety of
carvings in Chinese styles of different periods, Oberstein-Idar has
produced striking imitations of Maori carvings in New Zealand
greenstone.[119] Only an expert will be able to tell a genuine *tiki*
from a copy of the same material, the criteria being minute technical details. It is obvious that copies of such a high degree of
perfection may be sold as genuine.

Forgeries in the proper sense of this term, that is to say, false
archaeological or ethnographical objects made with a fraudulent
intention, are known from Mexico and Peru. In both countries,
forgeries of pre-Columbian pottery are more or less free imitations rather than accurate copies of the originals, and can easily
be distinguished by a student with a little experience. The Peruvian fakes are mostly in the late Chimu style.

The most frequent forgeries are those of Negro art, especially
wooden statuettes. I do not know whether European forgers of
African sculptures are still active nowadays, but they 'flourished'
during the first quarter of this century. There was a rumour that
fakes of Congo statuettes and masks came from a workshop
somewhere in Belgium. 'African' statuettes were also manufac-
tured in Germany, and the forgers did not bother about tropical
woods as raw material but simply used European timber. Several
methods were employed in the treatment of the surface, to produce the appearance of antiquity. The wood was stained in the
first place, then bathed in a greasy solution which was allowed to
penetrate as deep as possible into the wood, to make sure that
superficial scratching of the surface would not immediately reveal
the freshness of the material. Then the piece was allowed to dry
thoroughly, and afterwards it was 'smoked' over a wood fire to
produce a film of soot, which is indeed not uncommon on sculptures from the parklands of the Cameroons and elsewhere. A dry
polish followed to work the soot into the porous surface, and the

procedure could be repeated if necessary. This is only one of several methods, and I do not venture to suggest that others are not 'better'. Now as long as the forger is a bungler, the bad quality and wrong style of the carving will give him away at a glance, no matter how well he imitated the surface. Unfortunately, however, some really good artists, including even a very prominent sculptor, amused themselves with the production of 'Negro sculptures', allegedly 'for experimental purposes'. Suppose the wood is genuine, it is almost impossible for anyone to recognize a copy, or fake, in such a case. I do not suggest any fraudulent intention as far as those 'experimenting' artists are concerned; but the danger will naturally arise once the piece has changed hands.

After the introduction of European tools, the natives would have been very foolish if they had not availed themselves of these more effective implements. Their use, however, brought about a different, easier technique and, implicitly, a change of decorative styles. For example, the Australian aborigines originally used a hafted incisor of an opossum for engravings, and the fine old wooden shields of the natives of Victoria are, therefore, decorated with incised lines of a width exactly corresponding to the width of an opossum's tooth (compare Fig. 40, p. 167). Later pieces reveal the use of European iron tools, especially knives; the engraved lines are thinner, and straight lines often replace the curved ornaments of the original style. Generally speaking, the discarding of the ancient tools and methods, together with the radical changes of the economic, social, and intellectual life of the tribes, are responsible for the degeneration of primitive arts and crafts. One or two anthropologists have suggested that an artefact produced with European tools cannot be regarded as genuine, or, at its best, only as 'semi-genuine'. This view is, in my opinion, incorrect. The dynamic process of cultural evolution implies, among other factors, influences from outside (compare p. 31). There is no reason why the changes wrought by the import of European goods and methods should not be recognized as a formidable case of diffusion of culture. Therefore, works of primitive art made with European tools are at least documents of a historical development, although their artistic quality is inferior. Does this mean the end of primitive art? The answer is: not necessarily; as we have seen in Chapter XVIII, there may be a renaissance.

NOTES

1. The reader will find a particularly successful exposition of the connexion between art and history in Professor D. Talbot Rice's book *The Background of Art* (Discussion Books, ed. by Richard Wilson and A. J. J. Ratcliff, No. 64), London, 1939.

2. M. C. Burkitt 'Most Primitive Art', in *Early Man*, London (Ernest Benn), 1931, p. 84.

3. Herbert Read, *The Meaning of Art*, London (Faber & Faber), 1931, pp. 39–40.

4. G. A. Stevens, 'Educational Significance of Indigenous African Art', in *Arts and Crafts of West Africa*, ed. by Sir Michael Sadler, Oxford University Press, 1935, p. 13.

5. John Cansfield Ewers, *Plains Indian Painting. A Description of an Aboriginal American Art.* Stanford University Press, Stanford University, Cal.; Oxford University Press, 1939, p. 5.

6. Franz Boas, *Primitive Art* (Instituttet for Sammenlignende Kulturforskning, Series B, vol. viii); Oslo, London (Williams & Norgate), and Harvard University Press, 1927, pp. 155 f. There is now a new edition.

7. Eric Newton, 'Stamina in Painting: The Meaning of "Finish"' (*Sunday Times*, 30 July 1939).

8. A. L. Kroeber, Article 'Primitive Art', *Encyclopaedia of the Social Sciences*, Vol. ii, New York (Macmillan), 1935, pp. 226 ff.

9. L. Adam, 'Le portrait dans l'art de l'ancienne Amérique', in *Cahiers d'Art*, Paris, 1930; and 'L'animal dans l'art de l'ancienne Amérique', *ibid.*

10. William I. Thomas, *Source Book for Social Origins*, Chicago, 1909, p. 610.

11. F. Boas (*loc. cit. supra*, note 6), pp. 72 f.

12. A. C. Haddon, *Evolution in Art*, London, 1895, p. 122; A. L. Kroeber (note 8).

13. Max Schmidt, 'Ableitung südamerikanischer Geflechtsmuster aus der Technik'. *Zeitschrift f. Ethnologie*, Vol. 36, Berlin, 1904.

14. Hugo Obermaier, Article 'Kunst', in *Reallexikon der Vorgeschichte*, ed. by Max Ebert, vol. vii, Berlin, 1926, p. 136.

15. John Collier, *A Primer of Art*, London, 1882, p. 2.

16. E. Stephan, *Südseekunst*, Berlin, 1907, p. 35.

17. A. C. Haddon (*supra*, note 12), p. 216. The later stages through which alphabetic writing has passed are, according to Professor Haddon: *phonograms*, i.e., graphic symbols of sounds, usually developed out of conventionalized ideograms, which have been taken to represent sounds instead of things; *verbal signs*, representing entire words; *syllabic signs*, denoting the composing articulations of words; and *letters*, representing the elementary sounds into which the syllable can be resolved.

18. Reproduced by A. C. Haddon, *loc. cit.*, p. 124. The specimen is in the Ethnographical Museum at Berlin.

20. Elsie Clews Parsons, *Pueblo Indians' Religion*, The University of Chicago Press, 1939, 2 vols.

21. Sir Michael Sadler (see note 4), p. 4.

21a. An important critical essay on the subject is 'The Analysis of Mana: an Empirical Approach' by Professor Raymond Firth, *Journal of the Polynesian Society (Wellington, N. Z.)*, Vol. 49 (1940), pp. 483–512.

22. Various peoples show their deferential esteem towards an older person, or a person of high standing, by addressing him as 'father' or 'elder brother'; and this has probably led to the mistake that a *totem*, which is usually regarded with a certain amount of respect, must be an imaginary relative. Actually, this is not always the case.

23. James Johnson Sweeney, in his otherwise excellent introduction to his beautifully illustrated catalogue entitled *African Negro Art* (The Museum of Modern Art, New York, 1935).

24. Eckart von Sydow, *Primitive Kunst und Psychoanalyse* (Imago-Bücher, No. X), Leipzig, Vienna, Zurich (Internationaler Psychoanalytischer Verlag), 9927.

25. H. E. Gibson, 'Domesticated Animals of Shang and their Sacrifice', *Journ. of the North China Branch of the Royal Asiatic Soc.*, Vol. lxix, 1938; Shanghai, 1939, pp. 9–22.

26. Jackson Steward Lincoln, *The Dream in Primitive Cultures*, with introduction by C. G. Seligman, London, 1935; J. Winthuis, *Das Zweigeschlechterwesen*, Leipzig, 1928; G. Roheim, *Australian Totemism*, London, 1924; id., *The Eternal Ones of the Dream, a Psychoanalytical Interpretation of Australian Myth and Ritual*, New York, 1945 (reviewed by R. M. and C. H. Berndt in *Oceania*, vol. xvii, no. 1, Sept. 1946).

26a. Additional literature for Chapter V: Warner Muensterberger, 'Roots of Primitive Art' (in *Psychoanalysis and Culture*, New York, 1950); Ferdinand Herrmann, 'Die Bildnerei der Naturvölker und die Tiefenpsychologie' ('tribus', *Jahrbuch des Linden–Museums*, Stuttgart, 1952, 1953); id., 'Zur Beurteilung der Sexualsymbolik bei Naturvölkern' (*Studium Generale*, 6. Jahrgang, H. 6, 1953); Katesa Schlosser, *Der Signalismus in der Kunst der Naturvölker*, Kiel, 1952.

27. Hans Himmelheber, *Negerkünstler*, Stuttgart, 1935, pp. 8 ff.

28. The history of Haida art has been thoroughly studied by F. Boas and John R. Swanton. A modern, beautifully illustrated handbook on Northwest American art is *Art of the North-west Coast Indians* by Robert Bruce Inverarity (University of California Press, 1950).

29. Compare Karl Bücher's famous book, *Work and Rhythm*. We need not enter on a discussion of Prof. Bücher's theory that 'play is older than work, art older than production for use'.

30. Professor F. Boas, *Primitive Art* (*supra*, note 6), deals at length with rhythm in decorative art (pp. 40 ff.), primitive literature, music and dance (pp. 310 f.).

31. Huntington Cairns, *Law and the Social Sciences*. Foreword by Roscoe Pound, New York (Harcourt, Brace & Co.), London (Kegan Paul), 1935, p. 26.

32. Huntington Cairns, *op. cit.*, pp. 30 f.; Lowie, 'Incorporeal Property in Primitive Society', 37 *Yale Law Review*, 1928, p. 551; L. Adam, 'Inheritance Law in Primitive Cultures', *Iowa Law Review*, vol. xx (1935), p. 764.

33. A. L. Kroeber, *loc. cit. supra*, note 8.

34. Professor Koch-Grünberg (*Anfänge der Kunst im Urwald*, Berlin, 1905) has himself acknowledged this resemblance and refers to the very first work on children's drawings by Dr Siegfried Levinstein (*Kinderzeichnungen bis zum 14. Lebensjahr*, Leipzig, 1905). Parallels between children's art and primitive art have been drawn by Viktor Loewenfeld in his book *Nature of Creative Activity. Experimental and comparative studies of visual and non-visual sources of drawing, painting, and sculpture by means of the artistic products of weak sighted and blind subjects, and of the art of different epochs and cultures*, transl. by O. A. Oeser, London, 1939. The few examples of primitive art given by Loewenfeld are, however, insufficient, and the thesis could be documented by a wider selection of illustrations.

35. Comte Béguen et Norbert Casteret, in *Revue Anthropologique*, 1923, pp. 533 ff., and Comte Béguen, 'Les modelages en agile de la Caverne de Montespan (Haute Garonne)', in *Séance de l'Académie des Inscriptions, etc.*, de Toulouse, 1923.

36. H. Obermaier, in *Reallexikon der Vorgeschichte*, vol. vii, p. 147.

37. R. R. Marett convincingly suggests the following psychological stages in the evolution of the Aurignacian artist: ' —first, he scribbles; next he says, "This reminds me of a bear"; next he says, "I will draw a bear"; lastly, he draws a bear so near to life that folk exclaim. "This is Bruin himself!"' (*Faith, Hope and Charity in Primitive Religion*, Clarendon Press, 1932, p. 155).

38. Compare, for example, Sir Flinders Petrie, 'The Hill Figures of England', *Royal Anthrop. Inst. Occasional Papers*, 1926.

39. Some outstanding works on *European prehistoric art*: H. Breuil and M. C. Burkitt, *Rock Paintings of Southern Andalusia*, Oxford, 1929; H. Breuil and H. Obermaier, *The Cave of Altamira at Santillana del Mar, Spain*, Madrid, 1935; M. C. Burkitt, *Prehistory: a Study of Early Cultures in Europe and the Mediterranean Basin*, Cambridge, 1921; 2nd ed., 1925; *The Old Stone Age: A Study of Palaeolithic Times*, Cambridge, 1933; V. Gordon Childe, *Dawn of European Civilization*, 1925; H. Kuhn, *Kunst und Kultur der Vorzeit Europas*, vol. 1, 'Das Paläolithikum', Berlin, 1929; G. H. Luquet, *The Art and Religion of Fossil Man*, transl. by J. Townsend Russell, Yale University Press and Oxford University Press, 1930; Herbert Green Spearing, *The Childhood of Art*, 2nd ed. (2 vols.), London (Ernest Benn), 1930 (includes rich material from other areas). An excellent handbook is *The Prehistoric Foundation of Europe to the Mycenean Age*, by C. F. C. Hawkes, London (Methuen), 1940 (deals with all the important problems of prehistoric art study and is rich in bibliographical notes). The finds made near Montignac, Dordogne, are described and beautifully illustrated (partly in colour) in a volume *The*

NOTES

Lascaux Cave Paintings, by Fernand Windels, with a preface by C. F. C. Hawkes, a personal note by the Abbé Henri Breuil, and an introduction by A. Leroi-Gourhan. London (Faber & Faber), 1949. The latest publication (of which no copy had reached us by the end of December 1952) is by l'Abbé H. Breuil and is entitled *Four Hundred Centuries of Cave Art* (published by the Centre d'Études et de Documentation Préhistoriques, Montignac, Dordogne (France)), 1952. According to the prospectus, this work presents the chief paintings and engravings from the ninety decorated Old World caves discovered up to date.

40. Curtius, *Hist. Alex.*, IV, c. 7, sect. 12, first quoted by Ed. Hahn in *Reallexikon der Vorgeschichte*, vol. vi, p. 197.

41. Leo Frobenius and H. Obermaier, *Hadschra Maktuba*, Berlin, 1925; an analysis by Obermaier of the material published in *Hadschra Maktuba* is also in *Bushman Art, Rock-Paintings of South-West Africa*, by H. Obermaier and Herbert Kühn, Oxford University Press, 1930, pp. 33 ff. 'L'Art Rupestre Nord-Africain', par Raymond Vaufrey (*Archives de l'Institut de Paléontologie Humaine*, Mémoire 20), Paris (Masson et Cie), 1939.

42. L. Frobenius, *Ekade Ektab*, Berlin, 1937 (especially plates 75, 77, 79, 80, 82, 83).

43. *Art Rupestre au Hoggar* (*Haut Mertoutek*), by F. de Chasseloup Laubat, Paris (Librairie Plon), 1938. A summary of the book, with the principal illustrations, appeared in the *Illustrated London News*, January 1939.

44. For *primitive art in the Egyptian area*, especially Upper Egypt, I can only briefly refer to the discoveries made and published by G. Schweinfurth, J. de Morgan, G. Legrain, A. M. Hassanein Bey and Hans A. Winkler. Compare *Arch. Survey of Egypt, Rock-Drawings of Southern Upper Egypt*, I (Sir Robert Mond Desert Expedition), by Hans A. Winkler, London, 1938. A survey of the older discoveries is in Obermaier's work cited in note 41, pp. 31 f. Compare also *Primitive Art in Egypt*, by Jean Capart.

45. C. F. C. Hawkes (*supra*, note 39), p. 43.

46. *Principal literature on Bushman art: Bushman Paintings*, copied by M. Helen Tongue, with preface by Henry Balfour, Oxford University Press, 1909; O. Moszeik, *Die Malereien der Bushmänner*, Berlin, 1910; L. S. B. Leakey *Stone Age Africa*, Oxford University Press, 1936; *Rock Paintings in South Africa from Parts of the Eastern Province and Orange Free State*, copied by George William Stow, with illustrations by Dorothea F. Bleek, London (Methuen), 1930; M. C. Burkitt, *South Africa's Past in Stone and Paint*, Cambridge, 1928; Obermaier and Kühn, *Bushman Art* (see note 41); Miss Wilman, *The Rock Engravings of Griqualand West and Bechuanaland*, 1933; Miss Margaret Orford, 'The Rock Engravings of the Western Transvaal', in *Trabalhos do 1.o Congresso Nacional de Antropologia Colonial*, vol. ii, Porto, 1934, pp. 463–97. The latest publication on Bushman paintings is the first which is illustrated by reproductions of original colour photographs, whereas all the older polychrome reproductions are from painted copies. It is *Rock Paintings of the Drakensburg, Natal and Griqualand East* by A. R. Willcox, with a foreword by Prof. C. van Riet Lowe, London (Max Parish), 1956. Apart from the superb Polychrome illustrations,

229

this work is also distinguished by an excellent scientific text, dealing with the archaeological, ethnographical, and aesthetic aspects of the subject.

47. Felix von Luschan, 'Buschmann-Einritzungen auf Strausseneiern', *Zeitschrift f. Ethnologie*, vol. 55 (1923), pp. 31 ff.

48. The problem can be solved only when more prehistoric finds (of human relics and artefacts) are made in Africa, especially in the North.

49. A very good example of this diversity is the contrast between two peoples of the same linguistic stock: the Yoruba, with their highly developed plastic art, and the Nupe, whose art has no images at all. Compare 'Experiments on Culture Psychology', by S. F. Nadel, in *Africa*, vol. x, London, 1937, p. 424.

50. Monuments and Relics Act, 1936.

51. Roger Fry in his essay entitled 'Negro Sculpture', first published in *Athenaeum*, 1920, then reprinted in *Vision and Design*, 1920 (now in the Pelican Series, No. 20, pp. 87–91).

52. The observations on primitive art among the Guro and Atutu tribes are based on H. Himmelheber's excellent book, *Negerkünstler* (see note 27). Dr Himmelheber visited the Ivory Coast in 1933.

53. Compare J. Maes and H. Lavachery, *L'Art Nègre à l'exposition du palais des beaux-arts* (November 15–December 31, 1930), Brussels and Paris (Librairie Nationale d'art et d'histoire), 1930; E. Torday and T. A. Joyce, *Les Peuples Bakuba, Les Bushango*, Brussels, 1911; C. Kjersmeier, *Centres de Style de la Sculpture Nègre Africane*, 3 vols., Paris (Morancé); E. von Sydow, *Handbuch der afrikanischen Plastik*, vol. I: *Westafrikanische Plastik*, Berlin, 1930 – according to Sir Michael Sadler 'the most systematic account of West African sculpture'. Useful bibliographies [up till 1935] in Sir Michael Sadler's and Sweeney's publications (notes 4 and 23). The latest important publications include: Professor Melville J. Herskovits, *Dahomey, An Ancient West African Kingdom*, New York (J. J. Augustin), 1938. The second volume has three chapters on art (plastic and graphic; religious and secular). Most important plates 94–101, illustrating human statues and statuettes in wood, round-headed individuals, represented with the utmost simplicity of natural human forms. Dahomean sculpture has a monumental character and hardly a parallel in other African styles. Another publication by Professor Herskovits is his small but fundamentally important booklet *The Backgrounds of African Art* (A Cooke-Daniels Lecture, Denver Art Museum, 1945, 64 pp., 6 pl.). The standard work on Congo sculpture is now Professor Frans M. Olbrechts' *Plastiek van Kongo* (in Flemish) (N. V. Standaard Boekhandel, Antwerp–Brussels–Gent–Leuven, n.d.) Professor Olbrechts has introduced an excellent system of classification of the various plastic art styles in the area according to the forms of eyes, nose, mouth, and hair style preferred by the sculptors of the various art provinces. The author also reproduces a large number of the portrait statuettes of the (over 120) kings of the Bakuba, or Bushongo. One of the styles defined by Professor Olbrechts, the 'long-faced style of Buli', a Baluba sub-style, is illustrated on our Pl. 6.

Carl Kjersmeier's latest work is *African Negro Sculptures* (Copenhagen, 1947, Fischer's Forlag), numerous plates. A comprehensive survey of African Arts, based entirely on the collections in the Musée de l'Homme in Paris, is by Marcel Griaule, *Arts de l'Afrique Noire* (Arts du Monde, Collection dirigée par Georges de Miré, photographs by Emmanuel Sougez. Paris, Les Éditions du Chêne, 1947). There exists an English translation with the same illustrations (some in colour). A well-illustrated monograph is F.-H. Lem, *Sudanese Sculpture* (Paris, 1949), dealing with the country south of the upper Niger and on the Volta river, mainly the Dogon and Bambara tribes. Professor Paul S. Wingert of Columbia University is the author of a small but comprehensive and well-illustrated handbook, *The Sculpture of Negro Africa* (Columbia University Press, New York, 1950). The characteristics of the principal styles are admirably defined, and there is a useful map. J.-P. Lebeuf and Mme Annie Masson-Detourbet presented us with an account of their excavations (comp. Pl. 1(*b*)) under the title *La Civilisation du Tchad*, Paris (Payot), 1950. It is the prehistoric civilization of the Sao people, and the principal site is Tago. The book is illustrated by line-blocks only, the beautiful photographs by M. Sougez have appeared elsewhere. An English translation of the fascinating book is desirable, but not without the photographs. For the art of Ashanti (Ghana) comp. Eva L. Meyerowitz, *The Sacred State of the Akan*, London, 1951, with beautiful illustrations of Ashanti metal work (brass and gold), furniture (stools), and some architecture. One of the more recent publications on Negro sculpture generally is *African Sculpture Speaks* by Ladislas Segy, New York, 1952, with 250 illustrations of African sculptures in wood, stone, clay, and metal. This remarkable work gives a comprehensive survey of nearly all the important styles of West Africa and the Congo Basin, and an interesting, though controversial, introduction to the aesthetic understanding of primitive sculpture.

54. The British Museum possesses old original coral ornaments of this type.

55. C. H. Read and O. M. Dalton, *Antiquities from the City of Benin and from other parts of West Africa in the British Museum*, London, 1899; Felix von Luschan, *Die Altertümer von Benin*, 3 vols., Berlin, 1919; Bernhard Struck, 'Chronologie der Benin-Altertümer', *Zeitschrift für Ethnologie*, vol. 55 (1923), pp. 113–66. Professor von Luschan has drawn up a chronology suggesting several stages in the gradual developments of Benin art. Other epochs have been proposed by Struck. Eckart von Sydow ('Zur Chronologie von Benin-Ornamenten', *Ethnol. Anzeiger*, vol. 4, 1935) has made a valuable contribution, establishing a chronological order according to certain designs, arrangements, and technical details. A chief of the Bini, Jacob U. Egharevba, has published a remarkable *Short History of Benin* (Church Missionary Society Bookshop, Lagos, 1936), containing, among other interesting dates, some important information about the history of Benin art.

56. *Cire-perdue* technique: the method which is applied in Benin today has been described at length by Chief Egharevba in the journal *Nigeria*, No. 18, 1939. The technique used in Ashanti can be seen from Dr R. S. Rattray's book, *Religion and Art in Ashanti*, Oxford University Press, 1927.

57. E. H. Duckworth, 'Recent Archaeological Discoveries in the Ancient City of Ife', *Nigeria* (Lagos), No. 14 (1938), pp. 101 ff.

58. According to another theory it represents a god. There are several heads wearing this type of ornament but otherwise different, so that both interpretations may be correct. In a brilliant technological examination of the Olokun head (which is in the possession of the present Oni), William Fagg and Leon Underwood have shown that this piece is not an original but actually a cast ('An Examination of the so-called "Olokun" Head of Ife, Nigeria', *Man* (London), No. 1/1949, with Pls. A and B). Their arguments are regarded as convincing, among others, by a competent former member of the Department of Metallurgy in the University of Melbourne. The discovery is not surprising, since replicas, made with, or without, moulds are a common and well-known feature of the religious art of India, throughout the sphere of Buddhism, and also during the Aztec period of Mexico. It is in fact one of the details pointing to an Oriental origin of West African metal casting. W. Fagg and Underwood believe that their discovery implies the evidence that the head is a modern reproduction, but I think that this is still obscure. The question has, of course, nothing to do with the antiquity of the Ife bronzes as such. Where there is a cast, clearly there must be, or have been, an original.

59. P. Amaury Talbot, *The Peoples of Southern Nigeria*, Oxford University Press, 1926, vol. iii, fig. 227 (opposite p. 926), Nos. 1 and 7.

59a. For the kind information about alloys of copper (bronze resp. brass) I am obliged to Prof. K. Worner (formerly Head of the Department of Metallurgy, University of Melbourne, and now Chief of the Research Department, Broken Hill Pty Ltd, Broken Hill, N. S. W.).

59b. The ancient civilization of Kaffa has been thoroughly studied by Friedrich J. Bieber. The results of his researches are laid down, first, in a series of articles published in the periodical *Globus* (Brunswick); and secondly in his work *Kaffa* (Anthropos-Bibliothek II, No. 2, two vols.). The original illustration of the sacred crown (*tate uko*) of the emperor of Kaffa, showing a forehead-ornament of three parallel phalli, is in *Globus* XCIII (1908), p. 167, fig. 3. The illustration of the *kallatcho* (gentleman's membrum), a (fairly large) forehead-ornament mounted at 45° on a twisted head-band of metal, decorated otherwise with chains and pendants, appeared *ibid.*, XCV, p. 216, fig. 3 (1909). Other places, or peoples, where phallic forehead-ornaments have been recorded, are mentioned in G. A. Wainwright's important article 'The Founders of the Zimbabwe Civilization' (*Man*, No. 80/1949).

60. A. C. Burns, *History of Nigeria* (Allen & Unwin, 1929), pp. 32 f.; Rev. Samuel Johnson, *The History of the Yorubas*, ed. by Dr O. Johnson, Lagos; London (Routledge), 1921, pp. 3 ff.

61. Wilfrid D. Hambly, *Ethnology of Africa*, Chicago, 1930, p. 196.

62. One of the recently excavated bronze heads from Ife, of the type shown here on pl. 10(*a*), is now in the British Museum, while two others were acquired by the North-western University, Evanston, Ill. Compare 'The

Legacy of an Unknown Nigerian Donatello', by William R. Bascom, *Illustrated London News*, 8 April, 1939, and 'Bronzes and Terracottas from Ile-Ife', by H. and V. Meyerowitz, in the *Burlington Magazine*, October 1939. It will be observed that some of the bronze heads are distinguished by extraordinarily long necks. As the proportions are otherwise perfectly natural, there must have been some purpose connected with the elongation. A parallel from India suggests that on certain occasions these heads might have been mounted on solid sticks covered with garments to represent a whole figure. At Ife no bodies in bronze, such as might be adjusted to the heads, have hitherto been discovered. But there exist some fragments of human figures modelled in clay, trunks and limbs, for example feet, sizes varying between two-fifths and half life-size. I am indebted to Mr R. L. V. Wilkes, sometime District Officer at Ife, for this information. Two complete bronze statues of a different type, evidently composed of several separately cast sections, have been found in the Nupe village on Jabba Island.

63. J. D. Clarke, 'The Stone Figures of Esie', in *Nigeria* (Lagos), No. 14, June 1938, pp. 106–8.

64. The finds of Chou Kou Tien, including illustrations of the stone implements, have been published by D. Black, Teilhard de Chardin, C. C. Young and W. C. Pei, 'Fossil Man in China'; *Geological Memoirs*, publ. by the Geological Survey of China, Series A, No. 11; Peiping (Peking), 1933.

65. Neil Gordon Munro, *Prehistoric Japan*, Yokohama and Edinburgh, 1911; H. Matsumoto 'Notes on the Stone Age People of Japan', in *American Anthropologist*, vol. xxiii (1911), pp. 50–76; Kurt Singer, 'Cowrie and Baubo in Early Japan', *Man* (London), 1940, 61 (with photograph showing an unusual neolithic figure).

66. G. von Merhart, 'The Palaeolithic Period in Siberia', *American Anthropologist* 1923; A. M. Tallgren, in *Reallexikon der Vorgeschichte* (ed. by M. Ebert), vol. xii (1928), p. 55; vol. iii, p. 224; Ellis H. Minns, 'Archaeology in Soviet Russia', *Man*, 1942, No. 24.

67. So far I am only able to quote from an article under the (not quite accurate) title 'First Finds of Prehistoric Painting in Soviet Asia' in the *Moscow News*, published by Mezhdunarodnaya Kniga, January 27, 1954.

68. *Scythian Art:* Ellis H. Minns, *Scythians and Greeks*, Cambridge, 1909; M. Ebert, *Südrussland im Altertum*, 1921; G. Borovka, *Scythian Art*, 1928; Rostovtseff, *Iranians and Greeks in South Russia*, 1923. A brief but very elucidative survey has been delivered by Professor D. Talbot Rice (see note 1) recently. For parallels in other areas compare Carl Hentze, *Objets Rituels, Croyances et Dieux de la Chine Antique et de l'Amérique*, Antwerp (De Sikkel), 1936.

69. D. H. Gordon, 'Indian Cave Paintings' in IPEK, *Annual Review of Prehistoric and Ethnographical Art*, Berlin and Leipzig, 1935, published in 1936. For other publications see Herbert Kühn's article, *ibid.* Fortunately, we now possess a comprehensive handbook of Indian prehistoric archaeology, viz., Professor Stuart Piggott's *Prehistoric India* (with many illustrations and bibliographical notes attached to each chapter), Pelican Books (Harmonds-

worth, 1950). For a new edition of this excellent work a larger and more detailed index would be appreciated by students.

70. Helmut de Terra, 'Stone Age Man in Ice Age India and Burma', in *Asia* (New York), March 1939, pp. 158–63.

71. Sir John Marshall, *Mohenjo-Daro and the Indus Civilization*, London, 1932, 3 vols.; Ernest Mackay, *The Indus Civilization*, London, 1935 (the best short introduction for the beginner), second edition, revised and enlarged by Dorothy Mackay under the title *Early Indus Civilizations*, London (Luzac & Co., Ltd), 1948.

72. Guillaume de Hévésy, 'The Easter Island and the Indus Valley Scripts', *Anthropos*, vol. xxxiii (1938), pp. 808–14. There exists already a large number of articles *pro* and *contra* Hévésy's theory. Only a few can be quoted here: R. von Heine-Geldern, 'Die Osterinselschrift', *Anthropos*, vol. xxxiii, pp. 815–909 (*pro* Hévésy); Alfred Métraux, 'The Proto-Indian Script and the Easter Island Tablets', *ibid.*, pp. 218–39; the same author, 'Two Easter Island Tablets in the Bernice Pauahi Bishop Museum, Honolulu', *Man* (London), 1938, No. 1 (*contra* H.). See also Hévésy's rejoinder in *Man*, 1938, No. 183.

73. Some of the finds from Tell Brak are illustrated in *The British Museum Quarterly*, vol. xiii, No. 3 (1939), Pl. xl.

74. *Tell Halaf, a new culture in oldest Mesopotamia*, by Max Baron von Oppenheim, transl. by Gerald Wheeler. London and New York (Putnam), being the enlarged English edition of *Der Tell Halaf, eine neue Kultur im ältesten Mesopotamien*, Leipzig (Brockhaus), 1931. – A brief account (not illustrated) of the excavations at Tell Halaf is in Sir Frederic Kenyon's book, *The Bible and Archaeology*, London, etc. (1940), pp. 151 ff.

75. C. Leonard Woolley, *The Development of Sumerian Art*, New York, 1935.

76. G. D. Hornblower, 'Early Dragon Forms', in *Man* (London), 1933 and 1936.

76a. W. G. Archer, *The Vertical Man. A Study in Primitive Indian Sculpture*, London (Allen & Unwin), 1947 (with beautiful illustrations; for the student of primitive art the best monograph on this subject).

77. Ajitcoomar Mookerji, *Folk Art in Bengal*, with a foreword by Sir W. Rothenstein, University of Calcutta, 1939.

78. J. H. Hutton, *The Angami Nagas*, London, 1921, pp. 65 ff.; J. P. Mills, *The Ao Nagas*, London, 1926, pp. 96 f.

78a. Additional literature for Chapter XIII, sect. 6.: G. L. Tichelman, *Batakse Kunst* (Royal Institute for the Indies, Mededeling No. LXXXVI, Afdeling Volkenkunde No. 33, Amsterdam, 1949); id. 'Batakse Kunst' (in Winkler Prins *Encyclopaedie*, Amsterdam & Brussels, vol. 3, pp. 351–4), both concise introductions to the massive and sombre art of the Batak peoples of Sumatra.

79. Illustrations of Koryak carvings in W. Jochelson, *The Koryak*, Jesup North Pacific Expedition, Vol. vi, Leiden and New York, 1905–8.

80. B. Laufer, *The Decorative Art of the Amur Tribes*, Jesup North Pacific Expedition, Vol. iv (1902).

81. J. Roeder, 'Rock-Pictures and Prehistoric Times in Dutch New Guinea', *Man*, London, 1939, No. 173; Henri Lavachery, *Les Pétroglyphes de l'Île de Pâques*, Antwerp (De Sikkel), 1939.

82. E. Banks, 'Some Megalithic Remains from the Kelabit Country in Sarawak', *Sarawak Museum Journal*, vol. iv, No. 15, July 1937, pp. 411–37.

83. *Some outstanding works on Oceanian arts:* (New Guinea): A. C. Haddon, *The Decorative Art of British New Guinea*, Dublin, 1894; Raymond Firth, *Art and Life in New Guinea*, London, 1936; (Melanesia): E. Stephan, *Südseekunst*, Berlin, 1907; Augustin Krämer, *Die Malanggane von Tombara*, Munich, 1925; Gladys A. Reichard, *Melanesian Design*, Columbia University Press, 1933; (Polynesia): Augustus Hamilton, *The Art Workmanship of the Maori Race in New Zealand*, Dunedin, N.Z., 1896 (the fifth part issued in 1900); H. D. Skinner, 'Evolution in Maori Art', *Journal Royal Anthropological Institute*, vol. xlvi, 1916; *id.*, 'Maori amulets in stone, bone, and shell', *Journal of the Polynesian Society*, vols. 41–45; 52 (Wellington N.Z., 1932–6; 1943); Gilbert Archey, 'Evolution of certain Maori carving patterns', *Journal of the Polynesian Society*, vol. 42 (1933); *id.*, 'Maori carving patterns', *ibid.*, Vol. 45 (1936). While Mr Archey regards Maori carving as 'an elaborate complex of human figures', developed entirely in New Zealand, Dr Skinner is on the side of those scholars who prefer to compare Maori art forms with similar motives outside New Zealand (Melanesia and, ultimately, Asia). It is not here possible to enter into a discussion of details. Two more recent publications must be mentioned: Gilbert Archey's *South Sea Folk* (2nd edition, Auckland War Memorial Museum, 1949), a guide book with beautiful illustrations, and *The Coming of the Maori* by the late Sir Peter Buck (Te Rangi Hiroa), Wellington, N.Z. (Whitcombe & Tombs Ltd, 1949), the last work of the author, with special consideration of technology and art forms. However, students of Maori art should first read Raymond Firth, 'The Maori Carver' (*Journal of the Polynesian Society*, vol. 34 (1925), pp. 277–91), still the best exposition of the social background as well as technical details of Maori carving. Karl von den Steinen, *Die Marquesaner und ihre Kunst*, 3 vols., Berlin, 1925–28; W. C. Handy, *L'Art des Iles Marquises*, Paris, 1938; *Bulletins of the Bern. P. Bishop Museum*, Honolulu. Beautiful photographs of works of art from various parts of *Oceania* are reproduced in the French periodical *Cahiers d'Art*, Paris, 1929, No. 2–3. A very successful concise outline of the characteristics of the various South Sea arts has been given by Dr Hans Nevermann, *Südseekunst*, Berlin, Staatl. Mus., 1933. A beautifully illustrated handbook is *Arts of the South Seas*, by Ralph Linton and Paul S. Wingert, in collaboration with Rene D'Harnoncourt, Museum of Modern Art, New York (distributed by Simon and Schuster), 1946.

84. A special study of the 'figure-stools' as he calls them, has been made by Jan Söderström of the Ethnographical Museum in Stockholm: *Die Figurenstühle vom Sepik-Fluss auf Neu-Guinea*, Statens Ethnografiska Museum, Stockholm, 1941. It is interesting that, according to the author, there are altogether forty-four of these stools in the European museums. Professor Felix

Speiser, however, believes that there are still more (cf. Speiser's review in *Anthropos*, vol. xxxv–vi, 1940–41).

85. E. Stephan, *Südseekunst*, pp. 35, 102.

86. For kind information about the technique of wood carving in Kiriwina, Trobriand Islands, to-day I am indebted to Mr John R. Neill, of Melbourne.

87. Henry Balfour, 'An Interesting Naga-Melanesian Culture-Link' (in *Custom is King*, Essays presented to R. R. Marett, ed. by L. H. Dudley Buxton, London, 1936, pp. 11–16).

88. Nevermann, *Südseekunst*, p. 44.

89. F. Boas, *Primitive Art*, p. 69, fig. 63.

90. Nevermann, *Südseekunst*, p. 27.

90*a*. The classical source of information about Easter Island, its population, native culture, and art is Alfred Métraux, 'Ethnology of Easter Island' (*Bernice P. Bishop Mus. Bulletin* No. 160, Honolulu, 1940). It is not superseded by the same author's latest work, *L'Île de Paques*, Paris, 1951.

91. For the study of Australian aboriginal art some outstanding ethnological publications should be studied first, which is indispensable for the understanding of the psychological background of primitive art: A. P. Elkin, *The Australian Aborigines: How to Understand Them*, Sydney and London, 1938 ff. (2nd ed., reprinted 1945); Herbert Basedow, *The Australian Aboriginal*, Adelaide, 1925 (with useful information about the material culture); A. P. Elkin, *Aboriginal Men of High Degree* (University of Queensland Publication), Sydney, 1946 (indispensable for the understanding of the emotional life, beliefs, and rituals); Sir Baldwin Spencer's and F. J. Gillen's works on the tribes of Central and North Australia; A. W. Howitt, *Native Tribes of South-East Australia*, London, 1904. Special publications on art: D. S. Davidson, *A Preliminary Consideration of Aboriginal Australian Art* (Memoirs of the American Philosophical Society, IX), Oxford, 1937; Fred S. Brockman, *Report on Exploration of North-West Kimberley*, 1901 (an official publication of Western Australia), Perth, 1902 (with the first reproduction, since Sir George Grey's discovery and first publication in 1839, of rock paintings in the Kimberleys); A. P. Elkin, 'Rock Paintings of North-West Australia', in *Oceania*, vol. i (1930); H. Basedow, 'Aboriginal Rock Carvings of Great Antiquity in Southern Australia', *Journal Royal Anthropological Institute, London*, vol. xliv, 1914; A. P. Elkin, 'Anthropology in Australia, 1939', *Oceania*, vol. x, No. 1, 1939; C. P. Mountford, *A Survey of the Petroglyphs of South Australia* (Report of the Melbourne 1935 Meeting of the Australian and New Zealand Association for the Advancement of Science). The following important for the study of symbolic designs, etc.: Carl Strehlow, *Die Aranda-und Loritja-Stämme in Zentral-Australien*, ed. by M. Frhr. v. Leonhardi, Frankfurt a. M., 1908, vol. i; C. P. Mountford, 'Aboriginal Crayon Drawings' (a series of papers relating to Central and Western Australia), *Transactions Royal Society of South Australia*, vols. lxi–lxiii (1937–39). The following important from the psychological point of view: id., 'Contrast in Drawings made by an Australian Aborigine before and after Initiation', *Records South Australian Museum*, vol. vi, Adelaide, 1938. (The following concerning Arnhem Land

and Groote Eylandt): Norman B. Tindale, 'Natives of Groote Eylandt and of the West Coast of the Gulf of Carpentaria', *Record South Australian Museum*, vol. iii (1925–28), especially pp. 166 ff.; Donald F. Thomson, 'Two Painted Skulls from Arnhem Land with Notes on the Totemic Significance of the Designs', *Man* (London), 1939, No. 1; Frederick Rose, 'Paintings of the Groote Eylandt Aborigines', *Oceania* (Sydney), vol. xiii (1943). A. P. Elkin, Catherine & Ronald Berndt, *Art in Arnhem Land*, Melbourne & London, 1950; L. Adam, 'The Bark Paintings of Groote Eylandt (Gulf of Carpentaria)' in *Südseestudien, Gedenkschrift zur Erinnerung an Felix Speiser*, Basel (Museum für Völkerkunde), 1951; *Burial Trees*, by Lindsay Black, Melbourne, 1941, deals with the carved trees of New South Wales mentioned in the text. A good introduction to the decorative art of all the recent tribes is *Australian Aboriginal Decorative Art*, by F. D. McCarthy, a publication of the Australian Museum, Sydney, 1938, 3rd ed. 1952 (with many illustrations). The same author's Records of 'Rock Engravings in the Sydney District' are published in *Mankind*, official journal of the Anthropological Societies of Australia (Sydney). A well-illustrated popular article by McCarthy on this subject will be found in the *Australian Museum Magazine* of 31 December 1938, pp. 401 ff. Some good photographs of representative, symbolic, and decorative art from various parts of Australia, ancient and recent, are in Charles Barrett's and R. H. Croll's book *Art of the Australian Aboriginal*, Melbourne, 1943.

91a. More details about the *mamariga* symbol are given by Mr Rose in his recent article entitled 'Malay Influence on Aboriginal Totemism in Northern Australia' (*Man* [London], October 1947, No. 142). There are actually three different wind-totem symbols, which are apparently conventionalized representations of three different shapes of a sail, as they were observed by the natives. Thus the south-east wind totem mentioned on p. 159 illustrates the sail with a moderate area of canvas exposed, because the south-east wind is 'strong and persistent, but no dangerous squalls are to be expected'. On the other hand, the north wind symbol is a very narrow sign indicating that 'the sail would be expected to be furled completely' because 'this wind is light, but during midsummer is often the immediate precursor of thunderstorms', etc.

92. Carl Strehlow, *Die Aranda- und Loritja-Stämme in Zentral-Australien*, ed. by M. Frhr. v. Leonhardi, Frankfurt a.M., 1908, Vol. i, Part ii, fig. 2.

92a. R. H. Goddard, *Aboriginal Sculpture*, Report 24th Meeting Australian and New Zealand Association for the Advancement of Science, Canberra; Sydney, 1939, pp. 160 ff.

93. Diamond Jenness, 'The Prehistory of the Canadian Indians', in *Custom is King*, Essays presented to R. R. Marett on his seventieth birthday, London (Hutchinson), 1936.

94. Franz Boas, *Relations between North-West America and North-East Asia*; Roland B. Dixon, 'Contacts with America across the Southern Pacific' (in *The American Aborigines, their Origin and Antiquity*, ed. by Diamond Jenness, University of Toronto Press, 1933); L. Adam, 'North-West American Indian Art and its Early Chinese Parallels', *Man*, London, 1936, No. 3.

95. W. D. Strong, *An Introduction to Nebraska Archaeology* (Smithsonian Miscellaneous Collections, vol. 93, No. 10), Washington, 1935; Albert E. Jenks, *Pleistocene Man in Minnesota*, University of Minnesota Press, Minneapolis, 1936. (Critical): G. M. Morant in *Man* (London), 1938, No. 75; Kirk Bryan and Paul McClintock, 'What is Implied by "Disturbance" at the Site of Minnesota Man?' *Journal of Geology* (*U.S.A.*), vol. xlvi, No. 3, Part i (1938).

95a. Willard F. Libby, *Radiocarbon Dating* (Chicago, 1952), p. 82.

96. H. J. Spinden, 'Origin of Civilizations in Central America and Mexico', in *The American Aborigines*, ed. by D. Jenness.

96a. Ancient Eskimo art and archaeology: Henry B. Collins, Jr., *Prehistoric Art of the Alaskan Eskimo* (Smithsonian Miscellaneous Collections, vol. 81, No. 14 (1930)), plates 3 ff. Helge Larsen and Froelich Rainey, 'Ipiutak and the Arctic Whale Hunting Culture' (*Anthropological Papers of the American Museum of Natural History*, Vol. 42, New York, 1948); the following are papers read at the 29th International Congress of Americanists and published in *Indian Tribes of Aboriginal America*, ed. by Sol Tax (The University of Chicago Press, 1952): Kaj Birket-Smith, *Present Status of the Eskimo Problem*, followed by a *Discussion* by Frederica de Laguna (*ibid.*, pp. 18 ff.); Helge Larsen, *The Ipiutak Culture: Its Origin and Relationships* (with a discussion by Diamond Jenness, pp. 30 ff.).

96b. Bishop White, 'Bone Culture of Ancient China' (*Museum Studies*, No. 4, University of Toronto Press, 1945), plates xcix to ciii, pp. 41, 209.

96c. Willard F. Libby, *Radiocarbon Dating* (1952), pp. 89 f.

97. F. Boas, *Primitive Art*, p. 65.

98. H. Himmelheber, *Eskimokünstler*, Stuttgart, 1938, pp. 33 ff.

99. T. A. Joyce, 'A Totem Pole in the British Museum', *Journal Royal Anthropological Institute*, vol. xxxiii (1903), pp. 90 ff.

100. Professor Boas' original essay, 'The Decorative Art of the Indians of the North Pacific Coast of America', appeared in *Bulletin American Museum of Natural History*, vol. ix (1897). It has been incorporated, in a revised form, in Boas' *Primitive Art* quoted in Note 6. Other outstanding contributions on North-West American art are by John R. Swanton and George T. Emmons.

101. Frederic H. Douglas and Rene D'Harnoncourt, *Indian Art of the United States* (Museum of Modern Art), New York, 1941, p. 157. Like the other excellent publications of this series, this book is based on an exhibition, and this particular exhibition had been prepared by the Indian Arts and Crafts Board of the United States Department of the Interior. The very existence of this Board is another wonderful proof of the enlightened and progressive spirit in which Indian affairs are now being conducted in the U.S.A. I wish we had an analogous institution in Australia. The book here referred to has good illustrations, including some colour plates, of Eskimo art and Indian art from all parts and periods of North America. There is also a large selected bibliography.

102. John Canfield Ewers, *Plains Indian Painting* (see note No. 5), pl. 22.

103. A. T. Jackson, 'Picture-Writing of Texas Indians', *University of Texas Publication*, No. 3809, Austin, 1938.

104. There exists a voluminous literature on Pueblo pottery. The latest publications are: Kenneth M. Chapman, *The Pottery of Santo Domingo Pueblo*, 1936; H. P. Mera, 'The "Rain Bird": A Study in Pueblo Design', 1937; *ibid.*, 'Style Trends in Pueblo Pottery', 1939 (*Memoirs of Laboratory of Anthropology*, vols. i, ii, iii, Santa Fe, New Mexico).

105. T. A. Joyce, *Guide to the Maudslay Collection of Maya Sculptures, British Museum*, 2nd ed., 1938, p. 53.

106. Compare, for example, *The Gilding Process and the Metallurgy of Copper and Lead among the Pre-Columbian Indians*, by Paul Bergsøe, translated from Danish by C. F. Reynolds, Copenhagen (Danmarks Naturvidenskabelige Samfund), 1938.

107. K. Th. Preuss, *Monumentale vorgeschichtliche Kunst, Ausgrabungen im Quellgebiet des Magdalena*, Göttingen, 1929, vol. i, p. 112.

108. Hermann von Walde-Waldegg, 'Stone Idols of the Andes Reveal a Vanished People', *National Geographic Magazine* (Washington, D.C.), vol. lxxvii (1940), pp. 627–47.

109. Erland Nordenskiöld, *L'Archéologie du bassin de l'Amazone* (Ars Americana I), Paris (G. van Oest), 1930.

110. A. C. Haddon, *The Decorative Art of British New Guinea*, p. 271.

111. Edwin Avery Park, in *Encyclopaedia of the Social Sciences* (New York, Macmillan), vol. ii, p. 257.

112. When Epstein's alabaster statue, 'Adam', inspired, it is understood, by Bethoven's Seventh Symphony, was on exhibition, raising both enthusiasm and a storm of emphatic criticism, Mr T. Sheppard, Director of the Hull Municipal Museums, sent a letter to *Picture Post*, including a photograph of a wood carving from Tahiti, very similar to the figures shown in Pl. 26(*b*). He explained that that figure, 'which had a remarkable resemblance to Epstein's "Adam"', was loked upon as a god and that is was 'quite possible it may be their idea of Adam'. Mr Sheppard ironically added that the natives of that far-away South Sea island 'cannot have obtained their inspiration from Epstein, as their figure was made first', and that he felt sure 'that the Tahitians would never have heard of Beethoven's symphony, so that they cannot have obtained their inspiration from Epstein's source'. Incidentally, the resemblance appears only in the profiles.

113. *Report of the Committee appointed in 1938 by the Governor of the Gold Coast Colony to inspect the Prince of Wales College, Achimota*, Accra and London, 1938, p. 108.

113*a*. 'Felix Idubar's Sculpture', *Illustrated London News*, 27 July 1957, p. 157.

114. *Indians at Work*, published by the U.S. Department of the Interior, Office of Indian Affairs, Washington, D.C., February 1940, pp. 27 ff.

115. *The Art of Albert Namatjira*, by C. P. Mountford, 79 pp., with 21 illustrations including colour plates. Melbourne, 1944.

116. Quoted from the *Seventeenth Annual Report of the Victorian Aboriginal Group*, 1946 (Melbourne, 1947), p. 10.

117. *Prähistorische Fälschungen. Eine Rundfrage.* Edited and with introduction by Dr Siegfried Türkel (Scientific Publications of the Criminological Laboratory of the Metropolitan Police of Vienna), Graz, 1927, p. 48. This book consists largely of fourteen articles contributed by prehistoric archaeologists, ethnographers, mineralogists, geologists, technologists, chemists, and metallurgists.

118. *Prähistorische Fälschungen*, p. 1 ff., Pl. i and ii.

119. Technical details of ethnographical forgeries are discussed at length in F. Gräbner's *Methode der Ethnologie*, Heidelberg, 1911. A monograph on the nephrite industry of Oberstein-Idar is 'Die Nephritindustrie in Oberstein-Idar' by Richard Andree (in *Zeitschrift f. Ethnologie*, vol. xxxix, 1907, pp. 943 ff.). Abstracts of both in Dr Türkel's book quoted in Note 117.

INDEX

(References given in the 'Notes' are not included in this index except for a few more detailed quotations. These references are marked with the letter N and printed in italics.)

Magic 50, 51, 74, 84
Makerere College 212
malanggans, malanggane 150
Malays 131
Malekula 151
Mallowan, M. E. L. 126
mana 54, 144
manaia 155
Mangaia (Hervey Island) 155
Maori 155, 210
Maps 48
Maracá 204
Marajó 203
Marble vases, Honduras 197, Pl.
  38(*b*)
Marett, R. R. *N.37*
Marquesas Islands 153, 156
Marriage toys 129
Marshall, Sir John 123
Masks 99
— composite 176
— principal areas 52
— African 100
— Alaska Eskimo 175 f., 178
— European palaeolithic 84
— Iroquois 184 f.
— N.W. American 61, 180
— New Britain 150
— New Guinea 141, 143
Massim area 139, 145 f.
Masson-Detourbet, Annie 109
Material, influence of form and
  colour of ... 42 f.
Maurya dynasty 123, 126
Maya 120, 171 f., 196 f.
Mediterranean influence in Ni-
  geria, problematic 107
Megalithic culture of Colombia
  200 ff.
Melanesia 44, 131, 137, 148 ff., 161
Mentawei Islands 133
Mera, H. P. 191, 193
mereshú 42 f.
Meroe 112
Mesopotamia 123, 125 f.
Metal technique, S. America 199

Meteorite gods, Egypt and Nubia
  109
Métraux, Alfred, 124
Mexico 187 f., 195 ff.
Meyerowitz, H. V. 44, *N.62*
— Eva, L. R. 109
Micronesia 131, 153 f.
Mini-Mini 163
Minnesota man 172 f.
Minusinsk 116
Mirzapur 121
Mississippi valey 185
mithan 130
Modigliani 207
Mohenjo-Daro 122 ff.
Monckton, C. A. W. 144
Mongolians, Mongoloids 135
Montespan, Caverne de ... 80
Morals, primitive 62
Morant, G. M. 173
Moszeik, O. 92, 95 f.
Mound-builders 172, 185 ff., 189
Moutford, C. P. 61, 165, 213
Mousterian 77
Mounthless figures 131, 160, 198
Mythical world 61

Nadel, S. F. *N. 49*
Nagas (Assam) 130 f.
Namatjira, Albert 213
Nanaimo (Vancouver Island) 178
Naturalism 34, 39 f., 158, 178 ff.
Nature, symbolic representations
  in Melanesia 44, 146 f.
Navajos 194
Nazca 193, 198
Nebraska 172
Negro art 58, centres of ... 98
Neolithic period
— America 173, 202
— China 115
— Siberia 117
Neuhauss, R. 144
Neurotics, art of ... 58
Nevermann, H. 149 f., 152
New Britain (*Birara*) 150

New Caledonia 153 f.
New Guinea 138 ff., 160
New Hebrides 151
New Ireland (*Tombara*) 148 ff.,
— X-ray drawings 40 (Fig. 3)
New Mexico 192 ff.
Newton, Eric 37
Ngandong skulls 114
Nias 131, 154
Nicobar Islands 132 (Fig. 28)
Nicoya 197
Nigeria 102, 109 ff.
Nilgiri Hills 128
Nisbett, Hume, 205
Nok 111
Nordenskiöld, Erland Baron 204
Nordmark, Olaf E. 212
North Asia 133 f.
North-west America 39 f., 60 f.,
65, 67 ff., 71, 84, 119 f., 178 ff.
Nubia 109
Nukuoro (Caroline Islands) 131,
153 f.
Nupe *N.49*, *N.62*

Obermaier, H. 78, 79, 83
Ohio 186 ff.
Ohio valley 185
Okladnikov, Prof. 117
Okvik 175
Old Bering Sea culture 175
Oni of Life 105
Oppenheim, Max Freiherr v. 126
Ordos, Land of the ..., and
bronzes 115
Oriental influences in prehistoric
Europe 84
Orissa 128
Ostiaks 135 f.
Otomi 195

Painting, see under Graphic art,
Rock art
Palaeoasiatics 135, 137
Palaeolithic, upper 27, 77 ff.
— in different continents 30

— America 172
Palaeolithic, China 114
— Siberia 116 ff.
Papuans 138, 141, 153, 205
Pareroultja, Edwin 213
Parsons, Elsie Clews 51
Parvati 125
Passek, Tatyana 117
Patters, curvilinear, angular 134
Peasant art 71 f., 129 f., 196
Pechstein, Max 206
Pelew (Palau) Islands 153 f.
Perriman, H. L. 164
Perspective 37 f., 75, 82, 96
Peru 186, 193, 195
Petrie, Sir Flinders 107
Philippine Islands 131, 133, 154
Picasso 207 f.
Pictographs, 47, 58, 84, 91
— North America 191
— Australia 166
— Chinese, 63, 120 f.
— Indus valley 124
Pipe-heads (mounds, N. America)
186
pithecanthropus erectus 114 f.
Pole sculpture 99, 131, 137, 150 f.
180 ff., 194
Polynesians 28, 138, 154 ff.
Porcupine quills, embroidery with
... 184
Portraiture
— Africa:
— Bushongo, Congo 46
— Ife, Nigeria 105
— West Africa generally 64, 101 f.,
110
— America:
— North-west 53, 180
— Mexico 195
— Mound-builders 186
Portraiture
— Asia:
— Nagas, Assam 130; Indo-China
131
— South Seas:

— Malekula 152
— Maori (*schematic*) 38
— Sepik area, N. Guinea 64, 141
— Solomon Islands 151
— Yap, Micronesia 154
Portuguese influence, West Africa 103 f.
Pottery
— Colima, Mexico 188
— Maya 197
— New Guinea 141
— Peru 186, 193
— Prehistoric N. America 186, 190
— Pueblo 192 ff.
Prehistoric, in terms of ethnology 144 f.
Prehistoric man, in Europe 30, 77
— — in other continents 30
— — America 172 f.
— — Asia 114 ff.
Preuss, Konrad Theodor 202,
Primitive mentality 57 f., 69
Primitiveness, meaning of ... 27 ff., 31 ff., 39, 207 f.
Profiles, symmetrical, in Chinese and American art styles 120, 182
Property, in primitive law 69
— incorporeal 70
Proportions, arbitrary 38
— incorrect, dependent on material 99 f.
— incorrect, Mexico 196
Proto-Australoid race 123 f.
Proto-Elamites 123
Psycho-analysis 60 ff.
Pueblo Indians 192 ff.
Punuk Island 175
Purari delta 139

Quartz, stools carved in ... (Ife) 105
Quimbaya 198 f.

Radiocarbon dating 24, 82, 173, 188

Rain-snake, rainbow-snake 160, 191
Rainey, F. 175
rakshasas 102
Ram, sacred animal of Amun and Shango 109
Ramu river 139, 142 ff.
Rattray, R. S. 15, *N.56*
Read, Herbert 33
Realism, intellectual 39
Rebirth, Australia 62
Reindeer 136 ff.
Reisner 112
Religion 28, 49 ff,. 58
Replicas 32, 71
Rhythm 68, 165 f.
Rice, Talbot 207, *N. 1*, *N. 68*
Rivers, W. H. R. 129
Rock art
— Australia 158
— N.W. America 178 f.
— Oceania 138 f.
— Sarawak 139
— U.S.A. 190 f.
— see also under Africa (northern), Atlas, Bushman art, Palaeolithic
Róheim, Géza 64
Rose, Frederic 164
Rostovcev, M. I. 128

Sadler, Sir Michael 52, 58, *N.53*
Sahara 85 ff.
Saint Périer, Count 79
Sakhalin 137
San Agustín 200 ff.
Sand paintings, Navajo 194
Santarem 204
Sarawak 133, 139
Saunders, Chas. F. 193
Scenic representations, Palaeolithic 82 ff.
— — Australia 161
— — Benin 102
Schmidt, Max 42
Schmidt, P. Wilhelm 50
Sculpture (see also Stone sculpture, Pole sculpture)

Tell Brak 126
Tell Halaf 126
Tennessee 186
Teotihuacan 195
Terra-cotta heads of Ife 105
Texas 190 f.
Thruston, General 187
Thunder-bird, N. W. America 52;
Pl. 35(*a*); 180
tiki 155
Tindale, Norman B. 163
ting (Chinese bronze tripod) 115
tjuringa 164 ff.
Tlingit 67, 180
Todas 128 f.
Toltecs 195
Tombara (Native name of New
Ireland) 148
toromiro wood 156
totem, totemism 54 f., 58, *N.22*;
polygenetic 57
Totem designs (Groote Eylandt) 164
Totem poles 178, 180
Toys, West Africa 101
— 'marriage toys', India 129
Trade routes, prehistoric 69
Tripods (Honan pottery of period II,
Yang Chao) 115
Trobriand Islands 140, 145 ff.
Trowell, Mrs Margaret 212

Uhe *see* Ife
uli (New Ireland) 148 f.
Uluá, Rio (Honduras) 120
ulurí 42
Underwood, Leon 231
Ur 127
Utah 191
Utilitarian art 46 ff., 143, 186, 189,
197
Uzbekistan 117 ff.

Vancouver Island 178 ff.
Vandalism 96
Vatchivokoe 102
Venezuela 198 f.
Vision 37 f., 213
Voyevodsky, Mikhail 118

Wadjak skulls 114
Wainwright, G. A. 109, *N.59a*
Walde-Waldegg, H. von 202
Walrus ivory 137, 175
wampum 184
White, Bishop 176
Wilkes, R. L. V. *N.62*
Willendorf, the so-called 'Venus
of ...' 59, 79 f.; (ill.) 78 (Fig. 13)
Wilson, Thomas 186
Wilton group, of Bushman art 94
Wingert, Paul S. *N.53*
Winthuis, J. 64
Wiradjuri 167
Women artists 65
wondjina 131, 159 f.
Woolley, Sir Leonard 123, 127
Worms, Ernest, Very Rev. Fr 160,
163

X-ray drawings 39; 40 (Fig. 3);
62 f.; 161; 162 (Fig. 38); 182
— — in Siberia 119
X-ray, parallel in children's art 75

Yakutsk 117 f.
Yap 153 f.
Yelch, Yetl 180 ff.
Yoruba 100, 102, 104 f., 108 f., *N.49*

Zaraut-Saya Gorge (Uzbekistan) 118
Zervos, Christian 208